Nicholas Senn

War Correspondence

Hispano-American War

Nicholas Senn

War Correspondence
Hispano-American War

ISBN/EAN: 9783337405090

Printed in Europe, USA, Canada, Australia, Japan

Cover: Foto ©ninafisch / pixelio.de

More available books at **www.hansebooks.com**

WAR CORRESPONDENCE

(*HISPANO-AMERICAN WAR*)

LETTERS FROM

DR. NICHOLAS SENN
CHIEF SURGEON U.S. VOLUNTEERS,
CHIEF OF OPERATING STAFF WITH THE ARMY IN THE FIELD.

REPRINTED FROM THE
JOURNAL OF THE AMERICAN MEDICAL ASSOCIATION.

CHICAGO:
AMERICAN MEDICAL ASSOCIATION PRESS.
1899.

CONTENTS.

War Correspondence....	1
An Old Battle Ground.....	24
Letter from Camp George H. Thomas....	31
Assigned to a New Field...	41
The Floating Hospitals..	50
The Medical Department of the Army in the Cuban Campaign..........................	55
The Qualifications and Duties of the Military Surgeon..	61
The Invasion of Porto Rico from a Medical Standpoint..	79
Typhoid Fever in the Porto Rican Campaign.......	95
The Returning Army...............	101
The National Cry..................	108
Our Relief Societies................	115
The Wounded of the Porto Rican Campaign	122
On the Frequency of Cryptorchism and its Results. ...	131
The Seat of War and our Military Surgeons.......	133
Headquarters Fifth Army Corps............	138
Recent Experiences in Military Surgery after the Battle of Santiago........................	146
The Surgery of Camp Wikoff...............	183
Empyema in Camp George H. Thomas..........	237
Esculapius on the Field of Battle............	255
Nurses and Nursing in War..............	265

WAR CORRESPONDENCE.

The beating of the drum, the measured tread of an armed host are again heard throughout the land and have aroused the patriotic spirit of the American people. For a fifth time our nation is face to face with a war the gravity of which it is impossible to estimate at the present time. The first war brought us our liberty and independence; the second established our reputation on the sea; the third taught our Mexican neighbor respect for our country; the fourth saved the Union, and the fifth, which is now being waged, was provoked in the cause of humanity.

For centuries the beautiful neighboring island of Cuba has been in the greedy grasp of a foreign nation. The people to whom this gem of the ocean belongs have been downtrodden, tyrannized over and abused by the cold iron hand of an effete monarchy. The humane liberty-loving people of the United States have heard the cry of the oppressed starving Cubans for years, and have done all in their power, short of resort to the sword, to relieve their sufferings, but without avail. The ear of the proud, cowardly Spainard remained deaf to well-meant and most earnest appeals. The Chief Executive of the United States exhausted every resource to improve the condition of the native Cubans, the rightful owners of the unfortunate island, without bloodshed, but all his efforts were ignored and antagonized by the brutal oppressors.

War is always a great calamity, but when entered upon for the sake of humanity, for the relief of the oppressed, it becomes a weapon in the hand of the Almighty. The issue before us is a righteous one, and it is not difficult to forecast the ultimate result. Justice and humanity are on our side; corruption and oppression on the other. On our part the struggle is purely unselfish; on the other it is a desperate but vain attempt to ignore the claims of an enslaved people. Such are the conditions of the present war with Spain, at the same time our people will now and for all time come "Remember the Maine."

The war has begun, the deafening roar of cannon has been heard in different Spanish ports, the hero of Manila has planted the Stars and Stripes, the emblem of liberty and equality, on the shores of the distant Philippine Islands; there it will remain until the unhappy inhabitants breathe the bracing air of independence. No war was ever undertaken in which the government had such a firm and enthusiastic support from the mass of the people regardless of politics, religion, nationality and position in life.

The policy laid out, advised and carried in effect by President McKinley, meets with the undivided support of the reunited nation. The gray is eager and anxious to don the blue in his country's cause. Federal and Confederate meet again to talk over the memories of the past at a common camp fire during the campaign against a common foe, who has been permitted far too long a time to abstract the life blood of an innocent people, the legitimate owners of one of God's most beautiful islands so close to our own great, forever free and united country.

ILLINOIS ARMY.

Illinois has always been in the front when our country was in danger. Its record during the War of the Rebellion stands foremost in the history of the nation. It gave to the nation Abraham Lincoln, who, during the dark days of the Rebellion, guided the Ship of State through many a storm and many a danger into a harbor of safety and gave freedom to a despised and degraded race. It gave to the nation Grant, who led the army from victory to victory, until the misguided but determined foe was willing to sue for peace and accept the terms offered by its conqueror. It gave the nation a Logan, whose heroic and gallant deeds brought terror to the enemy. It gave the nation an army of soldiers who took an honorable and heroic part in the deadly conflict. It gave the nation Dick Oglesby, the intimate friend of Lincoln, who happened to be in Washington on the memorable night of Lincoln's assassination. The moment the fatal shot was fired he was summoned, and when he arrived at the entrance of the house to which Lincoln had been taken, he was confronted by an armed guard who refused him admission. There was no time for argument; the sturdy Governor grasped the guard by his collar and pushed him aside like a

J. N. Reece, Adjutant-General.

toy, with the words, "I am the Governor of Illinois, get out of my way!"

Illinois will do her share in the present conflict. When the War Department called for troops, the message was received by Governor Tanner on April 26. After a brief consultation with Adjutant-General Reece, the button was touched flashing the order over the wires to the regimental commanders in different parts of the State, and in less than thirty six hours 10,000 men were at the State Fair Grounds at Springfield ready to do their duty. General Barkley, the senior Brigadier General, was placed in command of the post, which he named Camp Tanner, and thanks to his foresight, energy and knowledge of military art, the troops received proper shelter and were assigned to their quarters immediately upon their arrival. Adjutant-General Reece demonstrated by every act that he was master of the situation. There was probably never a time when upon such short notice a temporary camp for so large a force was made more comfortable and efficient. Both of these officers, as well as their subordinates, are entitled to great credit and to the thanks of the good people of Illinois for having acted so promptly and wisely to efficiently meet such an emergency. The newspaper reporters and visitors to the camp were astonished by the fact that no complaints were made either by officers or men. Considering the limitations of equipment, the number of men in the camp, the unprecedentedly disagreeable weather and the short notice, this must certainly appear as the most satisfactory proof of the intense patriotism which animated every man and made him ignore his physical requirements in the thought that he was called upon to discharge a duty to his country.

A few days after the arrival of the seven regiments of infantry and the First Regiment of Cavalry, Captain Yeager of Battery A, First Artillery, appeared in camp with a splendid body of well drilled men, which added much to the military appearance of the camp. The representatives of the United States army, Lieutenant-Colonel Roberts, Captain Swift and Lieutenants Ballou, Cole and Davis were on the field early and rendered invaluable service in the organization and mustering in of the troops. It was indeed pleasant to observe the harmony in word and action which prevailed between these officers of the regular army and the officers and men of the National Guard. This war will do much in cementing together more closely the professional and citizen soldier. In less than four weeks all of the troops were examined, mustered into the United States service and turned over to the Government.

Lieutenant-Colonel Roberts.

The Fifth and Third Regiments of Infantry were the first to leave Camp Tanner amid the cheers of their comrades left behind. In due time they reached their appointed station, Camp George H. Thomas, Chickamauga, Ga. The Sixth Infantry was next ordered to Camp Alger, Falls Church, Va., near Washington, and the First Infantry a few days later joined their comrades of the Third and Fifth Regiments at Chickamauga. The Second Infantry was then ordered to Tampa, but en route received notice to report at Jacksonville, Fla. The Fourth Infantry, after considerable delay, was ordered to Tampa, the Seventh Infantry to Virginia, and the First Cavalry is now on its way to Camp Thomas, Chickamauga.

GOVERNOR TANNER.

The office of governor of a State is always important and responsible, but especially so in time of war. The citizens of Illinois have reason to congratulate themselves that during the last election their choice fell upon the right man at the right time. Governor Tanner has shown that he is made of the right metal for an effective and wise war governor. His experience during the late war as a private has been of great value to him in meeting the duties of the hour. He knows what it is to serve in the ranks, and has therefore taken the deepest interest in the welfare and comfort of every soldier who has come to the camp. He is a staunch friend of the common people (the backbone of the nation), and has catered but little if any, to the whims and fancies of the silk stocking element. He is now more popular than ever with the National Guard. He takes pride in his army. He imbues every soldier with the idea that the highest position is within his reach if he devotes himself to his legitimate duties. He has strained every nerve in bringing his troops to the front, and has had the satisfaction of seeing an Illinois regiment the first to be mustered into the volunteer service of the United States, and that the State he represents has thus taken the lead as regards promptitude and dispatch in answering the call of the President for volunteers.

Our Governor is intensely patriotic; he has shown this in every act in the organization and equipment of the troops. It is not generally known that Governor Tanner is a great orator; the speech which he made at a banquet he gave to the officers of his staff and of the regiments in camp, was a revelation to every one present. He seemed to be inspired ; his eyes flashed : every nerve and muscle responded to his intense emotion; every word and thought found a hearty response in the hearts of his profoundly interested audience. I doubt very much if he will ever be able to duplicate that speech, because such an occasion comes but once during a man's life. It was a speech which left a deep and permanent impression, a speech calculated to make a man better and more devoted to his country and his country's flag.

John R. Tanner, Governor of Illinois.

The Governor has visited the camp daily and always has a cheerful word and a pleasing smile for every one he meets, privates and officers alike. John R. Tanner will go down in history as a famous war governor, a worthy successor to Governors Yates and Oglesby.

MRS. TANNER.

The beautiful, youthful and accomplished wife of our Governor came to the Executive Mansion at the right time. She takes great interest in the work of her distinguished husband.

Mrs. John R. Tanner.

She is a great favorite with the people of Springfield. She is ready in conversation and quick in perception. She visits the camp frequently and takes an active interest in the care of the sick. Her cheerful disposition and her tender care of her husband have done much to lighten the heavy burden and many perplexities, which have been resting upon the shoulders of our overtaxed Governor since he assumed the duties of his office, and more particularly since the declaration of war with Spain.

THE CAMP GROUND.

When the sudden call for troops came it was an important matter to select a camp centrally located and adapted for the season of the year. The officers of the State Agricultural Society came to the rescue of the military authorities and

Brigadier-General James H. Barkley, Senior Commander of the Camp.

offered gratuitously the State Fair Grounds for the use of the troops during mobilization. The grounds occupy 160 acres of land, north of the city limits, and are easily accessible by a line of electric cars. The surface of the ground is undulating and divided by several ravines well adapted for effective surface drainage with a little expenditure of time and money. The subsoil is of clay, which in combination with the continued rains made the streets pools of mud for more than a week, a destroyer of foot gear and a rich harvest for the bootblack.

The permanent buildings were well adapted for temporary quarters for the imperfectly equipped soldier. For two weeks two of the regiments lived in tents. The camp was supplied with filtered water from the Sangamon River. A specimen of the water was sent for analysis to Dr. A. W. Palmer, professor of chemistry at the State University, who pronounced it wholesome and practically pure.

A sufficient number of sinks were dug and boarded in and the dejecta were daily covered with dry earth. Fresh straw was furnished in abundance. The rations were satisfactory both in quantity and quality.

EXAMINATION OF SURGEONS FOR THE UNITED STATES VOLUNTEER SERVICE.

Soon after the troops reached Camp Tanner an order was sent from the War Department to Governor Tanner, making provision for the formation of an Examining Board. This board was to consist of one surgeon from the United States Army and two National Guard surgeons. The Government detailed Capt. H. P. Birmingham, U. S. A., stationed at Chicago, and Governor Tanner appointed Surgeon General Senn and Brigade Surgeon C. C. Carter of Rock Island, as members of the board. The duties of this board were to consist in the examination both as to physical condition and professional attainments of applicants for commissions in the Medical Department of the United States volunteers and the National Guard volunteer forces. The board was organized at once and proceeded to examine applicants for the Medical Department. The following blank was drawn up, typewritten, and presented to each applicant to fill out:

Applicants for the volunteer service are respectfully requested to fill out carefully the following blanks:

1. Name ——. 2. Age ——. 3. Height ——. 4. Weight ——. 5. Family history ——. 6. Physical defects, if any, either of congenital or acquired sources ——. 7. Residence and P. O. address ——. 8. Command, if any ——. 9. Place and date of graduation ——. 10. Professional or scientific study and investigation, other than military ——. 11. Foreign languages studied ——; *a*, able to speak ——; *b*, able to translate ——.

Surgeons of the National Guard and Illinois Volunteers.

12. Subjects or titles of books written or published, essays prepared, lectures delivered or papers read, when and where ——; *a*, No. ——; *b*, ——; *c*, ——. Remarks ——.

The physical examination was made in a very thorough manner, the man being stripped, and demonstrated that the candidates for commissions in the Medical Department compared favorably with the line and field officers. Out of the whole number only three were rejected.

It was the intention of the Board, in view of the fact that most of the candidates had done good service in the National Guard for a longer or shorter period, to make the examination as broad and practical as possible. The following are some of the subjects on which the examination was conducted:

Anatomy and Surgery.—1. Give the origin and distribution of the pneumogastric nerve. 2. Mention the bones of the carpus and give their relative locations by illustration. 3. Describe the innominate artery and give its relations to surrounding structures. 4. Enumerate the different hemostatic measures and describe their technic and indications. 5. Detail the treatment of recent compound fracture of the leg. 6. Describe the different amputations through and below the ankle joint and mention the names of the surgeons who devised them.

Hygiene.—1. Give your ideas on the selection and sanitation of camps. 2. The prophylaxis and treatment of sunstroke. 3. How would you determine, in the field, in a general way, the salubrity of the water-supply, and what measures would you take for preventing its pollution?

Military surgery.—1. Give method of treating (temporary) gunshot fracture of the thigh, on the field, and when and how would you remove the patient? 2. What is the effect produced by modern small jacketed bullet, compared with the old large caliber missile? 3. Give method of procedure in rendering first aid to, and removal of, wounded from fighting line to field hospital.

Practice of medicine.—1. Describe pneumonia: Definition, etiology, morbid anatomy, symptoms, complications, prognosis, termination, diagnosis, treatment. 2. Describe cerebrospinal meningitis: Cause, pathology, symptoms, diagnosis, prognosis, treatment. 3. Describe diseases most liable to occur in tropical countries, with short description of causes, symptoms, pathology, prophylaxis, diagnosis and treatment.

Materia medica.—1. What are the more common forms of mercury used in medicine? Write prescriptions for four. 2. Mention the comparative advantages of ether and chloroform as anesthetics. 3. Indications for the use of emetics, cathartics and alcohol.

The minimum standard was fixed at 70. It was a source of great gratification to the Board that, notwithstanding the fact that many of the applicants had been busy practitioners for years, the papers they turned in were of a high character. The result of the examination shows that in these applicants the State had desirable material for service in the volunteer regiments.

The fact that the revised code of the Illinois National Guard made provision for five surgeons to each regiment and the regulation for the United States Volunteer Service called for

Group of Hospital Stewards Illinois Volunteers.

only three, made it necessary for the junior assistant surgeons of some of the regiments to return unwillingly to their respective homes.

As soon as the results of the examination were announced, the assignments were made. The following is a list of the medical officers of the volunteer forces of Illinois:

First Infantry. Surgeon, W. G. Willard; Assistant Surgeons, T. E. Roberts and C. B. Walls.

Second Infantry. Surgeon, G. F. Lydston; Assistant Surgeons, J. G. Byrne and G. P. Marquis.

Third Infantry. Surgeon, J. B. Shaw; Assistant Surgeons, A. F. Lemke and C. E. Starrett.

Fourth Infantry. Surgeon, T. C. McCord; Assistant Surgeons, C. M. Galbraith and G. E. Hilgard.

Fifth Infantry. Surgeon, M. R. Keeley; Assistant Surgeons, E. A. Ames and J. L. Bevans.

Sixth Infantry. Surgeon, F. Anthony; Assistant Surgeons, C. A. Robbins and L. S. Cole.

Seventh Infantry. Surgeon, T. J. Sullivan; Assistant Surgeons, G. W. Mahoney and F. P. St. Clair.

First Cavalry. Surgeon, W. Cuthbertson; Assistant Surgeons, T. J. Robeson and J. Rowe.

Battery A, First Artillery. Hospital Steward, Dr. Jackson.

PHYSICAL EXAMINATION OF FIELD AND LINE OFFICERS AND ENLISTED MEN.

The examinations were conducted at the Senate Chamber of the State House from 9 A.M. to 6 P.M. daily, with an interval of an hour for lunch. The Board of Examiners was assisted by the regimental surgeon of each regiment and his assistants. The officers were examined separately in the Lieutenant-Governor's room. One of the assistant surgeons took the chest expansion, another examined the eyes and ears and a third the head, mouth, pharynx and neck. The Surgeon-General examined the lower extremities and abdomen, and Captain Birmingham the chest and the general aptitude for active service. Colonel Carter acted as clerk in conjunction with a number of the field and line officers.

The following blanks for physical examination were drawn up, and 10,000 copies were printed and distributed to the various regiments:

PHYSICAL EXAMINATION.

Name ——. Rank ——. Co. ——. Regiment ——. Age ——. Residence ——. Chest Expansion ——. Inspiration ——. Expiration ——. Are you subject to coughs or colds? ——. Have you ever had any serious illness? ——. Are you subject to sore throat? ——. Discharge of the ear? ——. Rheumatism? ——. Stiffening of the joints? ——. Hemorrhoids or piles? ——. Fistula? ——. Diarrhea or dysentery? ——. Do you believe you are sound and well now? ——.

Soon after the arrival of the Surgeon-General an order was issued instructing the regimental medical officers to make a preliminary physical examination of the recruits, which resulted in the return to their homes of several hundred men phys-

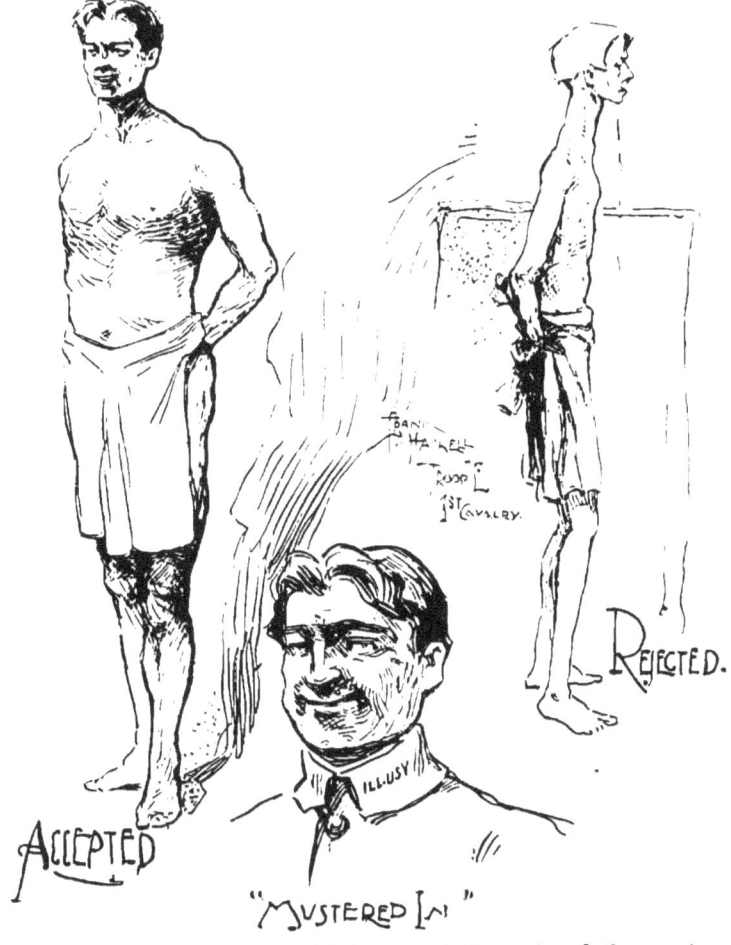

ically unfit for duty and which materially assisted the work of final examination. The most unenviable part of the examination fell upon the shoulders of the Surgeon-General, who for the purpose of quickening and lightening his duties devised

Company B, 7th Regiment Illinois Volunteers, after the medical examination.

the following commands: Heels together! Turn around! Turn back! Cough! Cough harder! which commands afterward became a favorite and familiar chorus among the men who passed the final ordeal to the satisfaction of the Board. On an average, it was found possible by following the thorough system adopted, to examine from 800 to 950 recruits a day. In all, 9899 men were examined.

The most common causes for rejection were hernia, varicose veins of the lower extremities, poor physique, heart disease, imperfect chest expansion, loss of teeth and flat foot. The presence of varicocele of different degrees in men otherwise apparenly in good health was marked. It was found that nearly 25 per cent. of all those examined presented a condition of varicocele of some degree. Only two recruits were rejected for this cause, as in their cases the varicocele appeared to be an acknowledged source of pain. In all the rest the statement was plainly made either that the applicant had no knowledge of the condition, or that it gave rise to no inconvenience. In probably one-half of all the cases the subjects were ignorant of the existence of this condition. The same remark may apply to flat foot as a cause of rejection, inasmuch as the deformity appeared to be extremely common, but only in a few isolated cases was it a cause of pain and consequently of disability for the volunteer service. The rejections for good and substantial causes were less than 10 per cent. This was influenced somewhat by the thoroughness with which the preliminary examinations had been conducted. The proportion of rejections was, on the whole, larger in the country regiments than in those made up of Chicago men. A great many men who passed the physical examination returned unwillingly to their homes by reason of the regulation reducing the number of men to a company from 109 to 84.

The intensity of the patriotic feeling which pervaded the men in camp is best shown by the illustrations which accompany this communication. The word "rejected" in many instances seemed to make a more profound impression than would a death sentence. The disappointment would be such that the soldier was often speechless, pale, staggering, and in not a few instances hot tears would roll down the bronzed checks as the best evidence of the deep regret of the recruit

Illinois Volunteer mustered in and fully equipped.

in being deprived of the great privilege of defending the honor of his country. On the other hand, the successful soldier would accept active service with a smiling countenance and would bound away into the dressing-room like a deer pursued by hounds.

SCHOOL OF INSTRUCTION FOR MEDICAL OFFICERS.

The second day after the Surgeon-General arrived at the Camp, he sent a telegram to Professor A. D. Bevan of Rush Medical College, Chicago, requesting him to send by the earliest train a cadaver for anatomic demonstration, and a course of operative surgery. The cadaver arrived promptly and a small amphitheater was extemporized in the Assembly Hall, which served as headquarters for the Third and Sixth Infantry. The hours between 8 and 10 P.M. were utilized in giving lectures, anatomic demonstrations, and a course in operative surgery. In this course not only the medical officers, but the members of the hospital corps took an active interest. The Surgeon-General demonstrated on the cadaver emergency operations with especial reference to military surgery; one of the assistant surgeons made a dissection every day, and in the evening demonstrated his work to the class. Among the demonstrations made were the following:

Major Lydston, operations on the urethra and bladder. Major Cuthbertson, hernia operations. Major Adams, osteoplastic resection of the skull. Colonel Kreider gave a lecture at St. John's Hospital, Springfield, on Sterilization in Surgery, demonstrating his remarks by the exhibition of the means employed in the hospital for this purpose. Among the lecturers were the following: Colonel C. C. Carter, "Prescribing in Military Practice." Major Adams, "Shock and Sunstroke, and Temporary Hemostasis." Major Sullivan, "Temporary Dressing of Fractures." Major McCord, "Prevention and Treatment of Camp Diarrhea." Captain Mahoney, "Prevention and Treatment of Gonorrheal Ophthalmia." Lieutenant Hilgard, "Treatment of Dysentery." Lieutenant Stanton, "Administration of Anesthetics." This School of Instruction was continued for nearly four weeks, and was found to be interesting, useful and well calculated to prepare the medical officers for their future work in the field. Those who took an active part in the teaching had the moral support

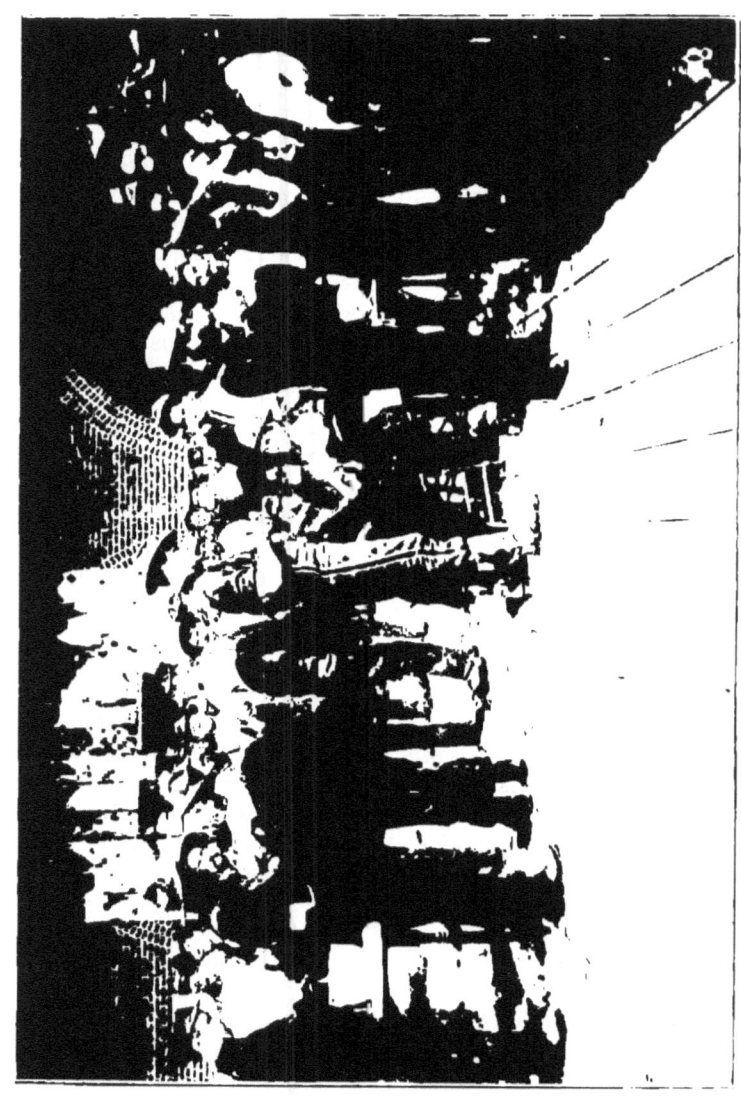

of both field and line officers, who did everything in their power to encourage them in their work.

LECTURES ON FIRST AID.

On May 10, the Surgeon-General issued the following order: "Regimental surgeons are requested to give officers and men in their commands instruction in first aid or self help, as the case may be, in the following subjects: Diet and drink in health and disease. Care of the person, bathing, clothing, feet, etc. What to do in sunstroke. Temporary treatment of fractures. Temporary arrest of hemorrhage. Transport of injured men. Application of first aid dressings. The illustrated triangular bandage will be furnished, to be displayed in a conspicuous place in company quarters so that every man may understand its application."

These lectures were well attended and proved of signal value in preparing the line officers and men in the use of the first aid package, and in the prevention and treatment of hemorrhage, as well as enlightening them on the subjects of hygiene and sanitation.

VACCINATION.

On May 12, the Surgeon-General issued the following order:
"To all surgeons and assistant surgeons:

"Vaccination by regiments will take place as soon as they are mustered. You are directed to operate according to the following rules, assisted by your hospital stewards:

"1. The left arm is to be bared. A space four inches square at the outer border of the deltoid midway between its origin and insertion is to be thoroughly scrubbed with warm water and potash soap, then cleansed with alcohol and finally washed with pure water and dried with a pledget of absorbent cotton.

"2. The arm is to be lightly scarified where cleansed for a space of one-half inch square. Both ends of the vaccin tube are to be broken off, and the virus blown on the wound with the rubber bulb furnished, and thoroughly rubbed in with the point of the lancet. The lancet is to be cleansed with alcohol after each scarification.

"3. The arm is to be left exposed until thoroughly dry. A pledget of sterile cotton two inches square, is to be placed over the wound and held in place by an adhesive strap one-half inch wide and four inches long."

There is reason to believe that the above specific directions did much in the prevention of septic complications.

CAMP DISEASES.

The season of the year at which the troops were called out, the crowded condition of the camp, the imperfect equipment of the men, the continuous rain for over a week, and the changeable temperature were influences well calculated to test the strength and power of resistance to disease of the men who sought the service of the Government.

The appearance of cerebro-spinal meningitis on the first day the troops were in camp in the case of a man of K troop, First Cavalry, excited much interest, and as this was followed in rapid succession by three additional cases in other commands, led to a thorough investigation as to the origin and spread of this disease. This investigation was conducted by Lieutenant Colonel Kreider pursuant to an order from the Surgeon-General. Colonel Kreider presented the following report:

CAMP TANNER, SPRINGFIELD, May 23, 1898.
COLONEL N. SENN,

Surgeon-General, I. N. G., Camp Tanner, Ill.

Sir: -Pursuant to your order to investigate the origin and spread of the cases of cerebro-spinal meningitis which have occurred at this camp, I have the honor to report that up to this time three cases have appeared, all of which have resulted fatally.

1. Ernest Royal Parish, of Troop K, First Cavalry. On my request, Major William Cuthbertson assigned to the First Cavalry made the following report: "He was ailing for some days prior to enlistment. While waiting at Tattersall's at Chicago I have ascertained that he was compelled to lie down, but was up and able to pass inspection. He was taken violently ill on the train on the way down, with chills and vomiting. On reaching Springfield in the morning he was unable to walk and was removed to the Post Hospital on a stretcher. As soon as possible he was transferred from there to St. John's Hospital, where he now lies. I have just learned that another case of this disease exists at Western Springs, the patient's home." Parish died May 1. As stated in Surgeon Cuthbertson's report, he had not placed a foot on the camp ground, and his stay there did not exceed half an hour.

22

2. Edward B. Beebe, of the Third Infantry, residing at Elgin, was sent to the Hospital May 13 by the Surgeon of the Regiment on the eve of its departure, and was first seen by me on the following morning. In the afternoon I found him delirious, so that he required restraint and constant watching, which was given by a hospital steward of the Second Infantry. He died May 15.

3. Robert Leland, of Third Infantry, residing at Ottawa, was first seen by me at the camp at 6 P.M., May 14, and, as all ambulances were in use, was conveyed in my buggy to the Hospital. Assistant Surgeon Lemke writes of the onset of the disease as follows: "I saw him at noon, when he was complaining of intense headache. He became delirious the same night, although he was rational when aroused." The disease ran a very rapid course and death occurred May 17 at 11 P.M. From his family physician I have learned that a sister aged 20 and a brother aged 15 had died of tuberculosis. As ordered, I had intended holding a postmortem on this case, but the body was removed from the Hospital at 2 A.M. by his father.

The disease in the first case may be traced to other cases in his home town. He was not associated in any way with the men of the Third Regiment, and it seems hardly probable that the disease could have been transmitted from him to the others. It seems probable that the disease in the Third Infantry was caused by the crowded and poorly ventilated quarters which this regiment occupied, or by the damp straw on which they slept. Each of these conditions was caused by the weather prevailing during the stay of this regiment at the camp. Because of the rains the men did not leave the building during the day, and thus the rooms became foul. I called the attention of the Surgeon of the Regiment to this foul odor early in the tour; because of the rain also, the straw was brought in damp and may have figured in causing the trouble.

Respectfully,

[Signed] GEORGE N. KREIDER, Post-Surgeon.

Among the other camp diseases must be mentioned pneumonia, measles and mumps. The pneumonia contracted in the camp proved to be of an unusually malignant type. Of the thirty-two cases only two died, a mortality of about 6 per cent.

Upon the outbreak of measles an isolated part of camp

ground was selected for an isolation hospital, and placed under guard with a yellow flag in front of the hospital tent. Three cases of measles and three or four cases of mumps occurred. The patients were placed in separate hospital tents, and as soon as they recovered from the illness were subjected to a thorough disinfection and their clothing disinfected before they were allowed to return to duty. This isolation of patients suffering from infectious diseases proved effectual in the prevention of a further spread of the diseases.

The ranks of the medical department were broken at an early date by the untimely death from pneumonia of Assistant-Surgeon Cole of the Sixth Infantry, who was taken ill while en route with his regiment to Washington, and died at Fort Wayne, Ind. Upon receipt of the news of his death the medical officers drew up the following resolutions:

WHEREAS, By the untimely death of our comrade, Lieutenant L. S. Cole, Assistant Surgeon, Sixth Illinois Infantry, U. U. A., a career of brilliant promise has been cut short, be it

Resolved, That in the death of Lieutenant Cole the State of Illinois has lost a valuable medical officer and the medical profession an efficient and able member.

Resolved, That we, the members of the Medical Department, of the Illinois National Guard and United States Volunteers at Camp Tanner, extend to his bereaved family and friends our condolence and sincere sympathy.

Resolved, That copies of these resolutions be sent to his mother, and to his regiment.

(Signed)
T. J. SULLIVAN, Major and Surgeon Seventh Infantry.
T. C. McCORD, Major and Surgeon Fourth Infantry.
Wm. CUTHBERTSON, Major and Surgeon First Cavalry.
S. C. STANTON, First Lieut. and Ass't.-Surgeon, I.N.G.
Committee.

With this communication my official connection with the National Guard of Illinois is temporarily severed, as I have been mustered in as Lieutenant-Colonel and Chief Surgeon, Sixth Army Corps, U.S.V., to be assigned to the command of Major-General Wilson, Camp George H. Thomas, Chickamauga, Ga.

AN OLD BATTLE GROUND.

CHICKAMAUGA, June 3, 1898.

Chickamauga! What a terrible name to the reunited nation! Here was enacted one of the bloodiest dramas in American history. It is here where one of the most desperate battles of the War of the Rebellion was fought. Almost every foot of soil of this great National Park was stained with the blood of heroes on both sides. What a grand spectacle this beautiful park must have presented when it was the scene of one of the greatest battles known to history! Two great armies composed of the same flesh and blood, face to face, engaged in a deadly conflict. Upon the issue depended much on both sides, hence the heroism displayed and the terrible sacrifice of life. It seems to me I can hear now the beat of the drum, the shrill voice of the fife, the thundering roar of cannon, the rattle of musketry, the shouts of command, the groans of the wounded and the labored breathing of the dying. The bullet-riddled trees, the innumerable cannon occupying the same position as when they vomited forth fire, death and destruction, the many beautiful monuments and tablets commemorating the position of troops during action, and the places where distinguished leaders fell, are the silent witnesses of those awful days when our Nation was threatened by disruption and even death. It was no fault of our valiant enemy that the star spangled banner triumphed. The victory was dearly bought. Thousands of brave soldiers are resting in yonder cemetery. Many wounds inflicted still remain. Many an aged mother and father have had their life saddened by an irreparable loss sustained in that battle. Many an empty chair has remained in numerous lonely households. It will take more than another generation to wipe out the immediate consequences of the horrors of that battle. Let the present and all coming generations remember with veneration and true gratitude the heroic deeds enacted here. Years have gone by and this great park has become again the camping ground of a large army. Within a few weeks nearly fifty thousand men have pitched their tents and are making active preparations for war. The hills, fields, woods and ravines are swarming with soldiers. Mounted officers are galloping in all directions in clouds of dust. Brigades, regiments, companies

LEITER HOSPITAL, CHICKAMAUGA, GA.

and squads are hard at drill under the burning sun. Sentries are stationed everywhere to preserve order, protect property and learn the art of watch dogs to protect the troops during the active campaign along the coast and in distant islands, the

the prospective fields of warfare. Almost every day new regiments arrive from every part of the country, often without arms and uniforms, but eager and ready to be instructed in the art of war. Our patriotic citizen soldiers in civilian dress envy their more fortunate comrades in showy blue, and impatiently await their turn to don the soldier's garb. It is refreshing and interesting to observe what patriotism will do in antagonizing the imperfections and hardships of camp life. Do you imagine you could hire many of these soldiers to do ordinary work under similar conditions at $5 per day? No! Give them a uniform, a gun, and an opportunity to fight for the honor of their country and the glorious stars and stripes, and they rush to the front without a word of complaint, unconscious of the privations and hardships incident to the life of the soldier.

SANITARY CONDITIONS.

Chickamauga Park is admirably adapted for a large camp. It embraces several square miles. The forest trees furnish protection against the burning rays of the semitropical sun and the many open places and fields are utilized as drill grounds. Humus is scanty and the subsoil is of clay. The surface is somewhat undulating and is cut up here and there by ravines, which add much to the beauty of the scenery. An ample supply of pure water is obtained from numerous wells, from 15 to 65 feet in depth, recently supplemented by a pumping station which derives the water from the river, a short distance below Crawfish Springs, and distributes the water to different parts of the park through iron pipes. The vastness of the grounds are realized by the visitor as soon as he reaches George H. Thomas camp, which at the present time is occupied by nearly 50,000 men, and yet seldom more than one regiment can be seen at one and the same time. In the past, Chickamauga has had an unenviable reputation as a health resort. The Indian name Chickamauga signifies literally "River of death." Along the banks of the Chickamauga river, which flows through the park, malaria was very prevalent years ago, which probably had something to do in inducing the Indians to designate this river by such a terrifying name. At the present time malaria has nearly disappeared from this part of the country, except a very localized district north of Crawfish Springs. The malaria contracted in this circumscribed locality has been of a mild form and is probably due to the draining of a little pond on the south side of Park Hotel.

An adequate number of sinks from four to eight feet in depth have been dug a safe distance from tents and field hospitals, all of which are boarded in. Three times a day the deposits in the sinks are covered with dry earth and ashes from the stoves and camp fires. One of the difficulties so constantly prevailing in camps has been the introduction of harmful articles of diet by interested friends and enterprising merchants. The regulations governing this evil are becoming more and more stringent and are more effectively carried out, so that the danger from this source is diminishing progressively.

PREVAILING CAMP DISEASES.

The most common disease affecting the troops at this time is diarrhea. The continuous heat, the change and often imprudence in diet and sleeping on the ground are the most important etiologic elements. The last mentioned cause becomes apparent from the fact that the privates are much more frequently affected proportionately than the commissioned officers, most of whom enjoy the luxury of a cot. A number of deaths have occurred from cerebro-spinal meningitis, more especially among the Illinois troops. In my first communication I traced the disease to Camp Tanner, where it originated from a case brought there by the first regiment of cavalry. A few days ago Capt. Lemke, 3rd Regiment Illinois Volunteers, made a postmortem examination at the 1st Division Hospital, 1st Army Corps, which demonstrated the pathological appearances of the disease to perfection. There was a difference of opinion in reference to the location and nature of the disease, as during the early history of the case the symptoms referable to the cerebro-spinal centers were conspicuous, while later a complicating pneumonia masked the manifestations of the original disease. The examination showed croupous pneumonia involving one lobe of the lung, of recent origin, while the meninges of the brain and spinal cord presented all the evidences of an acute inflammation. The lining membranes of all the ventricles were involved. The pathological changes were most marked at the base of the brain and more especially the pons Varolii and medulla oblongata. In these localities the meninges were found infiltrated and covered with a plastic exudate.

The remaining portions of the membranes enveloping the brain and cord were extremely vascular and in some places presented an opalescent appearance. A considerable quantity of turbid serum was found in the ventricles and subarachnoid space. It was evident from the postmortem appearances that the primary disease involved the nervous centers and that the lobar pneumonia set in later as a complication and contributed toward an early fatal termination. Two cases of cerebro-spinal meningitis, presenting grave symptoms observed in Camp Tanner, improved promptly after lumbar puncture and I have been subsequently informed that both of these cases ultimately recovered. The first tapping was made by Lieut. Rowe of the 1st Illinois Cavalry. All cases of cerebro-spinal meningitis that have been sent to the Division Hospital have been placed in isolation tents for the purpose of preventing further spread of the disease. Measles has broken out in the camp and all patients suffering from this disease, about twenty in number, at the present time are under guard in isolation tents. The disease is mild in type, the patients as a rule being confined to bed not longer than four or five days. Pneumonia has been prevalent, especially among the regiments from the northern States. Delirium is usually absent although the disease otherwise has assumed a grave type. In several fatal cases the postmortem changes indicated that death resulted from secondary streptococcus infection. At the present time there are only three or four cases of typhoid fever in camp and in most of them it is more than probable that the disease was contracted before the patients reached the camp. Considering the inadequate clothing of many of the volunteers, the heavy dew and the chilliness experienced some nights, it is remarkable that so few suffer from rheumatism and bronchitis. Sunstroke and heat exhaustion have so far not visited the camp, although heavy marching and active drilling often take place with the sun high up in the horizon. On the whole the health of the troops is excellent.

A TIMELY BENEFACTRESS.

As soon as I arrived at Camp George H. Thomas I called on Lieut. Col. Hartsuff, U. S. A., who received me very kindly and spent nearly half a day in showing me the location of regiments and field hospitals. His experience since he took charge of the medical affairs of the camp had taught him that the hospital facilities even with the limited number of sick at the present time were entirely inadequate. Near the park and on

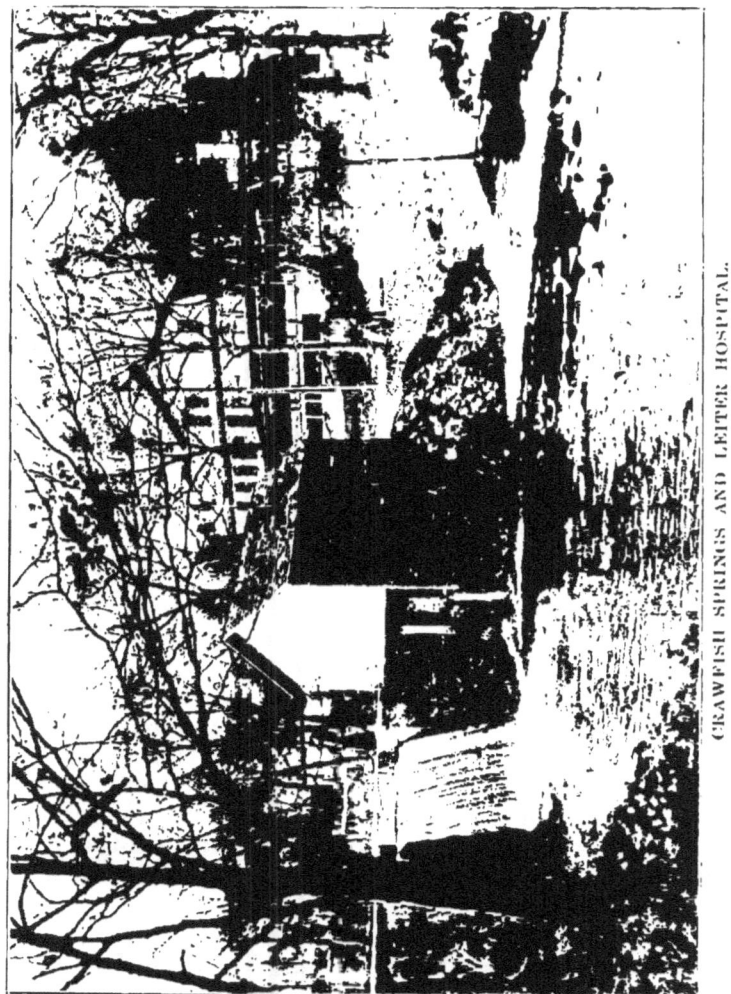

CRAWFISH SPRINGS AND LEITER HOSPITAL.

the south side of it, adjacent to the famous Crawford Springs is a large well built hotel containing seventy rooms, which had recently been evacuated and on which he had an option for a few days, purchase price $10,000. The building alone cost $65,000 and as the purchase price included the entire furniture, water privilege and four acres of land, and the building was in a condition that it could be occupied at once without much repair he had strongly recommended its purchase for hospital purposes to the Surgeon-General. There was no question as to the desirability of acquiring the property to better and increase the hospital facilities; neither could there be any doubt of the government's willingness to buy it to meet the existing emergency, but past experience satisfied all concerned that it would take weeks, and perhaps months, before the building could be made available by relying on the routine way in acquiring the property. Recognizing the necessity for immediate action in the premises and the fact that the option was open only for a few days, at the expiration of which the owners intended to reopen the hotel, I asked permission of Col. Hartsuff to allow me to make an attempt to secure the building by donation and later present it to the Government. This request was willingly granted. I telegraphed to Mrs. L. Z. Leiter, Washington, D. C., the condition of affairs and in due time received the pleasing information by wire from her husband that I should proceed at once and draw on him for the amount. After overcoming some of the technical difficulties in the way of securing the necessary water supply from the adjacent Crawfish Springs, the purchase was made and the 'Leiter Hospital" has become a beautiful monument to the memory of a distinguished family that has given the first large donation for the benefit of our sick citizen soldiers at the very beginning of the Spanish-American war. May this noble example find many imitators!

CHICKAMAUGA, GA., June 22, 1898.
CAMP GEORGE H. THOMAS.

From early dawn until taps, Camp Thomas is the scene of a busy, active life. It is the gathering point of the largest army concentrated in one place since the War of the Rebellion. It is at the present time the temporary home of 45,000 men representing almost every State in the Union. Many of the regiments are short of their quota, and recruits to the number of 500 on an average arrive daily to complete the organization of the regiments now in camp. The commander of the whole army in camp is Major General John R. Brooke, General in Chief in charge of the Department of the Lakes. He came here from Chicago with his entire staff. He enjoys the reputation of being a strict disciplinarian who does everything through the legitimate military channels. The greatest sources of confusion and consternation to the officers of the volunteers from civil life are these mysterious military channels which extend from the General's tent to the heads of the many departments in Washington. One of the blue books in constant use by officers, high and low, young and old, is the U. S. Army Regulations, 1895. The thousands of questions asked the professional soldier daily by his less informed volunteer officer are answered more often than otherwise by "Study the Regulations, *Study the Regulations*, STUDY THE REGULATIONS." Such advice, as a rule, is more easy to give than to follow with any expectation of approval at headquarters. The experience here has satisfied me more than ever that the National Guard officers need more thorough training in executive, clerical work, so essential in the efficient management of troops at home and in the field. One of the common sights in camp is to see an officer hide himself away under a solitary tree and pore over a work on tactics or the much feared "Regulations." If this war does nothing else but demonstrate to our people and to the legislators, State and National, the necessity of a well-organized militia it will have accomplished a great deal. If we had in this country, as we ought to have, a well organized, well equipped militia force of 200,000 men, we would have been in possession of all the Spanish islands and Spain itself, if we wanted it, long ago. As it is, it takes two millions a day and the hardest kind of work to bring our volunteers into fighting trim. The officers of the regular army have reason to be thankful to Spain for having given them a chance to fight. They have been looking a long time anxiously for such an opportunity. They are the recognized salt of the army. The Government has fully recognized their claims. Nearly every day the newspapers bring columns of names of lucky officers who have been advanced in rank, in fact it seems almost impossible for any one of them to escape promotion of some kind. This is probably as it should be, but occasionally such promotions lead to giddy heights. To make a lieutenant-colonel out of a second lieutenant of very limited practical experience is a transition of doubtful propriety and often followed by the most detrimental results, both to the over-ambitious officer and the over-confiding troops placed under his charge. Officers thus honored by promotion and assigned to the army of volunteers are, as a rule, more anxious to change the shoulder straps than to add the V. to the U. S. on the collar of the blouse. On the whole, the regular army officers are perfect gentlemen and great favorites in the camp, and the feeling between them and the officers from civil life is of a most cordial nature.

The First Army Corps under General Brooke is nearly completed. The Third Army Corps under command of Major-General Wade is nearing completion. The Sixth Army Corps is soon to be organized under Major-General James H. Wilson. General Wilson gained an enviable reputation during the late war as a dashing cavalry officer and will undoubtedly make a creditable record during the present war if it lasts long enough to bring his army into the field. Lieut.-Colonel Hartsuff, an experienced medical officer of the regular army, is Surgeon-in-Chief of the army gathered here, and as such is attached to the staff of General Brooke. Lieut.-Colonel Van Hoff is Chief Surgeon of the Third Army Corps, and has worked incessantly in completing the organization of the medical department under his supervision. He is regarded as one of the ablest executive officers of the medical service, and is known as a warm friend of the medical officers of the National Guard. He has from the very beginning taken a deep and active interest in the work of the Association of Military Surgeons of the United States. Every medical officer of the Third Army Corps should con-

Major-General John R. Brooke.
General in Chief in charge of the Department of the Lakes.

sider it a great privilege to serve under Lieut.-Colonel Van Hoff. The medical department of the First Army Corps is in charge of Lieut.-Colonel Heidekoper of New York, a hard-working, conscientious officer. Major Kimball of Marion, Ind., and Major Woodbury of New York, have reported here and are awaiting with the writer the formation of the Sixth Army Corps. At present my time is profitably occupied by consultations in the camp and by performing operations in the Leiter General Hospital and the St. Vincent's Hospital, Chattanooga. The evenings are occupied by giving lectures on first aid to the Hospital corps. St. Vincent's Hospital has been used as a temporary hospital for the troops until the Leiter Hospital was in condition to receive patients. The abandonment of regimental hospitals meets with the same opposition here as elsewhere, but the wisdom of such a course must be apparent to all who have had experience in the field. Major E. C. Carter, U. S. A., is now in charge of the Leiter General Hospital. He is one of the busiest men in the camp. He is in every way admirably adapted for the position he now occupies. He is straining every nerve to improve and equip the building for the accommodation of from 300 to 500 patients. He has the hearty co-operation of the Surgeon-General and Colonel Hartsuff in pushing the work. About thirty patients are at present in the hospital and in less than two weeks the number of patients will exceed one hundred. Hospital furniture and supplies are arriving every day, and in the course of two weeks the hospital will be fully equipped. The value of this hospital to our sick soldiers can not be overestimated. Mrs. Leiter will have the respect and sincere gratitude of every one of the inmates and of hundreds yet to come. Chickamauga is a quiet little country hamlet where our patients can enjoy to the fullest extent what they are so much in need of, rest and quietude. Six trained nurses have been sent by the Surgeon-General and are now on duty. With the increase in the humber of patients more will be sent. A corner room in the tower on the second story has been set aside as an operating room and is now undergoing the necessary repairs to adapt it for this purpose. The first operation performed in this hospital was for empyema following pneumonia. Two additional cases await a similar operation during the course of the week.

CRAWFISH SPRINGS.

One of the great attractions near the National Park and adjacent to the Leiter General Hospital is the famous Crawfish Springs. At the end of a large basin and at the base of a rock a large volume of water, as clear as a crystal, is poured out with considerable force. This spring yields 62,000,000 gallons of water in twenty-four hours. The temperature of the water is 56 degrees F., summer and winter alike. The dam a little

Major-General James H. Wilson.

below the springs, utilized to furnish water power for the hotel, has been removed for the reason that it interfered with the supply of water, deviating it evidently through subterranean channels in another direction. As soon as the property was transferred to Mrs. Leiter for Government use I had the basin cleaned out of moss and dirt by a detail of soldiers furnished by the Fifth Illinois Infantry. The sides of the hill around the basin were ditched a few feet above the level of the water for the surpose of draining the surface water to a safe distance below the springs. The Hospital is supplied with water from this spring. Besides, hundreds of barrels of water are brought daily into the camp by mule teams. The water is wholesome and palatable.

The following is the result of a chemical analysis made by a competent chemist:

ANALYSIS OF CRAWFISH SPRINGS WATER.

Bicarbonate of lime	0.6753
Bicarbonate of magnesia	0.4544
Sodium chlorid	0.856
Potassium chlorid	0.048
Silica	0.0537
Free ammonia	0.0029
Albuminoid ammonia	0.0025
Oxygen absorbed	0.031

The presence of free ammonia and albuminoid of ammonia, although small in quantity, led us to suspicion the presence of organic matter which might possibly prove to be a source of danger. For the purpose of testing the water still further as to its fitness for hospital and camp use, samples were sent at three different times to the professor of chemistry in the Chattanooga Medical College. Dr. H. Berlin made a very careful chemic analysis and bacteriologic examination with the result that he pronounced the water free from dangerous organic matter and pathogenic microbes. The only microbe which he was able to cultivate was the colon bacillus, and the presence of this microbe could be readily accounted for by the blocking of the sewer pipe, an evil which was promptly removed. The springs would furnish an ample water-supply for the whole army if the Government would only erect a pumping station near it, a project which is now under serious consideration. With such an improvement Camp George H. Thomas would be one of the most salubrious camping places in the United States for a large army. The intake now is some distance below the springs where the flow of water is impeded by a dam two miles and a half below the springs. Above the dam is a narrow beautiful lake two miles and a half in length, extending to near the springs, which is leased by the Chickamauga Fishing Club.

CHATTANOOGA MEDICAL SOCIETY.

This medical society meets twice every month, on the first and third Friday. At the last meeting the subject selected by the committee was "The Modern Treatment of Gunshot

Major-General Joseph C. Breckinridge.

Wounds in Military Practice." The writer was invited to open the discussion. After a brief résumé of the character of wounds inflicted by the modern bullet, the treatment was considered in detail. Special stress was placed upon the inutility of the ordinary and Nélaton's probe in locating and finding bullets lodged in the body. Attention was called to the value of the

X-ray as a substitute for the probe in making a reliable diagnosis. The use of the bullet probe on the battlefield was condemned and the advice given that bullet wounds should be hermetically sealed with the first aid package, which should contain an antiseptic powder composed of boracic acid and salicylic acid (4:1), and no exploration made until the patient reaches the field hospital, where all facilities for aseptic surgery and the necessary instruments for diagnosis and operation should be at hand. A new bullet probe and bullet forceps devised by the writer were exhibited and their manner of use explained. The balance of the paper treated of gunshot wounds of the extremities, cranium, chest and abdomen. For want of time consideration of the last subject, "Gunshot Wounds of the Abdomen," was postponed until the next meeting. Invitations to attend the meeting were sent to the military surgeons in camp, consequently the attendance was large and the discussion became general and proved of interest to all present. Considering that Chattanooga has only 40,000 inhabitants and that the average attendance at these meetings on ordinary occasions is never less than from thirty-five to forty, is the surest indications that our colleagues in this city take an active interest in the scientific work of the profession.

AMUSEMENTS.

The civilian soldier finds it difficult to satisfy his mind and body with what is required of him in camp life. But a few weeks ago he was a professional man, a clerk, teacher, or left the school, workshop and plow, and now it is hard for him to imagine that he should not be kept busy from sunrise to sunset. He is only too anxious to drill in sunshine or rain, and considers it a privilege to do guard duty, where his power and military significance can be made to appear at greatest advantage. He finds it difficult to occupy his many leisure hours in a profitable manner. To the credit of our soldiers it must be said that evidences of intemperance are rarely seen in camp. Temperance canteens are common and are better patronized than those in which beer is sold. I have not seen an intoxicated soldier since I arrived in camp. The more common amusement of the soldiers during the heat of the day, between 10 A.M. and 3 P.M., between drill hours, consists in reading, writing letters, playing cards, and the college boys are bound to play base- or football. The chaplains make themselves useful not only in caring for the spiritual welfare of their soldiers, but they also look after their intellectual interests. They extemporize reading-rooms and supply them with writing and reading material. These reading tents are very popular, and when the men are off duty they are always crowded. The many regimental bands furnish excellent music, which does so much in cheering up and amusing the soldiers. Two theaters have sprung up in the camp, mushroom-like. Performances are given in the afternoon and evening. The admission fee is twenty-five cents, box seats fifty cents. I have been told by those who have been in the habit of attending that the plays are good and that the patrons are made to feel that they have received their money's worth.

RED CROSS ASSOCIATION.

The Medical Department during the present war is in a condition fairly well prepared to supply the sick and wounded with the necessary instruments, medicines and food. There will be only a very limited field of usefulness for the Red Cross Association to fill in defects here and there as occasion and circumstances may require. The work of the Red Cross Association is, however, recognized by the War Department, as becomes evident from a circular letter received a few days ago from the Surgeon-General:

SURGEON-GENERAL'S OFFICE, WASHINGTON, June 9, 1898.

Lieutenant-Colonel Nicholas Senn, Chief Surgeon U. S. Volunteers, Sixth Army Corps, Chickamauga Park, Ga.

Sir:—The Secretary of War has approved the following proposition made by the American National Red Cross Association, and the chief surgeons of the Army corps and divisions will co-operate with the authorized agents of this Association for the purposes indicated :

" We can put any desired amount of hospital supplies—ice, malted milk, condensed milk, Mellin's food, etc., into any of the volunteer camps in a few hours. Will you be kind enough to bring this letter to the attention of Secretary Alger and ask him if there is any objection to our appointing a Red Cross representative to report to the commanding officer and the chief surgeon in every camp, confer with them as to their immediate needs and, if anything of any kind is wanting, open there a Red Cross station and send in the supplies. We can do this, not in a few weeks or a few days, but in a few hours, and can furnish any quantity of any desired luxury or delicacy for hospital use. We hereby tender our aid and put our organ-

ization at the War Department's service for co-operation in the field."
 Very respectfully,
GEO. M. STERNBERG, Surgeon-General U. S. A.

It was prudent and wise that the Surgeon-General and the Secretary of War granted this modest request. Dr. Gill of New York represents the Red Cross Association here. He arrived a few days ago and intends to erect a frame building near the general headquarters as a storehouse for the supplies. He possesses excellent executive abilities combined with modesty, which will ensure him a wide avenue of usefulness and the hearty appreciation of the medical officers. In my next communication I will speak of the hospital corps, its organization and scope of work in actual warfare.

ASSIGNED TO A NEW FIELD.

War always has been and always will be a cruel thing. The very object of war is to kill, disable, maim and starve until the result of the contest shall decide the issue by demonstrating the superiority of one army over the other in number, courage or skill of warfare. "The battle is the Lord's," but victory is not always on the side of justice. The Lord teaches, rules and benefits the children of men now, as during the time of the prophets, as often by defeat as victory. The God of battles has ways and means often impossible to comprehend, but they always lead to results beneficial to mankind. The terrors and sufferings of war are the prices paid for defeat as well as victory. The wonderful improvements made in weapons and projectiles during the last quarter of a century have made modern warfare more destructive if not less cruel. It is difficult to foretell the relative number of dead and wounded in the engagements of the future. Reliable information on the subject must come from actual observation on a large scale on the battlefield and not from the results of experiments on the lower animals and the cadaver. Warfare has become a science and an art, and victory will depend as much on the skill and foresight in strategy of the commanding officers as the endurance and valor of the troops. The long range rifles and the better marksmanship of the average soldier will increase the distance between the fighting lines and give the commanding officers better opportunities for the exercise of their skill in maneuvering the troops. In every respect war will and must assume more scientific aspects for the display of skill. What the improvements will be can only be determined by experience on a large scale. The rapid mobilization of troops, supply of ammunition along the line of battle, flank movements, the quick digging of shallow entrenchments for the protection of the soldiers in line of battle, are some of the important subjects which are engaging the minds of our wide awake military officers and which await a satisfactory solution by as yet an unknown second Napoleon. Let us hope that this important person is now in existence, an American citizen and now engaged in the present war with Spain.

HOSPITAL CORPS.

The humane side of the present methods of warfare is best shown by the organization of an efficient hospital and ambulance corps. The sick and wounded of the great war of the rebellion suffered indescribable pain and agony owing to inadequate provisions for transportation, first aid and nursing by

Private, hospital corps U.S. Army, field equipment (front view).   Private, hospital corps U.S. Army, field equipment (rear view).

men detailed for this special purpose. Our sick and wounded can look forward more hopefully for more prompt and efficient treatment. The Government, through the Surgeon-General and Secretary of War, is making ample preparations for the prompt and efficient treatment of those requiring medical or surgical aid. The prevention of disease by the employment of improved hygienic and sanitary measures will do much in minimizing the number of ignominious deaths in the field and general hospitals and in maintaining the full fighting force. The need of a well organized and well equipped hospital corps became apparent during our late war, but it was many years after the Union was restored before the necessary legislation was effected which brought it into existence. The Hospital Corps in the United States Army was created by an act of Congress approved March 1, 1887.

The law under which the Hospital Corps was established and as revised by March 16, 1895, and March 16, 1896, reads as follows:

(The Military Laws of the United States, 1897.)

"673. That the Hospital Corps of the United States Army shall consist of hospital stewards, acting hospital stewards and privates; and all necessary hospital services in garrison, camp or field (including ambulance service) shall be performed by the members thereof, who shall be regularly enlisted in the military service. Said Corps shall be permanently attached to the Medical Department, and shall not be included in the effective strength of the Army nor counted as a part of the enlisted force provided by law.

"674. That the Secretary of War is empowered to appoint as many hospital stewards as, in his judgment, the service may require; but not more than one hospital steward shall be stationed at any port or place without special authority of the Secretary of War. That there shall be no appointments of hospital stewards until the number of hospital stewards shall be reduced below one hundred, and thereafter the number of such officers shall not exceed one hundred.

"675. That the pay of the hospital stewards shall be forty-five dollars per month, with the increase on account of length of service as is now, or may hereafter be allowed, by length of service, as is now or may hereafter be allowed by law, to other enlisted men. They shall have rank with ordnance sergeants and be entitled to all the allowances appertaining to that grade.

"676. That no person shall be appointed a hospital steward unless he shall have passed a satisfactory examination before a board of one or more medical officers as to his qualification for the position, and demonstrated his fitness therefor by service of not less than twelve months as acting hospital steward; and no person shall be designated for such examination except by written authority of the Surgeon-General.

"677. That the Secretary of War is empowered to enlist or cause to be enlisted, as many privates of the Hospital Corps as the service may require, and to limit or fix the number, and make such regulations for their government as may be necessary; and any enlisted man in the army shall be eligible for transfer to the Hospital Corps as a private. They shall perform duty as wardmasters, cooks, nurses, and attendants in hospital, and as stretcher-bearers, litter-bearers and ambulance attendants in the field, and such other duties as may by proper authority be required of them.

"678. That the pay of privates of the Hospital Corps shall

Litter drill.

be eighteen dollars per month, with the increase on account of length of service as is now or may be hereafter allowed by law to other enlisted men; they shall be entitled to the same allowances as a corporal of the arm of service with which on duty.

"679. That privates of the Hospital Corps may be detailed as acting hospital stewards by the Secretary of War upon the recommendation of the Surgeon-General whenever the necessities of the service require it; and while so detailed their pay shall be twenty-five dollars per month, with increase as above stated. Acting hospital stewards, when educated in the duties of the position, may be eligible for examination for appointment as hospital stewards as above provided."

Since the original law providing for a hospital corps was passed many new features have been added which have made this branch of the military service more efficient.

The pay of members of the Hospital Corps is according to grade, as follows per month: Hospital steward, $45; acting hospital steward, $25; private, $18.

To the rates of pay enumerated above, 20 per cent. is added in time of war.

During the present war the commander of an army corps, or of a division, or of a brigade acting independently of a corps, has full control of enlistments for the Hospital Corps within his command, and of the detail of acting hospital stewards and the appointment of hospital stewards. The Hospital Corps force of the present war is made up three per cent. of the privates obtained by special enlistment or transfer from the line, that is, a regiment of 1000 men is entitled to 30 men for the Hospital Corps. The allowance for horses, wheel transportation and tentage is ample, as will be seen from the following order recently issued by the War Department:

GENERAL ORDERS. } HEADQUARTERS OF THE ARMY.
ADJUTANT GENERAL'S OFFICE,
No. 76. } WASHINGTON, June 22, 1898.

1.—By direction of the Secretary of War, the following allowance of horses for mounts, wheel transportation, tentage, etc., for the Medical Department of the Army in the field is authorized:

HORSES FOR MOUNTS.

	Hospital stewards.	Acting hospital stewards.	Privates.
To each regiment of infantry	1	......	1
To each artillery battalion (3 light batteries)	......	3	1
To each cavalry regiment	1	......	2
To each corps headquarters	1	......	2
To each division headquarters	1	......	1
To each brigade headquarters	1	......	1
To each division ambulance company	7	3	12
To each corps reserve ambulance company	7	3	12
To each division field hospital	2	2	6
To each corps reserve hospital	2	2	6

Wheel transportation.—One ambulance to 400 men of the effective force. One 4-horse wagon to 600 men of the effective force. One 4-horse wagon to each brigade.

Tentage.—For each ambulance company: 17 common tents for privates; 2 common tents for noncommissioned officers. For each division field hospital: 15 common tents for privates; 2 common tents for noncommissioned officers; 1 common tent for supplies. Hospital tents on a basis of 6 patients (beds) to each tent. Hand litters, with slings, to be furnished by the Quartermaster's Department: 1 for each company; 2 for each ambulance.

Requisitions for the necessary articles of camp and garrison equipage, tools, etc., will be based on the official allowances for companies of infantry.

Requisitions for the before mentioned supplies will be sent in separately for *divisions*, with statement whether or not the division organization is complete.

Horses and wheel transportation will be furnished by the Quartermaster's Department, and horse equipments by the Ordnance Department.

II.—Commanding Generals of Army Corps are directed to detail, upon the application of Chief Surgeons of Corps, two officers not above the grade of first lieutenant for duty as Acting Assistant Quartermasters with the medical service of each division.

BY COMMAND OF MAJOR GENERAL MILES:
H. C. CORBIN,
Adjutant General.

Litter drill.

As usual, many difficulties have presented themselves in the way of securing the necessary material both in quantity and quality, for the Hospital Corps during the present campaign.

The commanding officers are always averse to lose the most desirable men of the line. I have reason to believe that at the present time the importance of a good Hospital Corps is appre-

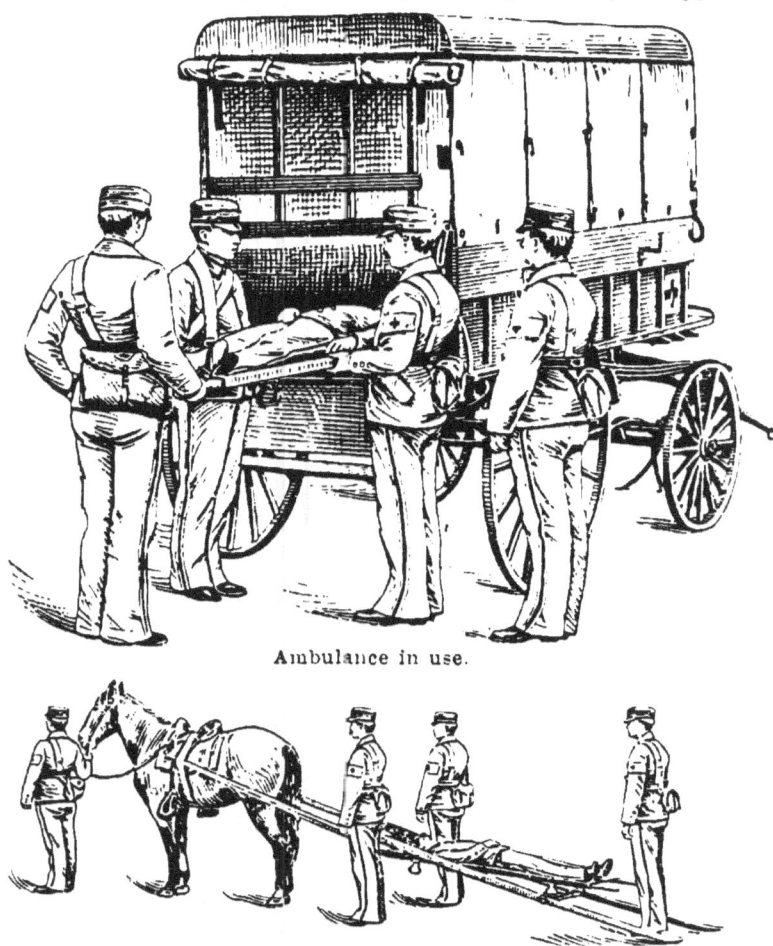

Ambulance in use.

Travois.

ciated more than ever by the commanding officers. The field officers have co-operated with the corps surgeons in the selection of the best men for this special service. The work of organization has progressed slowly, but on the whole in a satisfactory manner. The enormous demand for equipments and the sudden mobilization of troops have contributed much in retarding the organization and instruction of the Hospital Corps. The designation of the Corps as a Hospital Corps does not convey the proper meaning of the manifold purposes for which the men are enlisted and transferred, and has been the means of misleading many a patriotic doctor and medical student now engaged in this branch of military service. Many complaints are heard because instead of doing hospital duty proper the men are made to cook, drive ambulances, chop wood, dig sinks and haul water. There are today too many doctors and medical students in the Hospital Corps. The duties of the Hospital Corps are manifold, and in their proper discharge requires more skilled artisans than medical men. A good Hospital Corps should consist largely of young, bright, intelligent, robust men skilled as carpenters, cooks, blacksmiths, stenographers, photographers, ambulance drivers, tailors, shoemakers and other trades. Doctors and medical students should be in the minority, and ought not to exceed twenty-five per cent. of the non-combatant force. If the legitimate function of the Hospital Corps were better understood there would be fewer applications for this service on the part of professional men. The general impression prevails that the duties of the members of the Hospital Corps are less onerous than those of the private soldier of the line. It is difficult to conceive how such an idea could have originated. It is also understood that the non-combatant soldier is exposed to less risk of life than his comrade of the line, when the fact is apparent that in addition to the ordinary dangers incident to warfare, he is more exposed to the greatest source of danger—disease. The nursing in the field hospital is done exclusively by the Hospital Corps men, and involves much loss of sleep and constant care and attention. The transportation of sick and wounded is a task requiring good judgment, promptitude and care. A combination of firmness and gentleness, thoughtfulness of action and a determination to perform duty regardless of rest and comfort, is an essential element of success in the work of every Hospital Corps man. The climatic influence, the prevalence of tropical diseases will tax to the utmost the resources of the Hospital Corps during the present war with

Spain. That the work will be well and cheerfully done I have no doubt, judging from my observations during the last two months.

The American people expect that the sick and wounded of this war shall receive the best possible attention, and in this they will not be disappointed. The Government, although sometimes necessarily tardy, is willing and anxious to do all in its power to alleviate the horrors of this war, and in this humane intention it will receive the hearty co-operation of the Hospital Corps. The writer has been permanently detached from the Sixth Army Corps now at Chickamauga by a recent order, and is now on his way to Santiago de Cuba on special duty. He goes to the front as Chief of the Operating Staff with the troops in the field. For the purpose of informing my many friends among your readers what I am expected to do, I append a copy of the letter assigning me to my new field of labor.

HEADQUARTERS OF THE ARMY.
WASHINGTON, D. C., June 29, 1898.

Lieutenant-Colonel NICHOLAS SENN, U. S. V., Chief of the Operating Staff.

Sir:—In assigning you as Chief of the Operating Staff, the Major General Commanding the Army directs me to say that, at the several points to which you may be assigned to duty, you will confer with the Chief Surgeon of the Corps engaged as to the means by which you may consult with and advise the medical officers serving with that army regarding the clinical features of their professional work; that you will recommend such methods, either by lectures or operative demonstration, as may in your judgment be best suited to accomplishing the purpose in hand; that you will take the necessary steps for collecting data upon which the clinical and pathologic records of the field and hospital service may be classified, and from which the future medical and surgical history of this war may be prepared. Your present assignment will be for duty with the Fifth Army Corps, now operating before Santiago de Cuba, and at such future time as the General Commanding may decide, you will be transferred to other points where active military operations are progressing.

Very respectfully,
COL. CHAS. R. GREENLEAF,
Asst. Surg.-Genl. U. S. A., Chief Surgeon, Army in the Field.

I hope I will reach Santiago before surrender and enter it with our victorious troops. My address for the present will be
Fifth Army Corps, Santiago, Cuba.

My next communication will be from the seat of war.

THE FLOATING HOSPITALS.

OFF SANTIAGO DE CUBA, July 7, 1898.

The government, the different charitable societies, local, State and general, and the people, have from the very beginning of this war vied with each other in adopting and carrying into effect means and measures to provide comfort and efficient treatment for the sick and wounded. A commendable unity and harmony of action prevails throughout the entire country to bring about the best results. Desultory action, so common during the War of the Rebellion and that did so much in retarding the philanthropic work at that time, has largely given way to well organized, systematic efforts which will be sure to result in the greatest amount of good to all in need of such assistance. The patriotism of the people is only equaled by their generosity to those who are now engaged in the defense of the honor and dignity of their country. The outside world will watch the progress and extent of the humanitarian work displayed during this war with as keen an interest and degree of admiration as the victories of our army. The collection and distribution of funds, clothing, delicacies and hospital supplies is in the hands of responsible persons, and the liberal donors can be assured that the articles contributed will reach the intended destination. Many of the railway corporations have shown a laudable willingness to forward contributions of this kind at greatly reduced rates, a concession which will materially increase the usefulness of the various societies which have been or will be organized throughout the land for the distinct purpose of aiding the government in properly caring for those who have been disabled from injury or disease. Efforts in this direction are best calculated to stimulate the patriotism and heroism of our soldiers in the field. One of the noblest undertakings for this purpose is the action of the government in the recent purchase and outfitting of two large ocean vessels for hospital and ambulance use. The Navy has the *Solace*, and the *Relief*, now under sail for the seat of war, is intended for the Army. The seat of war makes the use of these ships an absolute necessity for the proper care of the sick and wounded. Both of these ships are floating hospitals supplied with all the facilities of a modern hospital.

The Hospital Ship "Relief."- -This communication is written on board the hospital ship *Relief*, on its first trip to the seat of war. The ship started from New York, July 2, and called at Fortress Monroe in the afternoon of the following day for the purpose of taking on board a number of surgeons, including the writer. Surgeon General Sternberg awaited her arrival, and made a thorough inspection before her departure. The name of the ship appears particularly appropriate from the conditions under which we left Fortress Monroe, Sunday, July 3. Shortly before leaving Fortress Monroe cable messages announced that fierce fighting was in progress on the third day of the battle of Santiago. They also announced to the anxious crowd that gathered around the bulletin boards at the hotel Chamberlin, that the number of killed and wounded on our side had reached the neighborhood of 1200, and that the enemy showed greater strength and resistance than had been anticipated. General Shafter, in command of the invading army, had sent a telegram to New York asking for the immediate despatch of the *Relief*. There can be no doubt but that the appearance of the boat is eagerly looked for at the seat of war, and that upon her arrival she will merit the name she bears. The *Relief* was formerly the John Englis, and was purchased by the Government, some six weeks ago, from the Maine Steamship Line, for $450,000. She was the sister ship of Horatio Hall, and was used a year and a half as a coast liner between New York and Portland, Maine. She was built by the Delaware River Iron Ship Building and Engine Works, Chester, Delaware, in 1896. She was well adapted for the coast service, and it was a rare opportunity when she was secured for Government service. The vessel is 300 feet in length, 46 feet in width, draws 15 feet of water forward and $16\frac{1}{2}$ feet aft, and has an average speed of 14 knots an hour. She carries two masts, one smoke-stack, and is supplied with large ventilators. The latter are of especial importance after her reconstruction into a hospital ship. Major Torrey, Surgeon U. S., formerly stationed at West Point, is in command of the ship, and had charge of the work of reconstruction in

making the necessary changes in adapting her for hospital use.
Many important changes in the interior of the ship had to be
made in transforming an ordinary passenger steamer into a
hospital ship. The major has spent six anxious, trying weeks
in accomplishing this. He availed himself of the valuable services of Naval Constructor Bowles. The work was done at the
foot of Ninth street, New York, and was watched with great
interest by the public and the medical profession in that city
and surrounding towns. Many of the staterooms had to be
removed to make space for five capacious wards. About 650
men were employed night and day in pushing the work to completion as rapidly as possible. American pluck and energy
were well displayed in completing the herculean task in four
weeks. The entire expense of reconstruction will reach nearly
$150,000, so that the ship costs the Government about $600,000.
I doubt if any other equal sum for any other purpose will do
so much for our army as this floating house for the disabled
soldiers.

The interior of the ship is so arranged that every nook and
corner can be utilized to advantage. On the hurricane deck
forward is the search-light on the pilot house, the pilot house,
pilot's and ship officers rooms. Center and aft are canopied
for convalescents, and are well supplied with long wooden
benches and steamer chairs. Eight life boats and four rafts
constitute the life-saving outfit. There are also two steam
launches 28 feet in length with a speed of nine knots an hour.
The upper saloon deck is intended for medical wards mainly.
Ward No. 1 is forward and has 82 beds. The iron bedsteads are
of special construction, securely fastened to the floor. The
cots in use are iron framed double-deck beds of single width,
with wire spring mattress and adjustable side rails. Cotton
mattress, linen sheet, two blankets and two horsehair pillows
constitute the bed proper. Each bed has a wire basket attached
for dressing material and medicines.

This ward is supplied with two toilet rooms, a stationary
bath tub and sink in middle of ward, with adjustable canvas
screen. Provision has also been made here for hot and cold
water shower bath. The room is lighted by four reflectors
with six incandescent burners to each, and a number of green
shaded incandescent burners. Four electric fans will prove a

source of comfort during hot weather. The center of this floor is devoted to state rooms for the female nurses, mess room for ward No. 1, and a large pantry containing tableware and facilities for preparing special diet. Ward No. 2 aft end of the ship with a capacity of 64 beds is connected by a hatchway with ward No. 4 below. Bath, toilet rooms, electric lighting and fans same as in ward No. 1. Forward on lower saloon deck are the sailor's quarters, offices, sleeping apartments and mess room for the medical officers, medical library and a small ward of 28 beds, well lighted and ventilated. In the center of this deck is the kitchen and mess room for the hospital corps and male nurses. At the entrance of the gangway and in a corner of the large surgical ward with 74 beds is the operating room. This room is large enough for all practical purposes, and contains two operating tables, a high pressure steam sterilizer, reagent and dressing cases, stationary wash stand, two instrument cases, two formalin sterilizers and two electric fans. The floor is made of interlocking rubber tiles. The fourth ward is well lighted and ventilated. On one side of this ward are stationed a static and X-ray apparatus under the management of Dr. Gray.

On the lower deck forward is the fireman's forecastle (27 beds), an ice machine with a capacity of a ton and a half a day, a refrigerator and an apparatus for manufacturing carbonated water at the rate of 100 bottles an hour, a water condenser (sixty gallons an hour) and a sterilizer (carriage 4 feet, 6 inches by 8 feet, 6 inches, which can be used for the disinfection of large articles by, a, steam under ten pounds of pressure at 240 F., b, formaldehyde, c, ammonia). In the center of this deck are the carpenter's and plumber's shop and a steam laundry of ample dimensions. Forward aft on this deck is ward No. 5 with forty beds, mess room and quarters for the hospital corps. A small laboratory for scientific work has been fitted up with many of the modern facilities and has been placed in charge of Dr. Gray of the Army Medical Museum. If Santiago has not been taken by the time we arrive the ship will be anchored at the most convenient point near the shore and the transfer of patients will be made by the use of the two steam launches on board. Arrangements have been made for taking patients aboard by canvas basket, by hoisting boat, or by stretcher up the stair gang, which for this purpose has been made much wider than usual. The ship is in charge of Capt. Frank Harding, First Officer C. W. Crocker, Second Officer Harksen, Engineer Charlton and a crew of sixty-eight men. Major Tomey is assisted by Major W. C. Gourgas and Major Bradley, both of the United States Army. Lieut. J. T. Crabbs, 8th U. S. Cavalry, is quartermaster and commissary, and Rev. George Robinson, U. S. A., and Rev. Father J. N. Connolly of New York, are the chaplains. Thre are sixteen trained nurses on board, ten male and six female, and a detachment of twenty-nine hospital corps men. The names of the female nurses are: Miss Elise H. Lampe, Miss Louise Jones Block, Miss Amy B. Furguhasson, Miss Lucy Ashby Sharp, Miss Amanda J. Armistead, Miss Esther Voorhes Hasson. The following contract surgeons have been assigned to duty on the ship: Drs. Myers, Schultz, Tierney, Jr., Williamson, Hartlock and Metcalf. The ship carries a large supply which will meet the immediate demands of the suffering troops. Every one on board is anxious to reach the destination to lend a helping hand. The female nurses have utilized the time in preparing the wards for the reception of patients. If it were not for the blue ocean, the waves and the motion of the ship, it would be difficult to realize that we are not in a well-regulated, well-equipped hospital on terra firma instead of a floating hospital. Tomorrow (July 7) the doors of this great floating institution will be thrown open for the benefit of those who have become incapacitated for duty in the field, and there is a great probability that every cot will be occupied in less than twenty-four hours after its arrival at the seat of action. The journey so far (July 6, 10 A.M., off San Salvador) has been a very pleasant and auspicious one. A stiff breeze from the south is fanning every room and cheering and invigorating its inmates. All is in readiness to fulfill the mission for which this messenger of mercy has been sent to the distant seat of war. Thousands of anxious hearts at home and in Cuba are following its course in thought and prayer and will be rejoiced when they know that its anchor has been dropped and its deck cleared for action.

THE MEDICAL DEPARTMENT OF THE ARMY IN THE CUBAN CAMPAIGN.

ON BOARD THE HOSPITAL SHIP "RELIEF," July 31, 1898.

In an editorial of the *Medical Record* of July 30, suspicions are thrown out reflecting on the efficiency, foresight and proper management of the Medical Department of the Army during the Cuban Campaign. The remarks made by the editor are based, as he himself asserts, almost exclusively on a correspondence which appeared in a recent issue of the *Sun*. In commenting on this article the editorial states: "If the report is true, and there seems to be no good reason for doubting it, the Army Medical Department appears in a very unenviable light. It is said that there was a total lack of everything necessary for the proper care of the stricken soldiers. Why this was so it is hard to explain, especially in view of the fact that the war department has constantly declared, in declining voluntary assistance from charitable organizations, that it was abundantly able to cope with any possible emergency in the field, and yet this is the result." The correspondent of the *Sun* made bold in saying: "It was evident that the Medical Department of the Army had failed absolutely to send hospital supplies, or by this time they would have been landed. On the one hand it was pitiful. On the other, it was negligence that could have been the result only of incompetence." I am sure if the editor of the *Medical Record* had been better informed he would not have been so willing to lend his ear to a newspaper correspondent whose success nowadays consists largely in tinging facts with more or less imagination and sensationalism. The medical men inside and outside the army have little, if any, influence over the lay press, but the editor of a medical journal of such high standing with the medical profession throughout the entire country as has been willingly accorded the *Medical Record*, should take the necessary pains to investigate more thoroughly the circumstances which dictated the editorial before casting any reflections whatsoever on the chief of the medical department. Dr. George M. Sternberg is no stranger to the medical profession and the American people. He occupies the exalted position of Surgeon-General of the United States Army, not by political preferment or gradual ascent by promotion, but by merit. President Cleveland made a wise selection when he made the appointment. It was a selection that met with the heartiest approval on all sides. General Sternberg knows from long and actual experience what it is to be a soldier in the field. He has been there. He served with distinction during the War of the Rebellion. He has followed the unruly and wily Indians over plains and mountains during many a campaign. He has investigated yellow fever at home and abroad, regardless of his own health and life. Since he has been placed in charge of the Medical Department of the Army he has been tireless in making many much-needed improvements.

The Army Medical School is one of the many fruits of his labors. He has taken special interest and pride in promoting the intellectual and professional advancement of his young army surgeons, assigning them for temporary duty in large cities, where they could enjoy clinical instruction and laboratory work. He has taken a deep and active interest in the organization and usefulness of the Association of Military Surgeons of the United States, and served most acceptably as president. Last year he was honored by the profession by election to the Presidency of the AMERICAN MEDICAL ASSOCIATION. The earnest devotion to his duties made it impossible for him, to his great regret, to attend the Denver meeting. The name of General Sternberg is often seen on the programs of scientific societies from the Atlantic to the Pacific and from Labrador to the Gulf. He crossed the Atlantic, last summer, to represent his Government at the International Congress, held in Moscow, Russia, and his work there added much to the luster of American medicine. The Surgeon-General, now so unjustly accused of incompetency, not only is accorded a well-deserved place in the front rank of the profession, but his administration shows executive talents which have served him well during the present campaign. He has shown good judgment in the selection of his advisers. Colonels Alden, Greenleaf and Smart, are all men of large experience and admirable executive abilities, as all can testify who have been brought in contact with them. The charge of incompetence and ignorance certainly lacks foundation in the case of General Sternberg and his administration. Now, as to facts. The correspondent of the *Sun* who furnished all the material for the editorial referred to goes on to say: "The wounded were carried back from the fighting line on stretchers, and laid on the ground to wait until the surgeons could reach them. Many

Brigadier-General George M. Sternberg, Surgeon-General of the Army.

were soon beyond the need of surgical treatment. There were four divisions of the army, and each division was supposed to have its hospital; but as a matter of fact there was but one, the division hospital of the Fifth Army Corps, under Major Wood. There were five surgeons, a hospital steward, and twenty assistants, to care for the wounded—several hundred. They had a number of operating tables, a small supply of medicines, but few bandages, and no food for sick or wounded men. It was comparatively easy to get supplies from the *State of Texas* ashore to the hospital here (Siboney), but there was no transportation to the front." In the opinion of the editor of the *Medical Record* and the correspondent of the *Sun* the Red Cross Association's work was the only redeeming feature of the whole campaign, to judge from the language of the latter: "God knows what we should have done here without the help of the Red Cross—your ship, your surgeons, and your nurses! and there is no other help for us at the front. Our wounded up there must have food, bandages, anything you can let us have in the line of hospital supplies." The editorial in the *Medical Record* brings matters to a focus in the closing extract: "It is right and proper that the Surgeon-General should resent any interference with his prerogatives, but he should not directly invite it by making possible such a condition of affairs as here described." This inference is entirely unwarranted by facts as they existed during and after the battle of Santiago.

The correspondent and editorial do not even mention the steamer *Olivette* we found July 7 anchored close to the shore before Siboney. This steamer, in command of Major Appel, U. S. A., was used as a hospital ship. This ship was in place and ready to receive the wounded during the battle. The steamer, at the time mentioned, had on board 300 wounded, who received the best surgical attention and nursing. The next day the steamer left for the United States, the medical staff being reinforced by the addition of Acting Assistant-Surgeon Brown of Chicago from the *Relief*. General Sternberg at an early date recognized the importance of hospital ships during this war. The *Olivette* was chartered for this special purpose, was well equipped and reached the seat of war in time. The hospital ship *Relief*, formerly the *John Englis*, under the supervision of its commander, Major Torrey, was transformed into an ideal floating hospital in less than six weeks and reached Siboney July 7, a day before the *Olivette* left for its home port. Do these things show either negligence or ignorance? Do they not rather demonstrate foresight and an earnest endeavor to better care for the sick and wounded in a way creditable to our country and the chief of the Medical Department? This question can safely be left for the wounded to answer. The Surgeon-General accepted the legitimate services of the Red Cross Association and had reason to expect aid from this source, should pressing emergencies present themselves. The medical officers, the wounded and the sick have every reason to be grateful to Miss Clara Barton, for what she did in furnishing ice, delicacies and medical supplies. The *State of Texas* did excellent work in aiding the Medical Department, but that is no reason why those connected with the Red Cross Association should claim all the credit and undertake to criticise a department of the government which has done all it possibly could in anticipating the requirements of a sudden emergency. It is a source of great regret that there should be any friction whatever between the Medical Department and the friends and supporters of the Red Cross Association. It must be clear to every unprejudiced mind that the treatment of the sick and wounded must remain under the direct care, control and management of the Medical Department, and that the function of Red Cross is rather auxiliary to it than as an independent organization if the greatest amount of good is to be realized from it. The hospital ship *Relief* brought an immense amount of medical supplies, delicacies, cots, pillows and blankets. When we arrived at Siboney we knew our presence was much needed, and looked in vain for some one to inform us where and how to land. The precipitous and rocky nature of the shore and the great depth of the ocean made it unfavorable to secure anchorage for several days. A single lighter attended to the demands of numerous transport ships. I am sure no one could blame the Medical Department for the unavoidable delay in unloading the supplies. The little steam launches did what could be done in bringing to the shore what was most needed. Major Torrey worked night and day in supplying the requisitions made by the surgeons in the field and hospitals. There was no red tape here, all they had to do was to inform him what was wanted and it was delivered as soon as it could be brought to the shore. The lack of proper transportation facilities from the landing to the front can not be charged to the Medical Department. It took more than a week of the hardest kind of work to land all of the supplies, and, considering the limited facilities available, it is and always must be regarded as a source of satisfaction that it was made possible at all. The *Relief* brought 1000 cots and an ample supply of bankets, which reached the hospitals with as little delay as possible.

Lieut. Crabbs of the 8th Cavalry, showed a creditable degree of ingenuity, energy and often of courage in landing the supplies. The complaint that the sick and wounded lacked medicines and dressing materials is true only to a certain extent. Some of the medicines were exhausted, owing to the unexpected enormous demand, but they were supplied as quickly as could be done under the existing circumstances. The writer had the privilege to operate in all of the hospitals and was always able to find the essential antiseptics and dressing materials required in military practice, and this was at a time when the supplies were at the lowest. There was no lack at any time of stimulants and anesthetics. There is no use in denying the fact that immediately after the battle the tentage and blanket supply were inadequate, but these defects were corrected promptly. War always has had its hardships and discomforts; it can not be prosecuted in parlor cars and clubhouses. Or soldiers expected deprivations and unavoidable discomforts, but on the whole they were subjected to less actual suffering than they had reason to look for. To the credit of the medical officers it must be said they shared the inevitable hardships with the soldiers. They lived on the same food, drank the same water and made the moist ground their beds. The writer will always cherish the memory of the hardships incident to a campaign in a foreign country, a tropical climate and among a strange people. The Cuban campaign was planned and executed so quickly that some omissions and defects had to be expected. It is a source of gratification to know that the complaints made against the medical department have come from newspaper correspondents and camp followers more than from the soldiers themselves. Among the thousands of sick and wounded with whom I have been brought in contact during the Cuban campaign I have seldom heard a complaint; on the contrary, I have heard nothing but words of praise for the hard-working, self-sacrificing medical officers and the department they represent in the field.

THE QUALIFICATIONS AND DUTIES OF THE MILITARY SURGEON.

Nearly five months of continuous service with the army in the camp and field has afforded me an excellent opportunity to make a practical study of the above subject. This time was spent in Camp Tanner, Springfield, Ill.; Camp George H. Thomas, Chickamauga, Ga., and the Cuban campaign, the time being about equally divided in the different places. The first four weeks were occupied in Camp Tanner, where I assisted in the capacity of Surgeon-General of the State in the organization of the State troops. This service brought me into closer contact with the National Guard of our State than at any time before. A physical and professional examination in which I took part brought out the shady as well as the sunny side of their qualifications. The result of my experience here convinced me that the average National Guard surgeon is a faithful doctor, with more than average professional ability, but, with few exceptions, lacking the necessary military training in performing satisfactorily his administrative duties. This is a part of his education that has been sadly neglected in the past and should receive more attention in the future. Very few States make provision for physical examination of the medical officers, consequently some of them have entered the service totally disqualified for participating in an active campaign. Two of the candidates for the volunteer service from the National Guard of Illinois were rejected on this ground. The four weeks' service at Camp George H. Thomas as chief surgeon of the Sixth Army Corps opened up a wide field for extended observations in making comparisons between the work done by the surgeons of the regular army and of the National Guard. The surgeons of the United States Army are all men of superior education, splendid physical development, and those who have been in the service for several years are well versed in the routine work of the Medical Department. However, in all matters pertaining to medicine and surgery the average National Guard surgeon more than holds his own. This superiority of the National Guard surgeon over his colleague of the regular army is no reflection on the latter; it is the natural outcome of circumstances, which made such a difference inevitable. The young army surgeon has to spend many years at small and often out-of-the-way posts, where the opportunities for clinical experience and intercourse with professional colleagues are necessarily limited. He naturally soon falls into the monotonous and routine work of the post life, with little or no inducements to continue his post-graduate, scientific and medical studies. When the time comes to pass an examination he wakes up from his lethargy sufficiently to go through the different compends to prepare himself for the coming ordeal. He breathes easy after he has reached the major's rank, as this promotion forever closes the door of the much-dreaded green room. From now on he is in the line of slow promotion without any extra exertions on his part. He receives his salary and looks confidently for assignments to posts where he can spend the balance of his life in ease and luxury. He has reached a time in life when he feels that he can avail himself of the work of his subordinates without interfering with his emoluments or his position in social and military life. He is conscious of the fact that he has reached a rank and a station in life where it is proper for him to look to his assistants to do the drudgery which he had become accustomed to in the past, and begin to enjoy the life before him. It is different with the military surgeon taken from civil life. He emerges from the turmoils of family practice. From the day of his graduation he has tasted the bitter fruit of active competition. His work has been watched with an envious eye and subjected to sharp criticism by his neighboring colleagues, old and young. He felt from the very beginning of his professional career that success depended upon his own exertions. The average American practitioner is a hustler. He is willing to work night and day to gain a lucrative practice and the social position which goes with it. With few exceptions he knows that what he has learned in college is but the entering wedge to a comprehensive knowledge of the practice of medicine and surgery. He knows that our profession has become a progressive one. His college education tells him what is new today will be old tomorrow. He looks with pity on his colleagues, advanced in years, whose language and practice convince him that they have fallen into a dangerous rut. He reads the numerous medical journals, the great avenues of recent medical literature. He spends his scanty income in purchasing new books and instruments for scientific investigations. All requisitions are made on himself and are honored only by writing his own checks. He joins medical societies, large and small, and attends their meetings regularly. He listens intently to the reading of papers and discussions to increase his store of knowledge and returns to his limited field of action better prepared to battle against disease. He mingles freely with the members of his profession, always ready to absorb and digest new ideas. He makes frequent pilgrimages to his alma mater or some post-graduate school to familiarize himself with the most recent advances in medicine and surgery. Social life has no attractions for him: he has entered the profession for the sole purpose of becoming an influential and successful practitioner. This is the kind of material our National Guard surgeon is made of. No wonder he outweighs the professional military surgeon in practical knowledge required in the treatment of injuries and disease.

The exacting and often onerous duties of the military surgeon in times of war require special qualifications to prepare and fit him for his work. He is not only expected to be well versed in theoretical and practical knowledge of everything pertaining to the practice of medicine and surgery, but he must be endowed with qualities both of mind and body upon which he can rely when engaged under the most trying circumstances. In field work he has often to perform the most difficult tasks with very limited resources. In such instances good common sense and deliberate action go much further in accomplishing what is desired than the finest scholarship and the most profound logical reasoning. The man who can in a few moments extemporize a well-fitting splint out of the simplest materials and perform with the contents of an ordinary pocket case the most difficult operation will do vastly better work on the battlefield than most professors of surgery and the most brilliant operators in civil practice. The surgeon who understands the principles and practice of good cooking is of more service to the troops than the one who can repeat, word for word, the contents of the most exhaustive treatise on materia medica and therapeutics. The medical officer with a full knowledge of hygiene and sanitation and endowed with the faculty of making a rational, practical use of it is preferable to the most expert clinician, as in military practice it is more important to prevent than to treat disease, no matter how successfully and scientifically the latter may be conducted. The all-around medical officer must be a good mechanic; he should know how to use the carpenter's and blacksmith's tools, how to row and sail a boat, how to make a raft and occasionally he will have reason to be thankful if he has learned how to pack a mule and drive an ambulance team. His miscellaneous knowledge of matters and things entirely outside of his legitimate province will be constantly drawn upon from different sources and the more he knows and is willing to impart the more he will be useful and popular. The man who enters the medical department of the army under an impression that he is only expected to treat wounds, set broken bones and prescribe for the ordinary camp ailments makes a serious mistake and will be surely a disappointment both to himself and to those he is expected to serve.

Physical condition.—The ideal military surgeon in possession of the necessary mental and physical qual-

Transfer of wounded to the hospital ship *Relief* at Arroya.

ities to make him so is seldom seen. The most active brains are often found in a frail body. I have often seen in civil life surgeons of great reputation struggling with disease or its effects, or the victims of some congenital or acquired defects, who were wonders in the operating amphitheatre in spite of such disability. I have seen more than once the saddest of all spectacles in professional life—a surgeon, himself the subject of an incurable disease, muster into service every particle of his reserve strength to perform a critical operation with a view of saving the life of another. Achievements of this kind are possible in private practice but are entirely out of the question in military service. The physical condition of the military surgeon must be as nearly perfect as possible. A physical examination as thorough and as painstaking as in the case of a private can only decide upon the necessary physical qualifications of candidates for commission in the medical service. For good reasons this rule is followed in the selection of medical officers for the regular army and there is no ground why the same requirement should not be exacted in the National Guard. During my service at Chickamauga and in the Cuban campaign, I saw more than one volunteer surgeon who ought to have been excluded from the service for physical disability. During a campaign the loss of a single medical officer may prove a great disaster. Of all commissioned officers the surgeon is the most indispensable. The vacant place of a line officer can be filled at a moment's notice without any serious loss to the service: not so with the surgeon. His position is one requiring special training and one that can not be filled without crippling the medical service at some other point. For this, if for no other reason, the medical officer must be in sound health and able to cope successfully with the hardships of a campaign. In battle, and during the prevalence of an endemic or epidemic disease, the medical officer is the one above all others whose strength and endurance are taxed to their utmost extent. His services are required by day and by night. He has no rest, and unless in possession of an iron constitution, his strength fails him and he becomes, if not a fit subject for the hospital, at least a physical wreck, who, if he persists in continuing his work, will often do more harm than good. A number of such instances came to my personal notice during the Cuban campaign. A medical officer should not only be in full possession of health and all that this implies, but he should have been in training to endure hardships of all kinds from early childhood. He need not necessarily be an athlete, but he should be able to walk twenty miles a day or ride forty without fatigue and then be ready to do a night's work should an emergency demand it. The dancing halls and club houses are poor training schools for a successful military career. The labor and hardships encountered in hunting are best calculated to prepare the body for a life of great activity and privation.

The Spanish military hospital in Ponce, Porto Rico.

Frugal living will not only prove conducive to the maintenance of health but will be the best means of initiating the surgeon to the uncertainties of the commissary department when on the march or in the field.

Let every one who chooses the military career dispense with unnecessary clothing and luxuries during early life in order to accustom and adapt himself for his life work, which in time of war will bring the inevitable amount of viscissitudes and even suffering.

The medical officer must be a good horseman, which here not only implies a good rider, but a knowledge of the usual ailments of horses, the treatment, feeding and care of the animals. To sum up, the military surgeon must be a man of vigor, made so by birth and training, with as few requirements in his habits of living as possible, in order that he may resist to the highest degree the influences of climate and disease and prepare himself for the hardships and privations incident to active warfare.

Mental qualifications. — A proper and adequate preliminary education is exacted of every surgeon in the regular army; without it he is not permitted to pass the medical examination. Statistics show that a large percentage of the candidates are dropped at this stage of the examination. This is a reflection on the system of medical education which continues to prevail in our country. About the only evidence of proficiency the National Guard surgeon in most of our States is required to show is his diploma. It makes but little difference when the diploma was obtained. Evidences of a satisfactory preliminary education are not required. In consequence of such an easy entrance into the medical service of our State troops, many of the men who receive commissions are illiterate. By hard post-graduate work they often become good physicians, but they seldom if ever make up for the early defects of their education, which seriously interfere with a successful military career. Is it to be wondered at that when such shortcomings are discovered by their colleagues and officers of the line, they do not command the respect their commissions, should entitle them to? The reports made out by such men speak for themselves, and appear as black stains upon the department they represent. The elevation of the standard of medical education by most of the medical schools throughout the country will gradually wipe out this blemish, but it will take many years before all of the diplomas can be accepted as sufficient proof that their possessors are entitled to recognition by the medical department of the different States. Let us hope that a speedy and radical reform may be instituted in the different States which will accomplish the desired object, and which will make the commission of a medical officer of greater import in showing a higher degree of preliminary and professional proficiency than the diploma of any of our medical colleges. This is a desideratum for the realization of which every one interested in

Ambulance train on the way to the hospital ship *Relief* in the harbor of Ponce.

the success and usefulness of the national guard should willingly use his influence. Fortunately, there are no specialties in military practice. The medical education of a military surgeon must be of the most liberal and broadest kind. His practice is so varied that he may have to be physician, surgeon, oculist, aurist, etc., the same day. The sphere of the regular army surgeon serving at a post includes in addition obstetrics, gynecology and diseases of children. Every military surgeon must be an expert in physical diagnosis and examination of the eye and ear. He must know something about dentistry, he must know how to extract teeth and how to put in a temporary filling in a carious tooth that can be saved. He must be familiar with neurology, the use and application of electricity as a diagnostic and therapeutic resource. In camp and field he is limited to his own resources in the diagnosis and treatment of all kinds of injuries and diseases. He must therefore be well equipped with a thorough knowledge of everything pertaining to surgery and medicine, and is often called upon to represent the different specialties. No amount of preliminary and professional education will make the military surgeon an efficient officer unless he is possessed of an inborn aptitude for the profession. He must be able to apply and make use of his knowledge. Many men of great learning never become successful practitioners. Their store of knowledge fails them when they come to apply it. The military surgeon in camp and field must be a man of quick perception. He must be able to recognize malingering as well as disease. In an emergency he must be in readiness to act intelligently at a moment's notice. Hesitation is dangerous both to the patient and the reputation and good standing of the surgeon. Indecision creates mistrust, procrastination disaster. Quick decision and prompt action are the essential prerequisites of successful emergency work. Successful action, however, must be preceded by thoughtful, systematic preparation. The most successful surgeon is the one who adopts and follows the watchword, *semper paratus*. He should never be caught napping. Careful preparation makes prompt action possible. The successful surgeon makes his plans ahead and supplies himself with the necessary outfit, medicine, dressing materials and instruments before the emergency arises, and when it does so he is fully prepared to meet it. A lack of forethought and systematic preparation accounts for many shortcomings of medical officers in the field and camp, with the necessary evil consequences for those entrusted to their care.

Military spirit.—Any one who enters the medical service of the army as a life avocation will be disappointed unless he does so imbued with a proper military spirit. The military surgeon must be a military man and an integral part of the army, if he wants to do justice to his calling and the department he represents. I fear it is a lack of the proper military spirit

Litter work in the court of the Spanish military hospital in Ponce.

in some of the medical officers in the regular army that is responsible for a well recognizable cleft between them and the officers of the line and field. If this is true in the regular army, it is only too obvious in the National Guard. The rank of the medical officers and their standing in military and social circles suffer when they are regarded and treated as an ordinary doctor. The West Point graduate, educated at the expense of the government, too often forgets that it takes more hard work and a longer time to make a good doctor than an officer. The officers of the National Guard, holding commission by the grace of their governor, do not realize sufficiently that their military surgeons have spent a small fortune and five years in acquiring a knowledge of their profession. They seem to forget, or at any rate often ignore, that when they go into camp or in the field they do so at a great personal and pecuniary sacrifice. Their absence from home, even for a short time, may cause a break in their practice difficult to repair. The medical officer is entitled to recognition as a military man, and if this is not accorded to him voluntarily, he must resort to measures that will enforce it. The lack of military dignity on part of the medical staff is due largely to a lack of the proper military spirit in the members which compose it, and to too great a familiarity between the surgeons and the officers and men. The correction of these evils can not be undertaken too soon, and when accomplished will add much to the dignity, influence and efficiency of the medical department of the army and State troops.

The medical officer who has enjoyed the advantages of an early military training in a military academy or the national guard, is the one best qualified to enforce military rules and assert the dignity of his position.

Punctuality.—The busiest men have always the most time to perform a duty or to meet an engagement at the appointed time. This rule holds good in all walks of life. The drones are always behind. In military life punctuality means everything and from this exaction the medical officer should never be excluded except for special and well founded reasons. In the regular army there is a way of disciplining the medical as well as other officers in coming to time in the performance of definite duties and in making out the reports. My long experience in the National Guard service has taught me, occasionally in a painful way, that the surgeons are often entirely oblivious to the matter of time, especially in the matter of making out and transmitting the regimental reports. It is the men who put off for tomorrow what should be done today, and who meet their engagements at one o'clock or thereafter instead of twelve, that render the life of their superior officers one of misery and full of disappointments. The men that accomplish the most are always ready and on time. The medical officers must be made to understand that a due regard for punctuality in performing their duties,

Court of the Spanish military hospital in Ponce.

in meeting appointments and in mapping out and forwarding reports is one of the most essential features of a successful military career.

Courage.—It is still the general belief that, in times of war the military surgeon is exposed to less danger than the soldiers and officers in command. That this is not so is shown by the statistics of all wars. Although the position of the military surgeon is behind the fighting line, he is usually near enough to the enemy when serving in the front to be reached by stray bullets and bursting shells. The number of surgeons killed and wounded in the performance of their duty in rendering first aid is by no means small in any war of magnitude. In active warfare, however, the greatest danger to the surgeons is to be found in their constant exposure to contagious and infectious diseases, which follow large armies in all climates and during all seasons of the year. To enter a yellow fever camp, to my mind, calls for more courage than to lead and command the troops in the battlefield. Disease always claims more victims than bullets, and this is especially true of the present war with Spain. The nation worships the heroism of those who fell before Santiago, but much less is said of the vastly greater number stricken down by disease, and who have lost their lives from disease, often after prolonged and intense suffering. To the credit of the medical officers of this and other wars it must be said that they showed no fear, either in facing the enemy or what is vastly worse—disease. When yellow fever made its appearance among the troops around Santiago, every man remained at his post and faced the danger without flinching. Men from the North who had never seen the disease accepted the detail for duty in the fever hospitals without a word of complaint. The medical officer must be endowed with more than ordinary courage to face the many dangers that surround him on all sides during every campaign. Patriotism begets heroism and I make a well-founded claim for both for the medical profession represented in the army.

Personal habits.—The old adage that "It is easier to preach than to practice," is a familiar one and should be made to apply with the same force to doctors as preachers. The first and most important duty of the military surgeon is to prevent disease. This can often be done more effectively by example than by precept. The military surgeon must guard the camp against disease. He is looked upon and must be regarded by those under his care as the one above all others who can give them advice in matters pertaining to their health. He is expected to do this by example as well as precept. He must become a permanent object lesson in inculcating the importance of cleanliness in person and in dress. His tent should be the cleanest and most orderly in camp. Temperance in eating and drinking can be taught more successfully by action than by words. A mili-

Transfer of patients to the lifeboat in the harbor of Ponce.

tary surgeon under the influence of liquor will do more harm in encouraging the vice of intemperance than can be undone by weeks of lecturing. Profanity is prevalent in every camp and while it is not the duty of the surgeon to supplant the chaplain in suppressing it, it should receive no encouragement by his example. In his conduct toward the men the surgeon should be firm and dignified, yet kind and sympathetic, especially to those in need of his professional services. An impetuous nature and an irritable temper create a rebellious spirit, which it is difficult to control by the most energetic measures. Proper questions should be answered willingly and with sufficient clearness and adequate length to furnish the desired information, and not gruffly and snappishly, as is occasionally done without any reason or provocation. Overwork and a disordered digestion are poor excuses for treating a subordinate in an undignified, ungentlemanly manner. The military surgeon must be known in camp as a gentleman, not only by the officers but by every man under his charge, if he expects to be respected and to do justice to his high calling and responsible position.

The military surgeon in war.—The true qualities of the military surgeon are crystallized and best known during an active campaign. It is in war that his ready resources will come to the surface and will be subjected to the severest tests. It is in battle and during the prevalence of devastating diseases that his moral courage and physical endurance will be most severely tried. It is under such circumstances that the troops will look to him most confidently as their protector and nearest and dearest friend. It is not in peace but in war that the bond of true comradeship becomes tighter and tighter between him and the officers and men. It is on the march, in camp, and on the battlefield that the important function of the military surgeon receives the recognition to which it is entitled. It is the wounded and the sick in a strange land that look to him for help and restoration to health. It is the surgeon who so often receives the last message of the dying.

The first and most important duty of the military surgeon during active warfare is to prevent disease and unnecessary suffering by giving early advice and resorting to timely precautions. The location of camps, policing of the same, the water-supply, food and clothing are subjects which must receive his early and earnest attention. In this work he should receive

the hearty co-operation of the officers in command
and if this is not the case he has the moral and military authority to demand it. It was not the medical
department, but the arrogance or stupidity of the commanding general of the invading army that is responsible for the extensive outbreak of yellow fever during
the Cuban campaign. This experience is sufficient to
teach commanding generals that it is unsafe in the
future to follow such an example, as an imprudence of
this kind, giving rise to inexcusable slaughter and indescribable suffering, will meet with universal indignation. The military surgeon is in reality the family
physician of the men placed under his charge. He
attends to the little ailments with the same care as
though he had been sent for by a wealthy family and
expected a handsome fee. To be successful in the
treatment of disease he resorts to the simplest medication. Complicated prescriptions are dangerous and
absolutely out of question in military practice. The
tablets containing drugs in the most concentrated form
are a great blessing to field practice and should be
relied upon almost exclusively in the treatment of disease. The remedies needed are few, and if well
chosen and applied will answer all indications. A
liberal supply of quinin, opium, calomel, strychnia,
camphor, iron, arsenic, bicarbonate of soda and bromid of potassium will leave but little to be desired.
Turpentine, castor oil, alcohol and the anesthetics are
about the only fluid medicines the military surgeon
has any use for. The breakage and waste in dispensing medicines in bottles are inexcusable in modern
field work. Fancy drugs and preparations should not
be tolerated. In the practice of surgery the military
surgeon who wishes to attain the maximum success
must be conservative. Strict asepsis and conservatism are the two things which are destined to make
miltary surgery successful. Every surgeon must have
special training in emergency work. He must be
perfectly familiar with the indications and technique
of every operation which may become necessary in

the field. He seldom will have an opportunity to cut for stone, extract a cataract, remove an ovarian tumor or operate for other benign and malignant growths, but he must know how to treat a compound fracture in the most modern and approved manner; he must be skillful in the treatment of wounds of all kinds, and he must be a master in performing an amputation and in ligating arteries in any part of the body. He must learn to perform all emergency operations with the simplest facilities and fewest instruments possible, in order to adapt himself in time to the exigencies of war. The surgeon who can extemporize an operating table in the field and who can secure asepsis with the use of the camp kettle, soft soap and carbolic acid or sublimate and who can perform the most difficult operations with the simplest and fewest instruments, with little or no assistance, is the one who will accomplish the most and who will obtain the best results in the field.

Ponce, Porto Rico, Aug. 8, 1898.

THE INVASION OF PORTO RICO FROM A MEDICAL STANDPOINT.

The occupation of Cuba and the Philippine Islands by our conquering navy and army in such rapid succession seemed to increase the desire of conquest and opportunities to test the strength of our arms. With the destruction of the weak navy of our enemy there was nothing in the way of sending troops to any of the many Spanish possessions. The fall of the heroic Cervera and his faithful little band, off the harbor of Santiago, before the murderous fire of our well-equipped fleet cleared the pathways of the ocean of further sources of danger. It was but natural that the beautiful island of Porto Rico, one of Spain's most valuable possessions, should have been selected by the military authorities as the next objective point for contention. Repeated attacks by our navy on its best stronghold, San Juan, had failed to bring about surrender and to gain a foothold on Porto Rican soil. So far the navy had taken the lead in bringing Spain to terms and the army was anxious to do its share in wresting from its greedy grasp another enslaved people. Major-General Miles, who conducted the invasion in person, decided to march upon San Juan from several directions, and, after uniting the forces, attack the city jointly. The experience gained in Cuba had taught us an important lesson in conducting the Porto Rican campaign. General Miles laid his plans wisely and with special reference to gain the desired object with as little suffering and loss of life as possible. Every movement in this campaign was made with a due regard for the welfare and success of our troops rather than a desire for personal gain and aggrandizement, which characterized the Cuban campaign, as every one knows. He was well aware of the depressing effects of the tropical climate on the unseasoned troops and of the necessity of resorting to timely and efficient precautions in preventing disease. From experience and personal observations, he recognized the fact that the unavoidable privations incident to warfare are multiplied many times when the seat of war is a strange and remote country presenting a climate and environments unaccustomed to by the invading force. His actions were clean-cut admissions that he was in need of a medical adviser and that they were influenced by the frequent consultations held with his chief surgeon. The war in Porto Rico was conducted upon the most humane principles, and although no great battles were fought, victory upon victory followed the footsteps of our army and in less than three weeks our flag floated over three of the largest cities of the island. Our troops love and respect their leader and have followed him without fear and grumbling under the scorching sun, full of confidence and trust. The news that peace had been declared reached the headquarters at Ponce, August 14, and the troops are now resting on their arms awaiting the final adjustment of the terms of peace. Eager to fight, yet every soldier in the field received this message of peace with joy and enthusiasm, fully satisfied that the army had done justice to the flag and country it represents. Col. Charles R. Greenleaf, chief surgeon of the army in the field, accompanied General Miles on his trip from Guantanamo to Porto Rico, and has been with the army ever since. He was long enough in Cuba to gain a full insight into the horrors created by infectious diseases, which so constantly follow large armies, especially in a war of invasion. He was amazed when he saw to what extent yellow fever had broken out in the few weeks the troops had been in Cuba. There was no difficulty in tracing the disease to a total lack of precaution on the part of the general in command.

General Nelson A. Miles, in command of the Army in Porto Rico.
By courtesy of "McClure's Magazine." Copyrighted 1898 by
S. S. McClure Co.

Col. Greenleaf had given his directions and advice before the army left Tampa, but they were not heeded. Owing to want of co-operation on part of General Shafter, the medical officers found themselves powerless in preventing and combating the dreaded disease. Col. Greenleaf's prompt and energetic action on his arrival in Cuba did much in repressing this disease, but it was too late too guard against a general outbreak. The many recent graves in Cuba containing the remains of the victims of this disease are the best proof of what will happen when the leader of an army ignores the health and comfort of his men. In planning the Porto Rican invasion, General Miles availed himself of the invaluable services of his chief surgeon. The expedition was well supplied with medicines, hospital stores and medical officers to meet all possible emergencies. The result has been that the army has been so far singularly exempt from disease, with the exception of typhoid fever and the effects of heat, both beyond the control of the medical officers. Since his arrival in Ponce, Col. Greenleaf has been the busiest man in the army. He has not been content in simply issuing his orders from headquarters, but he has attended in person to the execution of every detail. He has visited the camps and the hospitals and exercised personal oversight over the distribution of hospital supplies, instruments and medicines. Anxious to serve the sick and wounded, impatient when face to face with a slow, hesitating subordinate, he has more than once performed temporarily the duties of an ordinary hospital steward, to furnish a much-needed object-lesson. His work will justify the confidence reposed in him when he was appointed to the high and responsible position he holds during this war.

FIRST SKIRMISH.

General Miles landed with his expedition, which included a number of war vessels, at Guanica, Monday, July 25. The harbor was entered by the now famous

Col. Charles R. Greenleaf, Chief Surgeon of the Army in the Field.

little gunboat *Gloucester*, under the command of Lieut.-Commander Wainwright. A landing was effected by thirty sailors, the Spanish flag was hauled down, and the stars and stripes raised amid the cheers of the sailors, who knew well that what they had just witnessed meant liberty and freedom for the downtrodden people of the island of which they had just taken possession.

The planting of the flag and the deafening cheers which re-echoed from the hills of the liberated island were followed by a volley from the hidden enemy, which was promptly responded to by the guns of the *Gloucester* and a Colt rapid fire gun, which had been taken ashore. The Spaniards fled in confusion and sought shelter among the adjacent hills leaving four killed on the field, while our soldiers escaped without a scratch. The turn of the infantry came soon after landing, in the form of a lively skirmish, in which we lost one killed and fifteen wounded, of whom one died a day or two later. Most of the injuries were flesh wounds, which healed in a remarkably short time. A very interesting incident occurred during this skirmish. The day was hot, and our troops had to ascend a steep hill, from the crest of which the Spaniards defended themselves. One of the volunteer soldiers, outrunning his comrades advanced far ahead of his line and when he nearly had reached the Spanish position was overcome by heat. He fell in a semi-conscious state. A Spanish doctor rushed to his aid with a stretcher and two hospital corps men, administered the necessary restoratives and had him conveyed at once within our line. This one act alone goes to show that the Spaniards have often been unjustly accused of being cruel and inhuman. This certainly has not been the case during the present war. From my own observations I am sure that they have respected the Red Cross. In fact, the Red Cross people of Porto Rico, composed largely of Spaniards, have shown the greatest activity and interest in their humane work during the entire campaign. If anything, they have rather been overzealous, judging from the number of insignia displayed and worn. It was a common thing to see men wear a white cap with an immense red cross on top, another one in front, besides the brassard.

Ponce was taken and occupied without any resistance whatever. The citizens received our soldiers with enthusiasm and manifestations of joy. General Miles was hailed as a long-looked-for friend rather than a conqueror. The next engagement occurred

Fever patients in the court of the Spanish military hospital.

between Arroya and Guayama, between a small Spanish force in ambush and General Haines' brigade, and resulted in eleven wounded on our side. The only death following this skirmish was a soldier of the Third Illinois Infantry who was shot accidentally by an unknown man of the Fourth Pennsylvania regiment. The bullet caused an extensive non-penetrating injury of the chest, from the effects of which he died the next day. Such accidents have occurred too often during the present war, and to prevent repetition in the future this matter should be investigated, as was done in this instance, by the proper authorities. Among the injured was a man who was shot through the pelvis and another one the subject of a gunshot wound of the elbow joint, both of them doing well four days later when I examined the wounded in the brigade hospital at Guayama. The third skirmish took place between the advance column of General Wilson's division, on the march to San Juan, and a small Spanish force intrenched on the summit of a high and steep hill. Lieut. Haines, the son of General Haines, was the only one who was brought on board the *Relief* August 4. One of the wounded was operated on by Dr. Parkhill in an ambulance. The abdomen was torn open by a fragment of a shell, the intestines protruded and a resection had to be made of a loop for a tearing injury. It was reported that the patient rallied well from the immediate effects of the operation and that hopes were entertained of his recovery. Another engagement took place between the troops under command of General Schwan, on their way from Ponce to Mayaguez, and about 1000 Spaniards ambushed four miles from the latter city. This fight resulted in two killed and eighteen wounded on our side. All of the wounded were brought on board the hospital ship *Relief*, which called at Mayaguez on her way to New York, August 15. Such is a brief account of the casualties sustained by our army during the Porto Rican campaign. The experience here coincided with that gained in Cuba, to the effect of confirming the humane nature of the modern weapon. The proportion of killed to wounded is even smaller than in the Cuban war, as well as the number of seriously injured. Thanks to more elaborate preparations for the campaign, the wounded received prompt and efficient attention. The suffering of the well, sick, and wounded can not be compared with what I saw in Cuba. War is a great educator, and should we again be called upon to invade a foreign country, we shall profit by the experience of the past.

TYPHOID FEVER IN PORTO RICO.

The native doctors in Ponce, Porto Rico, gave us the assurance that not a single case of yellow fever had been seen in that city for the last three years. We were informed that in San Juan isolated cases occur from time to time. Malaria is present in all of the valleys, more especially in and around Ponce.

Fever patients in the court of the Spanish military hospital.

The large, pendulous abdomen, and the pale faces of the many little naked children in city and country, are the best witnesses in showing the prevalence of malarial intoxication.

Typhoid fever is endemic in certain localities, but at present Ponce is almost free from this disease. Having seen the destruction of life and the indescribable suffering caused by yellow fever in Cuba, Col. Greenleaf naturally turned his attention toward protecting our troops in Porto Rico against this scourge. The proximity of Porto Rico to Cuba, the many possible sources of infection, made such a course imperative. That this fear was not unfounded, and that the Chief Surgeon recognized the danger and made use of timely precautions are but shown by the contents of a letter addressed to the Adjutant-General, Headquarters of the Army, and Circular No. 1 issued before the army sailed from Guantanamo to Porto Rico, and a copy of the Quarantine Regulations formulated at the same time.

HEADQUARTERS OF THE ARMY,
ON BOARD U.S.S. "YALE," EN ROUTE TO PORTO RICO,
July 23, 1898.

To the Adjutant-General, Headquarters of the Army.

Sir:—I have the honor to submit the following recommendations for preventing as far as possible the introduction of yellow fever into the command now about to land on the island of Porto Rico:

The assignment of an officer of rank, to be placed in command of the base of supplies, with authority to indicate the sites to be occupied by the various supply depots and the hospital, and to enforce the regulations governing the health of the attachés of these departments and the persons who may visit them on business.

The assignment of a sanitary inspector whose duty it shall be to examine all vessels and persons arriving at our base from seaward ports, and to prepare sanitary regulations for the Government of all transportation and persons arriving and departing from the station by land. This officer should have authority to quarantine all suspicious persons and means of transportation, and to disinfect their belongings, either by fire or such other means as may be deemed necessary.

All persons connected with the Army are forbidden to enter any building whatever on the island without express authority from these headquarters, and all buildings in rural districts that may be suspected of harboring the germs of disease should be destroyed by fire or otherwise thoroughly disinfected.

As woven goods, particularly those of woolen fabric, are special carriers of disease, the purchase or acceptance of articles of this kind from stores or inhabitants of the island is strictly forbidden. Any such property found within the lines will be at once destroyed and the holder subjected to punishment.

That commanders of regiments be instructed to prepare their camping grounds with great care and maintain a rigid police in them; under no circumstances shall they camp on ground that has previously been occupied either by troops or by collective bodies of the inhabitants.

That medical officers be required to make frequent inspections of the commands to which they belong, and that any suspicious case of fever be immediately isolated and the fact of its occurrence reported to these headquarters.

Canteens should be filled daily with tea or coffee, and these beverages used habitually instead of water, unless that has been previously boiled. Very Respectfully,

CHAS. R. GREENLEAF, Colonel,
Asst. Surg-Genl. U.S.A., Chief Surg. Army in the Field.

Ward in the Spanish military hospital.

HEADQUARTERS OF THE ARMY,
OFFICE OF THE CHIEF SURGEON, ON BOARD U.S.S. "YALE,"
EN ROUTE TO PORTO RICO.

Circular No. 1. July 24, 1898.

1. Medical officers will, upon receipt of this circular, report to the Chief Surgeon of the Army the number of medical officers, hospital stewards, acting hospital stewards and privates of the Hospital Corps on duty with their command. Also the number of ambulances, litters and tents, and if medical supplies are insufficient, note the general character needed. This report will be made upon the following form:

Com- Med. Hosp. Actg. Priv- Lit- Ambu- Hosp. Character of Medical
mand. Offs. Stwds. H. S. ates. ters. lances. Tents. Supplies Needed.

2. A field hospital will be organized at the Army base as soon as possible after landing, and a depot of supplies will be connected with it. As we are widely separated from the source of our supplies a strict economy in their use is necessary; Surgeons of Divisions and Brigades will give their personal attention to this important subject.

3. Extreme vigilance is enjoined upon Medical Officers in the matter of camp sanitation; errors in this particular being promptly reported to the respective commanding officers.

4. The experience at Santiago has demonstrated the efficiency of properly applied first dressings to gunshot wounds; these should be left untouched until the patient arrives at the base hospital, unless the condition of the wound absolutely demands a redressing en route from the first dressing station. All diagnosis tags will be marked "Dressing not to be removed" or "Redressing required," as the condition demands. Unless an imperative necessity exists, surgical operations will not be attempted at the front. CHAS. R. GREENLEAF, Colonel, Asst. Surg.-Gen. U.S.A., Chief Surg. Army in the Field.

QUARANTINE REGULATIONS FOR THE BASE OF THE MILITARY EXPEDITION TO PORTO RICO.

1. Every vessel shall be officially visited by the inspector before communication is made with other vessels or with the shore.

2. A vessel having yellow fever or smallpox on board shall not be allowed to communicate with the shore, or with other vessels, but shall leave the island.

3. Vessels coming from sources of infection shall be detained five days without communicating either with the shore or with other vessels. If at the expiration of this time no cases of fever shall have developed, landing may be made under the following precautions:

All fomites shall be disinfected by one of the following methods: Immersion for one hour in 1-1000 solution bichlorid; sulphur fumigation in a chamber twenty four hours, four pounds of sulphur being used for each 1000 cubic feet of space; or boiling half an hour with complete immersion. The following need not be disinfected unless directly exposed to infection:

All new and dry material unpacked, all iron and steel implements, all goods in new and original packages, not having been broken or packed in an infected locality. Goods other than textile contained in textile material, such as coffee in sacks, bacon, spices, etc., kept dry and not broken in an infected locality do not require disinfection other than the container, which shall be treated as fomites as above. Fruits, sound, unless exposed in an infected locality need no disinfection. Live stock may be admitted.

Such ships shall be thoroughly cleaned and disinfected by the free use of 1-1000 solution of bichlorid, and by fumigation with sulphur before they may again receive men or supplies.

Ships quarantined shall display the usual flag, and those in detention shall be visited by the inspector daily until the time of quarantine shall have expired.

4. Vessels carrying passengers or having fomites from localities of infection, though they (the vessels) may hail from healthy ports, shall be subject to the same quarantine restrictions as vessels known to hail from infected localities.

5. Due precaution shall be taken to prevent infection of the base of supplies through communication with infected localities along the line of march by teamsters and others. As far as possible they should not be allowed to remain at the base

Ambulance train transporting the sick from the Division Hospital to the Spanish military hospital.

longer than necessary to load and unload, nor to come in such contact as to communicate infection. Stragglers, prisoners and strangers should be immediately sent away.

CHAS. R. GREENLEAF, Colonel,
Asst. Surg.-Gen. U.S.A., Chief Surg. Army in the Field.

Major Woodbury was appointed Sanitary Inspector. He met with the hearty co-operation of the city authorities of Ponce in the performance of his onerous and often unpleasant duties. The sanitary conditions of the city underwent a great improvement in a few days. The water-supply was found satisfactory. The absence of a sewerage system threw many obstacles in the way. The appearance of smallpox in a village some distance from Ponce made vaccination among the soldiers who were not protected against this disease and the natives necessary. An abundant supply of vaccine virus was on hand and was at once issued and used. When I arrived at Ponce, August 7, I found typhoid fever raging to an alarming extent. It was desirable to trace the origin of the disease. The absence of typhoid fever this season of the year, its outbreak in all the commands, and the short time that had intervened between leaving the United States and the landing in Porto Rico made it probable that the disease could be traced to the infected camps occupied by the troops before leaving for Porto Rico. General Miles was very anxious to obtain reliable information regarding the origin and spread of the disease. Pursuant to the following order I made an exhaustive and systematic investigation:

HEADQUARTERS OF THE ARMY, OFFICE OF THE CHIEF SURGEON.
PORT PONCE, PORTO RICO, Aug. 10, 1898.

Lieut.-Col. Nicholas Senn, Surgeon U. S. V., Chief of Operating Staff of the Army.

Sir:—You will proceed to the town of Ponce, visit the military and other hospitals in that town, and such of the camps in its vicinity as you may deem necessary, for the purpose of investigating and, if possible, determining the cause of typhoid and other fevers now prevailing in this army, and report the results of your investigation in writing to me. Should you find it necessary to have the services of an interpreter, or other civilian, to aid in your work, you are hereby authorized to employ him, sending the bill to this office for payment.

Very respectfully,
CHAS. R. GREENLEAF, Colonel,
Asst. Surg. Gen. U.S.A., Chief Surg. Army in the Field.

I obtained accurate information of two hundred fever patients, of which number more than 90 per cent. were well-marked typhoid fever, the balance malaria and the results of sunstroke. I estimated the whole number of fever patients in, and in the imme diate vicinity of, Ponce at 250. In extending my inquiries to General Brooke's command, with headquarters at Guayama, I found about 145 additional cases; however, in that locality malaria seemed to predominate. Most of the cases came from Chickamauga by way of Charleston and Newport News. The Second and Third Wisconsin Regiments furnished the largest contingent. Almost every soldier in the different hospitals belonging to either of these

Ambulance unloading the sick at the door of the Club House in Ponce used as a temporary hospital.

regiments suffered from typical typhoid fever, and what attracted my attention was that the disease appeared to be of a more serious type than in most of the men belonging to other regiments. The locality from which these regiments came, when encamped at Chickamauga, must have been badly infected. As the result of my investigations, I reported to Col. Greenleaf the number of cases found, and that in my opinion the disease was contracted in every instance before leaving the camps in the United States. In view of the fact that most of the cases came from Chickamauga, I suggested at the same time that the Medical Department should recommend immediate evacuation of that camp. In Ponce most of the cases found shelter and care in the Spanish military hospital, then in charge of Major Ten Eyck, U. S. A. The club-house and a school for girls, of the Sisters of Charity, were also placed at the disposal of the chief surgeon and were soon filled with patients. Miss Chancellor of New York did excellent service as a nurse in the former temporary hospital. A congestion which occurred in the military hospital, and which could not be prevented, took place when General Wilson's division moved forward and unloaded at the door all of the sick in the Division hospital, some 150 in number. The overcrowded condition was remedied the next day, when a large number of the more grave cases were sent on board the *Relief*, anchored in the harbor of Ponce. Medical supplies were in abundance at all times and were freely issued without any formality. The *Relief*, and later the yacht *May*, brought an additional supply, with many delicacies for the sick. Milk was bought and freely supplied to the sick. It is the intention of the chief surgeon to establish an extensive out-door receiving hospital as soon as the tentage arrives, which, according to information received from the Surgeon-General, is now on the way. The number of new cases of typhoid fever in the Porto Rican army will probably be a limited one, and if the troops are recalled as soon as the treaty of peace has been signed, we need to entertain little fear of the indigenous spread of the disease.

Arroya, Porto Rico, Aug. 12, 1898.

TYPHOID FEVER IN THE PORTO RICAN CAMPAIGN.

In Cuba our army met as its most formidable enemy one of the most dreaded of all infectious diseases—yellow fever. The Cuban invasion was characterized by hasty action, a lack of organization, and inadequate preparation. The last crippled the medical department and is responsible for the early and extensive outbreak of yellow fever. In less than two weeks after our army landed in Cuba, yellow fever made its appearance, and almost simultaneously attacked the troops from Siboney, the base of invasion, to the trenches before Santiago. In less than two weeks from its appearance nearly 500 fever cases, most of them yellow fever, impaired the fighting force and seriously taxed the limited resources of the medical department. Fortunately for the army, that type of the disease was mild, the number of deaths few as compared with some of the epidemics in the past. Under the circumstances, it was fortunate that Santiago surrendered in time, as the fighting force was being rapidly reduced by the invasion of yellow fever and the ever-present malaria. In planning the Porto Rican invasion the possible repetition of a similar experience was taken into due consideration, and timely precautions against such an occurrence were adopted and carried into effect. So far our troops in Porto Rico have escaped yellow fever, but soon after their landing, fever cases came into the hospitals at an alarming rate. Many of the soldiers were attacked on the transports or soon after landing. After landing in Ponce, August 8, I found at least 250 cases of fever in the different hospitals in the city and the division hospital near the city limits. Even a superficial examination sufficed to prove that most of the cases were typhoid fever. The time which intervened between the departure of the troops from the United States and the appearance of fever, made it more than probable that the infection did not have an indigenous origin. In some of the cases it was difficult, in others impossible, to make a differential diagnosis between malaria and typhoid fever without the use of the microscope, and this invaluable diagnostic resource in such cases was unfortunately not at hand. Another difficulty we had to contend with was the lack of recorded thermometric observations, which, when accurately made and systematically recorded, prove of such signal service in distinguishing between these two febrile conditions.

Pursuant to an order issued by Col. Greenleaf, chief surgeon of the army in the field, I investigated for two consecutive days all of the ·fever cases then in the hospitals, for the purpose of locating the origin of typhoid fever. In this work I availed myself of the kind and able assistance of Dr. M. O. Terry, Surgeon-General of the State of New York, and Acting Assistant-Surgeon Greenleaf, son of the chief surgeon. We made a careful examination of 200 cases of fever as they presented themselves, noted the principal symptoms and tabulated them (see appended table).

A careful study of these cases, as well as subsequent developments, furnished adequate proof that 90 per cent. of them were genuine typhoid fever. No further doubt could remain in tracing the infection to the camps occupied in the United States. The great prevalence of the disease among the troops, affecting as it did, more or less, all of the regiments, was a source of uneasiness and anxiety on the part of those who were in charge of the invasion. Measures were taken to secure ample hospital room and facilities for the accommodation and proper treatment of those on hand and such as might be brought in later. The order to General Wilson to take up the march toward

San Juan made it necessary to evacuate the division hospital. All of the patients were transferred to the Spanish military hospital in Ponce, which caused the temporary overcrowding to which I referred in a former communication. The Spanish military hospital is a substantial, square, one-story building with a large court in the center. It is built of stone, the floors being made of cement or brick tiling. It is on a high hill near the city limits, from which a magnificent view of the city, harbor and surrounding country can be obtained. It has a capacity for about 150 beds. It required a good deal of labor to make this building fit for the reception of patients. Major Dooly and his force worked persistently a whole day in removing the dirt and filth which the Spaniards had left, in their haste in evacuating the city, as an undesirable legacy. The hospital was at once supplied with cots, bedding and hospital stores. The club-house of the city, and a school for girls in charge of the Sisters of Charity, were offered to the authorities for hospital use, and courtesy was promptly accepted. For over a week the sick officers occupied the club-house and about fifty patients found comfortable quarters and excellent treatment in the school-house. Ponce has a large charity hospital, the "Tricoche," with 200 beds, under the care and management of the Sisters of Charity. The hospital is a model of cleanliness and comfort. Col. Greenleaf made arrangements with the city authorities to open the doors of this excellent institution for sick officers. I am sure that every one who will enjoy the kind treatment and excellent care of the Sisters in these great institutions of charity will have a good word for this ancient and worthy order. Out of the 200 cases of fever examined in the different hospitals in Ponce, and which appear in the table, the following diagnoses were made at the time: Gastric fever, 2; effects of sunstroke, 6; malaria, 9; doubtful, 21; typhoid fever, 162—total, 200.

I am satisfied that of the doubtful cases a sufficient number developed typhoid fever to bring the whole number of cases up to 280. In reference to the time the disease developed the following can be gleaned from the table: The first symptoms appeared before leaving the United States, 8; on transports, 86; within ten days after landing, 68, out of a total of 162.

As regards the place of infection the cases came from: Chickamauga, 90; Tampa, 48; Camp Alger, 23, Newport News, 1—total, 162.

The small number coming from Camp Alger, where the disease gained such a firm foothold, which led to the abandonment of the camp, is to be explained by the fact that a large number of fever cases, coming from that camp, were returned to the United States soon after landing, by order of Col. Greenleaf. All regiments were not affected alike by this disease. Among the troops in Porto Rico the typhoid fever cases were distributed as follows:

2d Wisconsin	42
3d Wisconsin	17
16th Pennsylvania	17
6th Massachusetts	15
19th U. S. Infantry	15
6th Illinois	11
3d Artillery	10
4th Artillery	5
11th U. S. Infantry	5
1st Provisional Corps	4
Hospital Corps	4
17th U. S. Infantry	3
2d Cavalry	3
5th Cavalry	3
3d Illinois	4
4th Pennsylvania	2
Signal Corps	2
5th Artillery	1
Total	162

In tabulating the symptoms the following facts appear:

Tongue.
- Dry, coated, red at tip and margin. 10.
- Coated, white fur. 21.
- Coated, pale, flabby. 17.
- Coated, red tip and margin. 56.
- Dry, brown and fissured. 20.
- Moist, glazed, red. 13.
- Sordes, lips and teeth. 12.

Abdomen.
- Tympanites. 29.
- Tenderness and gurgling right iliac fossa. 71.
- Rose spots. 37.
- Spleen enlarged. 141.
- Spleen markedly enlarged. 20.

Epistaxis during prodromal stage 28
Diarrhea 87
Intestinal hemorrhage. 3
Bronchitis 20
Delirium 1

The absence of delirium in all cases but one is remarkable, but it must not be forgotten that nearly all of the cases were examined during the early stages of the disease. In quite a number of cases this symptom appeared later. From the symptoms and the death-rate, ascertainable at this time, it is evident that the disease pursued a comparatively mild course. Nearly 200 of the more grave cases were transferred to the hospital ship *Relief*, which sailed from Ponce for New York August 15. Of this number fourteen died en route and twelve were buried at sea. In two of these cases death resulted from complications. In one case gangrene of the penis, which assumed a progressive form, was the direct cause of death. In one case a fatal termination threatened during the third week of the disease from laryngitis and lobular pneumonia. A metastatic abscess of the submaxillary gland, which developed in one case, deserves mention as a rare complication of typhoid fever.

RETURN OF THE HOSPITAL SHIP "RELIEF" FROM PORTO RICO.

The *Relief* sailed from Ponce, Porto Rico, August 15, for New York, and called on her way at Mayaguez to complete her precious cargo of sick and wounded. All of the wounded at the last port were taken on board. The entire number of patients on leaving Porto Rico was 255, the full capacity of the floating hospital. It is probably the first time in the history of the world that so many fever cases were treated on a hospital ship and conveyed from a foreign country to their homes. The first day out a brisk breeze caused considerable rolling and pitching of the ship, which induced some cases of seasickness among the patients, but did not seem to unfavorably influence the disease. The female nurses worked faithfully and proved of the utmost value to the sick. Fourteen of the more severe cases of typhoid fever died on the way to New York. Many of the patients improved rapidly during the voyage. The *Relief* has done all and more than was expected in serving as a temporary hospital and as an ambulance ship in the treatment and transportation of the sick and wounded.

New York, Aug. 20, 1898.

THE RETURNING ARMY.

The war is over and the heroes who freed the Western Continent from Spanish despotism are returning home. The first war of invasion on our part has been a short, decisive one. Only four months have passed by since the Chief Executive issued the first call to arms, and more than we expected has been accomplished. The outside world, which has sneered too long at our fighting strength as a nation, has been convinced that it is dangerous to trifle with Americans in matters of war. In less than two months after war was declared we had more than two hundred thousand men in the field, eager and anxious to face the dangers of active warfare. Less than one-half of this army took part in the invasion. The enemy's navy was entirely destroyed; not a single ship that came within range of our guns escaped. The proud Spanish fleet is a total wreck in American waters, a source of pride to our navy and a significant object lesson for all foreign nations. Santiago fell before our victorious army; Porto Rico yielded after a few skirmishes and Spain accepted our terms of peace without much argumentation, after the hopelessness of her cause had been demonstrated by our invincible army and navy. Peace has been restored, and the returning soldiers of the volunteer army will soon return to citizenship and resume their ordinary vocations of peaceful life.

What a contrast between the invading and returning army! This contrast has reference not only to size but also to appearance. Thousands have died from wounds and disease. Yellow fever, dysentery, malaria and typhoid fever have been and continue to be our most formidable enemies. We had no great difficulty in silencing the Spanish guns, but we have been less effective in preventing the origin and spread of these, the greatest terrors of camp life. We can calculate with some degree of precision the loss of life sustained in battle, but it is impossible today to estimate the ultimate damage inflicted by disease. The naval forces scored the greatest victories with little loss of life; they escaped disease and its consequences, to a large extent, and were subject to little or no privations. The invading armies suffered the brunt of privation and discomforts incident to an active campaign. The troops in camps who were denied the privilege of taking part in the invasion of Cuba and Porto Rico had their share of deaths, sickness and hardship. It is safe to say that not half of the soldiers engaged in this short war are in a fighting or working condition on their return home. It is a sad sight, indeed, to witness the disembarkment of a transport arriving from Cuba or Porto Rico. Every one of the vessels brings from fifty to one hundred and fifty disabled men requiring medical treatment. All of the men left on the outgoing transports in good health and cheerful mood; all who arrive show the effects of the campaign. Many have died in our new possessions, many have been consigned to the sea on their way home, others have reached the shore in a dying condition. The crowded transports, the inadequate provisions for proper food, have made the voyages to and from the seat of war a source of hardship instead of health and pleasure. The emaciated forms, the sunken eye, the hollow cheek, the pale, bronzed faces, the staggering gait, show only too plainly what can be done by disease, a tropic climate and improper food in disabling an army in a few weeks. In this respect our experience is a repetition of that of our enemy. It is well known that the Spanish army lost 50 per cent. of its fighting force from the same cause in two months after landing in Cuba. The Spanish surgeon I met inside of the lines of the enemy, four days before the surrender of Santiago, when we delivered to him, under a flag of truce, sixteen wounded Spanish soldiers, informed me that when his part of the army reached Cuba the men were all in good health, and that now many were sick and none well. He drew a sad picture of how their ranks were thinned out by yellow fever, malaria and dysentery. The outbreak and spread of typhoid fever in our home camps, so early during the campaign, is responsible for more deaths and suffering than any other cause. Many of our soldiers carried the infection with them to Cuba and Porto Rico, and were taken ill on the transports or soon after landing. It is much more difficult to keep typhoid fever out of the army than yellow fever. The yellow fever which our troops in Cuba encountered was of a mild type. Comparatively few died and most of the cases recovered after an illness of but a few days. Typhoid fever runs its typic course of three weeks or more, little influenced, as far as time is concerned, by medication. It is a disease which, above all others, requires careful nursing. The necessary attention to typhoid-fever patients in nursing and treatment is a matter difficult to obtain, even in a well-equipped hospital with all needful appliances. The management of such cases in field hospitals is necessarily attended by many difficulties which tax to the utmost the experience of the medical staff and nursing corps. Considering the limited resources at our command in the treatment of this disease, in our home camps and our new possessions, it is surprising that the mortality has not been greater. The Sisters of Charity and the trained female nurses from different cities, have done most satisfactory work in our home camps, crowded with typhoid fever patients. Many a soldier on his recovery from the disease will feel grateful for their faithful services.

CAMP WIKOFF.

Camp Wikoff is now a great hospital. It is located on Montauk Point, L. I., a narrow strip of land surrounded on both sides by salt water. The country is hilly and treeless and the sandy soil is covered with a scanty growth of grass. Between the hills are cup-shaped depressions with a marshy soil, which after rains are filled with stagnant water. These diminutive marshes threaten danger in case of a prolonged encampment. They are undoubtedly, all of them, the natural breeding-places of the plasmodium malariæ. They will soon become contaminated with the fecal discharge from hundreds of typhoid fever cases, as many of the sinks drain directly into them. I am told that the water-supply from the artesian wells, while not ample, is otherwise satisfactory. The small railroad which terminates here from New York, monopolizes the whole business of transportation, as this exclusive right was made conditional in securing the ground for camp purposes. This is greatly to be regretted, as steamer communication could be readily established, which would facilitate the present unusually large passenger and freight business between the camp and New York. Politics and personal interests have figured conspicuously in the management of the present war. Departments have been severely criticised, when a thorough investigation would often reveal a power behind the throne. If we had steamer traffic between here and New York we would not have to wait for days for the so much needed supplies. The little railroad has had sufficient influence in cutting off competition and in increasing correspondingly the value of its stock, and we here are suffering the consequences of this Judas Iscariot bargain. The whole little peninsula is a tented field. Regiment after regiment is arriving, day after day, seriously testing the quartermaster's department. All the troops that came from Cuba must land here to comply with the quarantine regulations. A detention hospital has been established near the landing, to which all suspects are consigned for the required length of time. Near the hospital a large disinfecting plant has been erected. So far no cases of yellow fever have been imported. The general hospital contains at the present time (August 26) nearly one thousand patients and all the sick in the camp will swell the number to 1500. The landing of so many sick in such a short time has brought about an overcrowding which, with the present facilities and resources could not have been prevented. Colonel Forwood, Assistant Surgeon-General, selected the camp site, and was the first man on the ground. His immense military experience, gained during the War of the Rebellion, fitted him in an admirable way for the difficult task imposed upon him. Colonel Forwood is an authority in military surgery and endowed with excellent administrative talents. His work here will be the crowning effort of his life. He has worked night and day since he has assumed his duties here. He is a friend of the soldier and will not leave a stone unturned to be of service to him. He has exclusive charge of the hospital construction, and his work was much admired by two staff surgeons of the German army, Drs. Steinbach and Wildemann, and by Lieutenant-Commander Tomatsuri of the Japanese navy, who came from New York to the camp with me. As they expressed themselves, the field hospitals here were the best they had ever seen. Colonel Forwood is ably assisted in his arduous duties by Majors Heitzmann, Brown, Nancrede and Wing and a large staff of acting assistant-surgeons. The writer, on his arrival, was placed in charge of the surgical work. An operating tent was erected and placed in working order with the assistance of two Sisters of Charity and Acting Assistant-Surgeon Greenleaf. The tent is floored and divided into four sections. The front part is the operating-room, with two side tables two feet in width the whole length of the room. The tables are covered with rubber cloth. An army operating-table and a few stands constitute the balance of the furnishing of the room. The next section is open on the sides to allow a free current of air and serves as an office. The next compartment is the preparation-room, fitted out with formaldehyde and steam sterilizers and sufficient shelf accommodations. The last section is used as a storeroom for dressings, splints, antiseptics and drugs necessary for the treatment of surgical cases.

Gen. Joseph Wheeler is in command of the camp, and although debilitated by the campaign and disease, he attends to his duties wtth a regularity and devotion which have characterized his whole military career. The sick are being cared for at the present time by fifty Sisters of Charity and sixty trained female nurses. One of the things that was greatly admired by the foreign military surgeons was the efficient work of the hospital corps. They were charmed with the way in which the patients were handled and the gentlemanly conduct of the litter-bearers. Less praise was bestowed on the military bearing of the men in camp. from the highest officers to the ordinary private. The military spirit seems to have been fully subdued in the enemy's country. The sentries move about sluggishly and seldom deem it worth while to come to a "present arms," no matter who may come within saluting distance. Men walk about in clothes showing only too distinctly the absence of whisk-broom or brush since they left Cuba. Guns, bayonets and scabbards have become rusty and show an entire lack of proper care. All drills are suspended and the whole camp presents more the appearance of a picnic ground than a military post. Officers and men are evidently impressed with the idea that their work is done, and while away their time in a way requiring the least amount of energy and exertion possible. In this respect our troops form a strong contrast with the German army when it entered Paris, after one of the most bloody wars and after a prolonged siege full of hardship and privations. On that occasion every soldier was in a condition to go on parade and to pass with credit the inspection of the most exacting officer. Such looseness of discipline as seen here at this time is not calculated to inspire the outgoing army with the proper military spirit that should be maintained and cultivated under the most adverse circumstances. Strict military bearing is also sadly lacking among the medical officers—a source of disappointment and surprise to the corps of acting assistant-surgeons, who entered the service with the full expectation that the reverse would be the case.

Camp Wikoff, Montauk, N. Y., Aug. 27, 1898.

THE NATIONAL CRY.

Unrest, criticism and grumbling are the accompaniments and heritage of every war. These symptoms of war fever have been unusually well developed during the war just ended, and they will be discussed for a long time after the treaty of peace has been signed. After an uninterrupted reign of peace for more than thirty years, the war cloud that came upon us so suddenly and unexpectedly provoked a commotion among the people unparalleled in degree and extent since the War of the Rebellion. All eyes were turned in the direction of the seat of war, and the contents of our enterprising and prolific newspapers were devoured with an eagerness unknown in any other country. It is strange that with all this great national unrest the current of commerce and business pursued its natural course. While our troops were engaged in war in foreign lands, the tilling of the soil, the hum of industry and the ordinary avocations of life continued as though harmony and peace reigned universal. The American never forgets that patriotism is not limited to the battlefield. The conscientious performance of duties at home, the fireside, the farms, the workshops, the manufacturing and business places, is one of the things essential in the successful prosecution of a war. This fact was recognized by our people, and the result has been that the prosperity of our country has suffered little, if any, during our first war of invasion. Criticism is a part of human nature. It is seen everywhere. It affects the educated as well as the ignorant, it extends from the cradle to the grave, it involves one sex as much as the other, it moves the well as much as the sick, it infects the pulpit as well as the stage, and it comes to the surface in the army from the commanding general down to the lowest of all privates. It is amusing to listen at a camp fire to the remarks made from all sources as to how the campaign should be conducted. The average private discusses the most complicated strategic problems with an ease as though he were repeating the multiplication table or the Lord's prayer. The generals high in command ease their conscience by criticising their subordinates most unmercifully, if any thing has gone wrong. Wise as well as ignorant men, a thousand miles away from the seat of war, have their convictions as to what should be done and are free to express them. Criticism increases in severity and extent in proportion as confidence is weakened and undermined. As we live in a free country criticism finds a fertile and productive soil everywhere and anywhere. The unbridled liberty of the press encourages and fosters it. Like swearing and other vices it is engendered by environments. Just and wrathful criticism is legitimate; criticism the outpouring of impure selfish motives is baneful. Our energetic, enthusiastic press is entitled to a great deal of credit in giving to the public the war news so promptly and completely, often at an enormous expense and severe danger to life. The American reporter has no equal in any country for obtaining news regardless of cost and risk. The reporters not only culled the news, but often took a hand in supplying the sick and wounded with fruit, tobacco, and delicacies. How quickly the reporters sniffed the latest news, I learned in Porto Rico. I arrived from Arroya in the harbor of Ponce, August 13. Rumors of peace were rife for a number of days. The *Herald* dispatch boat, then in the harbor, got up steam at about 3 o'clock in the afternoon. Soon the little craft put to sea, and I watched its course with intense interest. I said to my friends, if the boat, after leaving the harbor, turns in the direction of Arroya, it means war; if in an opposite direction, toward New York, peace has been declared. The proud little steamer turned its nose toward the United

States and made a bee line for New York. It was not until the next morning that the welcome news reached headquarters. This is only one of the many instances in which the reporters came in possession of the latest news before they reached the officials. The reporters were also instrumental in exposing many irregularities and defects of the military service from headquarters in Washington to the seat of war. I have no doubt that many wrongs were corrected under the pressure of the press.

It is not strange that many of our influential newspapers went a little too far in representing the grievances of the soldiers and in criticizing the action of departments and officers. A tinge of sensationalism is common more or less to all of our great dailies. Interviews that never occurred will continue to appear as long as the reputation of a reporter depends largely on his ability to satisfy the cravings of morbid curiosity. The statements made to reporters are always susceptible to more or less reconstruction. Again, it must be remembered that some men in the army, as elsewhere, are likely to exaggerate the true conditions, believing that by doing so, their services will be the better appreciated. As the result of my own observations. I can say without fear of contradiction that the best soldiers do the least grumbling. The most heroic and patriotic soldiers have the least to say of what they did and in relating hairbreadth escapes. It is the drone that does the complaining, and who rides in ambulances, and overcrowds the hospital, and puzzles and vexes the hard-working doctor. To the credit of the armies of invasion I must say that I heard but few complaints when the days were darkest and the food scantiest. One day I visited the fever camp near the division hospital of the army before Santiago, where I found two hundred patients literally lying in the mud, with nothing but a wet blanket, most of them under a shelter tent, some of them even without this slight protection against the pouring rains. Food was of the plainest kind, yet little or no complaint here. The men expected hardships, and when they came they were not disappointed. Grumbling became more marked and widespread with the progress of the war, after the men had become worn out by the campaign, and homesickness had gained a firm foothold. The severest complaints have originated with camp followers. The Medical Department has been criticized repeatedly, and yet it would be found very difficult to find among the returning soldiers any one who would be willing, or who would have reason to complain of the treatment he received at the hands of medical officers. In case of war, the machinery of our government is a very complicated one. The executive power of the Surgeon-General is indeed an extremely limited one. Everything of importance has to pass through the hands and by sanction of the Secretary of War. The Secretary of War is a busy man in keeping track of what is going in his department outside of the Surgeon-General's office. On the other hand the Medical Department depends entirely on the quartermaster's department in forwarding and distributing medical supplies. No wonder that many collisions between these departments occurred during the present war. Our experience has taught us in a most forcible way that the Medical Department should have charge of everything pertaining to the sick and wounded, in order to accomplish that for which it is intended. The Secretary of War is not supposed to have any knowledge of medicine or surgery or other wants of sick and wounded, and yet the Surgeon-General is powerless in the execution of his orders without his co-operation. If the forwarding and distribution of the medical and hospital supplies were directly under the control and management of the Medical Department we would have heard less of well-founded complaints of the scarcity of medicines and hospital supplies. To make a department strong and efficient it must be independent. It was not difficult to foresee when this war broke out that the greatest danger the troops had to expect was disease and not the Spaniards. The importance of the Medical Department was never more keenly apparent than at the present time, and yet what was done? The highest official in the Medical Department is a Brigadier-General, and only five medical officers with the rank of Colonel, and seven Lieutenant-Colonels. For the army major-generals were in abundance, brigadier-generals by the dozen, and colonels were turned out by the hundreds. Many of the brigadier-generals in brand new uniforms and glittering staffs never found a command, but their names remained on the pay roll just the same. Many of our newly fledged colonels could not handle a musket to save their lives and some of them even attempted the unusual feat of mounting the horse from the right side. In the face of all these appalling defects of army service the brunt of criticism continues to fall on the Surgeon-General and his hard working officers in the field. Much has been said of the mismanagement of Camp Wikoff. Considering the limited transportation facilities, and the fact that in less than three weeks more than 3,000 patients have been cared for, it is a source of gratification that so much has been accomplished, largely through the energy of the Chief Surgeon, Colonel Forwood, and Majors Brown and Heitzman. A corps of more than one hundred female nurses, including fifty Sisters of Charity, do the necessary nursing with a will and efficiency that astonish the many visitors. The hospital tents go up like mushrooms, day after day, and at the present time 2000 patients are well sheltered and well cared for. No lack of medical supplies at this time. The surgical ward in my charge was completed today and is already crowded with patients. The liberal contributions sent here by different relief societies supply the sick and well with an abundance of delicacies of all kinds. The diet of the convalescents is luxurious, much better than what is furnished by the officers' mess. The Red Cross is doing excellent work here, as elsewhere, in the distribution of clothing, medicines and delicacies. Mrs. A. Tscheppe, who represents a relief society of New York, is a familiar figure among the soldier patients and has been of much service in adding to their comfort and speedy recovery. Most of the patients are suffering from malaria, typhoid fever or dysentery. The number of deaths average from ten to fourteen daily, a small percentage considering the number of patients in the whole camp. The patients here enjoy fresh air, good nursing and excellent treatment, all of which will be conducive to rapid recovery. The conditions here for the successsul treatment of the fever cases are, in my opinion, far better than in any of the large hospitals in cities. It is to be hoped that the entire camp will be vacated in from four to five weeks, as after that time the soil will be thoroughly infected, in spite of all precautions, and the indigenous spread of typhoid fever would follow as an unavoidable sequence. The surgical work consists in the treatment of large abscesses, occurring in patients whose general health has been undermined by disease, or the hardships of the campaign, and operations for hemorrhoids and rectal fistula. Unjust and unnecessary criticism has a demoralizing effect on those directly or indirectly concerned. It is prone to intimidate and confuse those who are criticised and embolden those who look for undeserved sympathy. In this camp there is no further ground for complaint of any kind. It is generally known that the Medical Department was not consulted in locating the camps. For reasons known only to those in power, the camps were selected regardless of sanitary conditions. Our troops have been exposed to malaria since they left the State camps, and almost every man shows evidences of more or less malarial poisoning. As the essential cause of malaria enters the body by inhalation, malaria could not be avoided as long as the camps were located on a soil which breeds the plasmodium. Typhoid fever made its appearance in the State camps and followed the army to Chickamauga, Tampa, Alger, Cuba and Porto Rico. It is a repetition of what has happened during all campaigns under similar circumstances. Let the national cry subside now and let the press and people await the results of a thorough investigation by Congress, which will place the responsibility for any mismanagement where it belongs. The Medical Department courts such investigation, fully confident that the blame will be fixed outside of its legitimate jurisdiction.

Camp Wikoff, Aug. 31, 1898.

OUR RELIEF SOCIETIES.

War, pestilence, famine, floods and other great national calamities, are the most reliable tests to bring out the true philanthropic spirit of individuals as well as of nations. The good Samaritan is to be seen everywhere under ordinary conditions on his errands of mercy, following the footsteps of his Master in bringing comfort to the poor, the sick, the maimed and the oppressed, but his energies are taxed to the utmost, and his work is appreciated most keenly, when the masses are in distress. The American people are noted for their charitable disposition, and have gained a well-deserved reputation for humanitarian work. Our numerous ideal charitable institutions speak for themselves. Many national catastrophes have demonstrated the liberality and good-will of our people. The War of the Rebellion furnished an interesting object lesson to the outside world of the way in which patriotism is estimated here. During the war just ended many different relief societies have rivaled with each other in supplying our soldiers, sick and well, with many comforts of life beyond the limit of the government supplies. The government itself set a noble example by sending to the camps and the invading armies all kinds of supplies, unparalleled in quantity and quality in the history of the country. I am sure no one regrets more keenly than the government officials that these liberal supplies did not always reach their destination in time. The work of the many auxiliaries corrected many of these defects. Individuals as well as organized societies have labored incessantly and faithfully in coming to the aid of the government, in furnishing the troops with underclothing and delicacies usually beyond the reach of armies when engaged in active warfare. Miss Anabel Clarestes, a little girl in Lagrange, Ill., has been busy ever since the war commenced in preparing and sending to camps and the front home-made jellies, the product of her own hand. She had no difficulty in collecting money to purchase the necessary materials, but it was left for her to labor in the humble kitchen to prepare the incomparable delicacies for the soldiers in the field. This little American girl is a heroine worthy of the praise and admiration of the returning heroes who have been benefited by her modest, unselfish work. Many a patriotic woman, unknown to newspaper notoriety, has done her share in minimizing the sufferings of this war. It was not an uncommon thing for officers to receive a box containing the contributions of some female friend of the army who sent all she could spare for the alleviation of the troops in the field. In many such instances the name of the benefactress remained unknown to those who benefited by her donation. I have opened many such boxes, containing as a rule underclothing, bandages, reading and writing material, towels, handkerchiefs, and a few jars of jelly or canned fruit. The soldiers who were made the recipients of these gifts felt that they were remembered at home, an assurance which contributed much in intensifying their patriotism and in sustaining their courage under the most trying circumstances. The intense interest manifested by the government and the people in the care and comfort of the returning army remains unequaled in the history of our country. Every soldier was met with a reception given to an intimate and long-looked-for friend. The sick received the most tender care from all sides, and the well were given food that reminded them that they had reached home. The hospitals and many private houses threw the doors wide open to receive those who required medical treatment. Transportation home was made easy and comfortable by the active intervention of thousands of friends who were strangers when the troops left for the seat of war. In all large cities committees were organized to look after the comforts of the returning troops. In short, it may be safely stated that no army ever received a more enthusiastic, kind and cordial reception than the troops that have reached us from the seat of war.

RED CROSS SOCIETY.

Miss Clara Barton, President of the American Red Cross Society, has performed her onerous duties during the entire war with a devotion and earnestness that merit universal recognition at home and abroad. She has been tireless in her efforts to bring comfort to the soldiers at times when her services were most needed. The *Texas* and the little steamer *Red Cross*, under her command, made their appearance at Siboney at a time when outside help was most appreciated. Ice, medicines, dressings and hospital supplies were freely distributed among the sick and wounded. After the surrender of Santiago the *Texas* was the first vessel to enter its harbor on its errand of mercy in bringing food for the hungry Cubans and delicacies for the sick of the victorious and vanquished armies. The Red Cross Society established supply depots in all of the large camps and the good work done everywhere will live in the memories of all who were engaged in the conflict. Miss Barton has the confidence of the American people and she has sustained it through the present war by the thoughtful and timely distribution of the innumerable and liberal donations to the society she so well represents. An appropriate idea of what this Society has done can be gained from the fact that in Camp Wikoff alone two thousand dollars of supplies are distributed daily. Miss Barton has been assisted in her widespread humanitarian work by a large staff of physicians and nurses who came to the relief of the medical officers at times when their services were most needed. After peace was declared, Miss Clara Barton immediately sailed for Havana to bring much-needed aid to the starving reconcentrados of the long-besieged city, while her numerous helpers continued their faithful work in the home camps. The work of the Red Cross received the moral and substantial support of the charitably disposed citizens throughout the United States and liberal donations from abroad. Recent experience has again demonstrated that this society is the most important auxiliary in war as well as other natural disasters in bringing prompt relief to the sufferers.

WOMEN'S PATRIOTIC RELIEF ASSOCIATION, NEW YORK.

This benevolent Association has extended its work from the camps to the needy families of soldiers who enlisted and went to the front, leaving families behind them, worthy objects of well-deserved charity. It was founded in the City of New York at the outbreak of the war, at the residence of Mrs. Egbert Gurnsey, with Mrs. Howard Carroll as president and well-organized committees and ad.sory board, consisting of prominent business and professional men. The Association has provided food and house rent, as well as medical attendance, monthly, to no less than 2444 families. A free eatinghouse was established at 711 Eighth Avenue, where these families received food and clothing. Mrs. Charles Carroll, a member of the Association, was made president of the Naval Reserve Relief, and by contributions and a garden party given at her residence in New Brighton, Borough of Richmond, the sum of $2500 was secured, which was expended for the benefit of the New York Naval Reserves. This special function of the Association did much for the comfort and efficiency of this otherwise neglected branch of the military service. The hospital work of the Association has been under the management of Mrs. Charles Carroll, Mrs. Adolph Tscheppe and Mrs. Seymore. The ladies of the Association, with Mrs. William McDonald as chairman, gave an outing to the convalescent soldiers from the different hospitals in Central Park, which proved to be one of the most memorable occasions in

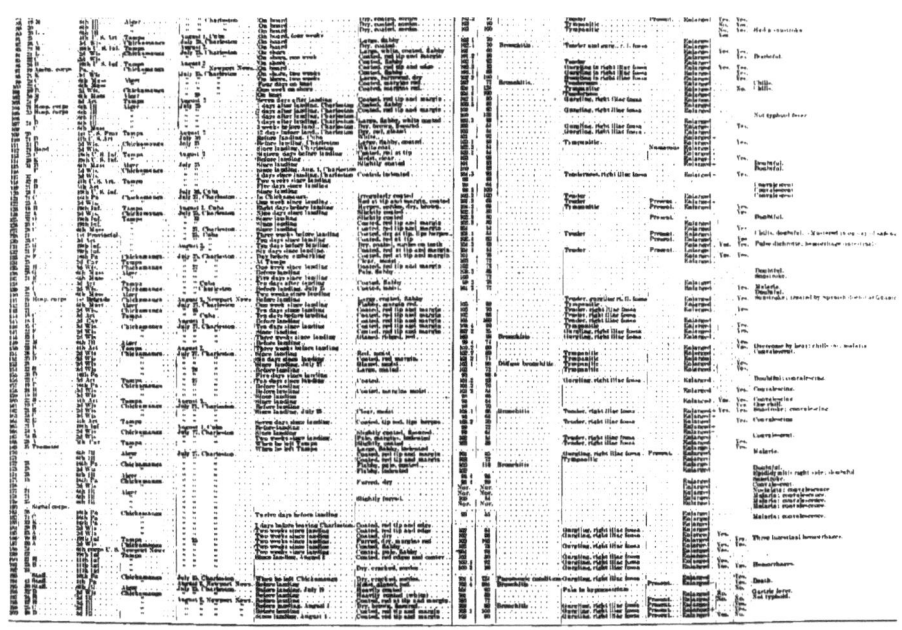

the annals of the history of this famous park. Mrs. Charles Carroll and Mrs. Tscheppe erected a tent in Camp Wikoff when the soldiers from Cuba commenced to return, and have been busy in distributing without any red tape an enormous amount of most valuable contributions among the sick and convalescents. Their donations of different stimulants and artificial waters have proved most acceptable and timely. From this tent ice cream has been furnished daily. A special messenger has done excellent service in distributing mail and in looking up soldiers inquired after by anxious relatives. So fertile have been the resources of this modest little tent that it has been designated "The Gold Mine." Mrs. Tscheppe represents the ladies of the "Liederkranz," and her popularity among the Germans of New York has brought not only the most liberal donations but likewise cash in large amounts. Only the other day she received from a single source a check for $500, which she was asked to use at her own discretion in the care of the sick and convalescent in the camp. The German press of New York has used its influence in supplying Mrs. Tscheppe with ample means on her errands of mercy.

ILLINOIS ARMY AND NAVY LEAGUE.

This relief association was organized soon after war was declared. It is composed of representative men and women throughout the State of Illinois, with headquarters in Chicago. The secretary, Dr. F. H. Wines, had an extensive experience in dispensing charity throughout the War of the Rebellion, and was consequently well prepared in assuming the laborious and trying duties of his office. While it was the principal intention of the association to look after the interests and comforts of the State Volunteers, many of the contributions reached soldiers outside of the Illinois troops. The State of Illinois, and the City of Chicago in particular, have been very active in minimizing the inevitable sufferings incident to active warfare by sending to the camps and the front large quantities of the most desirable articles of diet, delicacies, underclothing and medicines. The League made special arrangements for transportation at reduced rates, so that the donations reached their destination promptly and at small expense. The League has had from the very beginning a handsome bank account, and cash was sent to different points for the purchasing of the most necessary articles. The citizens of Illinois will have the satisfaction of showing that by concerted action of the members of the League the work of charity and benevolence has been accomplished in the most satisfactory manner.

MASSACHUSETTS VOLUNTEER AID ASSOCIATION.

There has been an impression prevailing among the regular troops, that while the soldiers of the regular army have fought the hardest and have been subjected to the greatest privations, they have not received the recognition to which they are entitled, and have been more or less ignored by the different relief associations. There is undoubtedly some truth concerning these statements. The Massachusetts Volunteer Aid Association has recognized the validity of this complaint, and has directed its surgeons toward correcting the oversight. The work of this association in this direction has been particularly notable in Camp Wikoff. A number of ladies representing this Association came to the camp, and have done all in their power to render the soldiers belonging to the regular army comfortable and happy.

A light diet kitchen was established, provided and equipped at the First Division Hospital, in charge of Major Wood, in conjunction with the Red Cross Society, under the superintendency of Mrs. M. H. Willard. The kitchen is an ideal one, and is presided over by a competent chef. Mrs. Dininger is the lady manager. The bountiful donation for the sick of the Regular Infantry Division was brought to the camp by

Mrs. Leach, wife of Major Smith S. Leach, of the Engineer Corps of the Regular Army, and was contributed by the ladies of New London, Conn., and the Pequot Society. It consisted of a well-assorted collection of soups, eggs, lemons, oranges, butter, crackers, sugar, barley, cocoa, farina, beef, ham, corn-starch, codfish, breakfast food, chocolate, gelatin, tobacco, pipes, keg of whisky, writing and reading material, towels, pajamas, night-shirts and underclothing. The light-diet kitchen is one of the attractions of the camp. The relief societies that I have mentioned are only a few of the hundreds organized throughout the United States for the same purpose, notably among them the "Daughters of the Revolution" and the "Colonial Dames," all of which did their good share in alleviating the sufferings of our army in camp and at the front. The charity that has been practiced so bountifully and so generally during the present war, must satisfy our victorious army that the patriotism they carried into the field has been cultivated at home in words and action to a degree and extent unparalleled in the history of the world. War in a just cause begets patriotism, and nothing can demonstrate this more clearly and forcibly than our experience in the field and at home during the last five months.

Camp Wikoff, Sept. 8, 1898.

THE WOUNDED OF THE PORTO RICAN CAMPAIGN.

The Cuban and Porto Rican invasions have confirmed the experience of the past in showing that the greatest horrors of war are caused by disease and its consequences rather than the implements of destruction. If the battle-grounds are in the extreme north or south, climate enters as an important factor in decimating the ranks and in increasing the sufferings of the contending armies. A war of invasion requires more preparation, foresight and forethought on the part of those who plan and conduct the campaign than one of defense, a fact we have been painfully made aware of during the last two months. The more remote the seat of conflict, the more difficult the task of providing food and clothing for the army, and the more serious becomes the problem of properly caring for the sick and wounded, and the greater becomes the difficulty in returning the survivors to their homes. Nostalgia, a very common affection among unseasoned troops, becomes more prevalent in proportion to the distance between home and the seat of war, as we had abundant opportunities to observe during the late war. The depressing effect of this common ailment has a decided influence in increasing the rate of mortality of the sick and wounded, and in impairing the effectiveness of the fighting line. Nostalgia is a contagious disease, not in the sense we use the word contagion ordinarily, but when once established in camp it increases rapidly by suggestion. The onset and spread of this common ailment of camp life are promoted by interruptions of the mail service, the only medium of communication between the soldier in the field and his distant home. Among the many sins of omission of those in charge of the management of the late war was a glaring neglect to provide for the much-needed and anxiously looked for mail facilities. If those who have the management of this branch of the government service in charge could be made to understand what an occasional letter will do in keeping up the spirit of the citizen soldier, nostalgia would have been less prevalent and its effects less disastrous during the late campaign. From the time I left Fortress Monroe for Cuba, July 3, and until I arrived in New York from Porto Rico, August 19, I received only two letters of the probable two hundred sent to me during this time. In summing up the casualties of the war just ended, it is safe to make the statement that the number of killed and the number of deaths resulting from the immediate effects of wounds will not exceed 280. The number of wounded will in all probability reach 1425. The number of deaths from malaria, dysentery, yellow fever and typhoid can not be estimated at this time, as these diseases are still prevailing and will claim many victims before the troops are recalled. The loss of life and the suffering as well as disability, as a claim for pension, caused by disease and the effects of climate will exceed by far those caused by Spanish bullets. During the Porto Rican campaign no pitched battle was fought. The force of the enemy in all of the skirmishes was small and in ambush. Only a few were killed and not more than forty were wounded. Among the wounded, bone injuries were rare, many of the wounds slight. All of these cases tend to confirm previous observations to the effect that the small caliber bullet of the Mauser rifle, the one used exclusively by the Spaniards, causes wounds of the soft parts, which if left alone under the first dressing, will heal by primary intention in the course of a week or two, unless complicated by serious visceral injuries. All of these cases corroborate the statement previously made that the small caliber bullet does not infect the wound and that it seldom carries with it into the tissues clothing or other infectious substances. This observation, so abundantly supported by substantial facts, is an extremely important one for future field service, as it must satisfy the military surgeons that such wounds will heal promptly if left alone under the first-aid antiseptic dressing. On the other hand, I have seen the evil consequences following meddlesome surgery in the form of unnecessary probing. Such wounds are very susceptible to secondary infection caused by the use of the probe. For the purpose of again calling attention to the humane nature of the modern weapon, and with a view of showing how rapidly wounds inflicted with the small caliber bullet will heal under the most conservative treatment, I will report briefly the nature of the wounds and the results of those wounded in the Porto Rican war:

Case 1.—Lieut. J. C. Byron, Troop F, Eighth Cavalry, wounded in the skirmish near Mayaguez, August 10. The bullet passed through the foot from side to side on the dorsal aspect, making a groove on the upper surface of the second and third metatarsal bones without fracturing them. Healing by primary intention under the first dressing. He was in the saddle when injured.

Case 2.—Lieut. John Haines, Battery F, Third Artillery, was wounded in the attack on Aibonito, August 13, and is probably the last man shot by the Spaniards during the invasion of Porto Rico. He was in the advance of the line, with his battery planted on a high hill in full view of the enemy. After firing the number of shots ordered, the gun was turned, and at this moment a bullet struck him in the left lumbar region, postaxillary line, and escaped about the sixth intercostal space, anterior axillary line, on the same side. No indications of bone injury or penetration of the chest. The wounds were dressed in the field and healed by primary intention. He was conveyed in an ambulance from the front to Ponce, a distance of twenty miles, and transferred to the hospital ship *Relief*. At no time has he suffered much from pain or even a sense of discomfort which could be referred to the wound. The patient must have been in a stooping position the moment the injury was received.

Case 3.—Lieut. T. H. Hunter, Battery B, Fifth Artillery, was accidentally shot by one of his own men by a Krag-Jorgensen bullet, which entered the right side of the ilium, passed downward and backward, emerging from the gluteal region on the same side below the ramus of the ischium. The course of the bullet excluded bone injury in this case. Notwithstanding the length and depth of the tubular wound it healed rapidly by primary intention. The indications are that the patient will recover without any functional impairment of the parts implicated in the injury.

Case 4.—William H. Walcutt, Company E, Fourth Ohio Infantry, was wounded in the skirmish near Guayamo, August 8. The bullet entered the plantar surface of the left foot between the first and second metatarsal bones, at the junction of the middle with the distal thirds, and escaped from the dorsal side, at a point a little nearer the distal side. From the course of the bullet it is clear that he was running in a direction opposite to the enemy when the shot was fired. The wounds were healed a week after the injury was received.

Case 5.—William J. Edgington, Company A, Fourth Ohio Infantry, was wounded during an engagement, August 8. The wound of entrance was at a point two inches to the left of the median line on a level with the sacro-coccygeal joint, the wound of exit at the base of the opposite thigh over its inner and middle aspect, directly over the adductor muscles. No evidence of any serious visceral injury of any of the pelvic organs. The temperature remained normal, the wounds healed by primary intention, and when I examined the patient in the hospital at Guayamo, five days after the injury was inflicted, the patient was free from pain and able to leave his cot without assistance. The course of this bullet explains the position of the patient at the time the bullet reached its unwilling, moving mark.

Case 6.—Noble W. Horlocker, Company C, Fourth Ohio Infantry, was wounded in the same skirmish. The bullet entered one inch in front of the right malleolus and escaped two and three-fourth inches below and a little behind the external malleolus. Although the bullet must have passed through the ankle joint and the astragalus, the injury was followed by very little pain, except on moving the ankle joint, and no indication of infection had set in five days after the injury was received. It is reasonable to expect that the wounds will heal by primary intention, and that the patient will recover with a useful, movable ankle joint.

Case 7.—Stewart J. Mercer, Company E, Fourth Ohio Infantry, was wounded August 5, in a skirmish on the way from Arroya to Guayamo. The bullet made a flesh wound over the inner margin of the left patella, and healed by primary intention in a few days.

Case 8.—Samuel T. Jones, Company C, Fourth Ohio Infantry, received a wound above the right patella, August 8. Wounds of entrance and exit one inch apart. Primary healing under the first dressing.

Case 9.—Edward O. Thompson, Corporal Company K, Fourth Ohio Infantry, was wounded near Guayamo, August 8. The bullet entered the forearm two-thirds of an inch above the wrist joint, on radial side, and after passing through the soft tissue in front of the bones, emerged from the inner aspect of the forearm just above the wrist joint. Wound healed by primary intention under the first dressing.

Case 10.—Harry Lee Haynes, Company C, Fourth Ohio Infantry, was lying down in a ditch at the time he was wounded, August 8. The bullet struck the arm two inches above the insertion of the deltoid muscle and emerged over the sterno-clavicular articulation on the same side. A third wound was found on a line with the course of the emerging bullet one inch below the mastoid process and in the direction of the sterno-cleido-mastoid muscle. A fourth wound, an inch and a half in length, one-quarter of an inch in depth and an inch in width, was found on the dorsum of the right forearm an inch above the elbow joint. All the wounds healed rapidly, caused but little suffering, and the patient was in a fair way to recovery when seen a few days after he was wounded.

Case 11.—Clarence W. Riffer, Company A, Fourth Ohio Infantry, was wounded August 8. The bullet entered the right thigh at a point five inches above the knee joint and about the middle of the external surface, passed through the soft tissues making its exit three inches to the left of the point of entrance. It re-entered the left thigh at a point two and a half inches above the knee joint, and an inch and a-half to the right of the posterior median line and emerged on the oposite side an inch and a-half above the knee joint. Both flesh wounds deep and long as they were healed primarily without suppuration.

Case 12.—John O. Cordner, Company C, Fourth Ohio Infantry, was wounded August 5. The bullet made a flesh wound at the lower border of the patella, the wounds of entrance and exit being separated by a space an inch and a half in length. Primary healing under first dressing.

Case 13.—William Rossiter, Company G, Eleventh U. S. Infantry, was wounded in the skirmish near Mayaguez, August 10. He was shot through the inferior maxilla. The bullet entered just below the margin of the bone on the right side about an inch in front of the angle and emerged over the angle of the bone on the opposite side, perforating the soft tissues of the neck in a transverse direction. The bullet appears to have passed through the bone without fracturing it. The only pain the patient complains of is produced when he undertakes to masticate food. Wounds of entrance and exit healed in a few days by primary intention.

Case 14.—Amos Wilkie, Eleventh U. S. Infantry, was on the march when wounded near Mayaguez, August 10. The bullet entered the right lumbar region just above the crest of the ilium, mid-axillary line, and emerged about two inches to the left of the spine and four inches above the left sacro-iliac synchondrosis. No indications of intra-abdominal complications.

He suffered considerable from cramping pains, which he attributes to cold and fever which he contracted by exposure to rain. A week after the injury was received, when the patient was an inmate of the Hospital Ship *Relief*, his condition warranted the hope of an early and complete recovery.

Case 15.—Harry C. Errick, Company C, Eleventh U. S. Infantry, was wounded August 10, in a charge on the enemy in ambush. Wound of entrance in left leg over the outer aspect of the middle third; the bullet passed downward and inward and emerged about five inches above the inner malleolus. Hemorrhage slight, no fracture. Wound healing rapidly under first dressing.

Case 16.—William H. Wheeler, Company A, Eleventh U. S. Infantry, was wounded August 10, near Mayaguez, when in a standing position with his side in the direction of the enemy, his gun down, ready to reload. The bullet struck the tenth intercostal space, left side, in the post axillary line and made its exit about four inches from the spine in the lumbar region close to the margin of the last rib. No serious complications followed the injury, and at the present time, August 14, the patient is improving rapidly.

Case 17.—George Curtis, Company D, Light Battery, Fifth Artillery, received a wound of the chest August 10, being in his saddle at the time. The bullet passed through the chest from the second left intercostal space in front to the middle of the outer border of the scapula on the same side. No hemoptysis or any other serious symptoms indicating the existence of the visceral wound of the lung. The only thing he complains of is a sense of numbness in the left arm. Primary union of both wounds.

Case 18.—Joseph P. Ryan, Corporal Company A, Eleventh U. S. Infantry, was wounded August 10. The bullet passed through the ankle joint. Wound of entrance over the internal malleolus of left leg, wound of exit two inches below the outer malleolus. No infection or signs of synovitis. Wounds healing by primary intention.

Case 19.—Samuel Copp, Company A, Eleventh U. S. Infantry, received a scalp wound, August 10, while he was lying on his abdomen on the summit of a hill. Wounds of entrance and exit about two inches apart, healed under the first dressing. He is suffering from a contusion of his abdomen he sustained by falling over an embankment during the same skirmish.

Case 20.—Arthur Sparks, Company C, Eleventh U. S. Infantry, received a wound of the lower third of the left thigh, August 10. Wound of entrance on external anterior aspect of thigh about five inches above patella. The bullet passed directly backward and came out on the opposite side on the same level without injuring the femur. Healing by primary intention.

Case 21.—George W. Whitlock, Company C, Sixteenth Pennsylvania Infantry, was in a kneeling position when wounded near Guayamo, August 9. The bullet entered the thigh near the perineum, over the adductor magnus muscle, passed in an outward and backward course and emerged from the gluteal region near or over the sciatic foramen. Hemorrhage slight. Paralysis of the foot and lower part of the leg points to injury of the sciatic nerve. Healing of wound without complications.

Case 22.—James Drummond, Company K, Sixteenth Massachusetts Infantry, was wounded near Guayamo, August 9. The bullet entered the neck on the left side, behind the sternocleido-mastoid muscle, two inches below the mastoid process. Wound of exit on the opposite side in front of the trapezius muscle. No immediate or remote complications. Wound healed by primary intention. Patient has suffered from slight attack of malarial fever.

Case 23.—Paul J. Mytzkie, Company D, Eleventh U. S. Infantry, was wounded in the skirmish near Mayaguez, August 10. The bullet made a flesh wound three inches above the external malleolus, which healed in a few days by primary intention under the first dressing.

Case 24.—Daniel J. Graves, Company M, Eleventh U. S. Infantry, received a gunshot wound of the thigh near Mayaguez, August 10. The bullet passed through the thigh in an antero posterior direction, fracturing the femur at the junction of the middle with the lower third. A week after the injury the patient was in excellent condition, the wounds remaining aseptic and healing rapidly.

Case 25.—Theodore H. Newbold, Company I, Sixteenth Pennsylvania Infantry, was shot while retreating during the skirmish near Guayamo, August 9. The bullet entered the right arm above the olecranon process and emerged from the extensor side of the forearm between the radius and the ulna. The olecranon process was broken off. The X-ray reveals the presence of a fragment of the bullet, or its mantel, lodged in the wound. Aseptic healing of the wound.

Case 26.—Clyde C. Frank, Company C, Sixteenth Pennsylvania Infantry, was injured near Guayamo, August 9. The bullet entered the inner surface of the middle of the right thigh, passed upward and backward, and in grazing the femur made a groove without fracturing the bone, emerging from the external and posterior aspect of the thigh. Both wounds healed by primary intention. In making a skiagraphic examination of the seat of injury a fragment of the bullet was discovered in the groove. The piece of lead, as well as a few loose fragments of bone, were removed August 17 by enlarging the wounds of entrance and exit. Operation by Dr. Shultze.

Case 27.—John L. Johnson, Company D, Eleventh U. S. Infantry, received a gunshot injury near Mayaguez, August 10. The bullet passed in an antero posterior direction through the middle third of the left leg, going through the space between the tibia and fibula. Hemorrhage slight. Healing by primary intention.

Case 28.—Samuel G. Frye, Company D, Fifth Artillery, was injured by a deflected bullet, as he stood by his cannon, near Mayaguez, August 10. The bullet passed through the soft tissues in the right anterior axillary fold without doing any further damage. The wound healed by primary intention.

Case 29.—Henry Gerrick, Company E, Eleventh U. S. Infantry, received a superficial wound over the pronator muscles, near Mayaguez, August 10. The wound healed promptly by granulation.

Case 30.—John Browning, Corporal, Battery D, Fifth Artillery, was wounded near Mayaguez, August 10. The bullet passed transversely through the soft tissues of the right forearm on a level with the wrist, in front of the radius and ulna. The bullet evidently cut the ulnar nerve and vein, as shown by the paralysis of the parts supplied by the nerve below the seat of the wound and the free venous hemorrhage which immediately followed the injury. Healing by primary intention.

The marked contrast in the results of the treatment of the wounded in Cuba and Porto Rico, I attribute entirely to the better preparations made for the last invasion, and not to any difference in the surgical skill of the medical officers. The surgeons engaged in the Cuban war were men exceptionally well prepared for their profession, and performed their onerous task with energy and enthusiasm. Ambulances were scarce, the fighting line far away from the base hospital, conditions which made it difficult to render timely and efficient first aid. Another circumstance which had its influence in interfering with the prompt and effective first aid to the wounded in Cuba was the large number of men who fell in battle in three days. The war in Cuba precipitated in a pitched battle; in Porto Rico it consisted in a number of skirmishes in which only a small number needed surgical attention. In Porto Rico the rear of the different armies was supplied with an adequate number of ambulances and Hospital Corps men. The first aid was rendered almost immediately after the wounds were received, after which the patients were conveyed to the hospital at once. A sufficient number of medical officers were on hand during each engagement to take immediate and proper care of the wounded. In most instances the wounds healed by primary intention under the first dressing. The value and importance of early surgical attention, and the first-aid dressing, became apparent in comparing the condition of the wounds, a week after the injuries were received, during the Cuban and Porto Rican campaigns.

ON THE FREQUENCY OF CRYPTORCHISM AND ITS RESULTS.

Cryptorchism and incomplete descent of the testicle are congenital defects, the frequency of which has never been established by reliable and extensive statistics. Undescended testicle, partial and complete, is frequently seen in infants and children, but becomes more rare with the development of the body to manhood. The writer has recently had an opportunity to make an accurate investigation into this subject by the examination of 9815 recruits for the Volunteer Service at Camp Tanner, Springfield, Ill. The ages of the men varied from 16 to 51. The following is the result of the examination with reference to the incomplete descent of the testicle :

Cryptorchism.—Right side, 12 ; left side, 22 ; both sides, 1.
Incomplete descent of testicle.—Right side, 10 ; with hernia, 1 ; left side, 14.

Total number of incomplete descent of the testicle in 9815 men, 59. Unilateral incomplete descent, the left side was affected 36 times, the right side 22. Out of 59 cases the defect was bilateral only once. In this case the inguinal canals were found completely obliterated, no trace of the testicle could be found. The man was in excellent health, married and father of several children. In only two instances was the incomplete descent of the organ complicated by a small hernia, in both cases on the right side. Both of these men were rejected. In all cases in which the testicle could be palpated the organ was found atrophic, seldom exceeding the size of a filbert or pigeon's egg, soft and not tender to touch. The testicles were most frequently found just within or below the external inguinal ring ; in the latter location it could be freely moved in all directions without causing any pain. None of the men thus afflicted complained of pain or even discomfort caused by the imperfectly developed and incompletely descended testicle. Recent scientific investigations appear to establish the fact that cryptorchism and incomplete descent of the testicle are attributed rather to an imperfect development of the organ than to a failure to reach its normal destination at the right time. The results of these researches as well as the deductions to be drawn from statistic material utilized in this paper seem to combine in teaching surgeons caution in undertaking early operations for cryptorchism for the purpose of transplanting the organ into its normal position and with a view of maintaining or increasing its functional activity. The congenital hernia which so constantly attends retarded descent of the testicle frequently disappears in the course of time without operative or truss pressure.

CHICKAMAUGA, June 25, 1898.

THE SEAT OF WAR AND OUR MILITARY SURGEONS.

At the time I am writing this communication I am at Fortress Monroe awaiting the arrival of the battleship *Yale* from Santiago de Cuba. Waiting is always tiresome, tedious, and often painful, but when it comes to waiting for a ship to take you to the seat of war, it is distressing. It has been the dream of my youth to take an active part in some great war, and now that I am in one, the very thought that I might not get near the fighting line is a source of keen disappointment. I have been in hopes that I would be present during the siege of Santiago de Cuba, but according to the messages that are being flashed (July 2) from the seat of war to the department in Washington, the stars and stripes will float over the doomed city in less than twenty-four hours. The *Yale* is expected to-day, but it will take at least two or three days for the troops to embark.

Our victories on land and sea will teach the crumbling monarchies of the old world that the American people are not only foremost in agriculture, commerce and the different industries, but that when forced to fight they know how to conduct a war. The heroic deeds of the American soldier have never been appreciated, except by those who were the means of giving him an opportunity of demonstrating his military qualities. England, Mexico and the native Indians, have been made to feel and are satisfied what the American soldiery can do. The proud Spaniards will be humuiliated in the eyes of the world as never before, and will soon plead for mercy and raise the white flag to negotiate for peace on any terms. Our people are now giving the world an object lesson in warfare that will not surely be forgotten. The military spirit is epidemic in our country; kindle it and it spreads like a flash of lightning, from North to South and East to West. We have the men, the muscle and the brains to bring into the field, at short notice, the best army in the world. Only sixty-five days have elapsed since the Chief Executive of the United States issued the first call for troops, and at the present time a fairly well equipped army of 200,000 men are in the field, eager and anxious to face the enemy. Our navy, the laughing-stock of haughty foreign countries, has grown with an astounding rapidity, and its achievements have already challenged the admiration of the world, and have become a source of pride to every loyal American citizen. Statesman and politicians may differ in their views regarding the propriety and advisability of extending our possessions beyond the present limits, but one thing remains sure, that our country—perhaps, less as matter of choice than of necessity—is destined to take an active part in the drama of international politics. The annexation of Hawaii and the present war with Spain—the latter provoked upon the most unselfish and purely humanitarian motives—have furnished the entering wedge into the field of foreign politics. Cuba should and must be owned by the United States. Cuba is the hot-bed, the breeding station of yellow fever, and always will remain so, whether under Spanish or Cuban rule. Yellow fever can be stamped out forever in less than two years after it has come into our possession. Yellow fever, always imported from Cuba, has retarded the prosperity of the South, and has ruined, at different times, the commerce of many of its otherwise flourishing cities, and has claimed the lives of more of our people than will be sacrificed in wiping out Spanish rule. Geographically and commercially, Cuba belongs to the United States. Cuban government would be only a repetition of what has always been going on in the neighboring islands and the republics of Central America—misrule and revolution. We want no such neighbors. Cuba must be freed from the Spanish yoke. The Cubans are not in a condition to establish and maintain a wise and prosperous self-government. Any such attempt would be little or no improvement over Spanish rule, either to its population or the people of the United States. The natural resources of the island are great, and are only awaiting a stable government for their development. The scourge of yellow fever, always a menace to the life and commerce of our people, more especially of the Southern States, must be quickly and permanently removed by effective sanitary measures, which can only be efficiently carried into effect by placing the island under the control of the government of the United States.

OUR MILITARY SURGEONS.

The medical profession of all countries has always been intensely patriotic in times of war. The doctors always have been and always will be the salt of the population. Their education and training are of a nature to ensure qualities necessary to citizenship of the highest type. The practice of their profession, even in times of peace, is admirably adapted to prepare them for the emergencies of war. In the exercise of their duties they encounter hardships and dangers foreign to the lives of the average citizens. They face epidemics far worse than bullets, as far as danger to life is concerned, without fear of death. In cities devastated by the scourge of yellow fever or cholera, when everybody else that can leaves for a place of safety, the doctors remain at their posts and minister to the sick and dying without any expectation of a substantial financial reward, or even the gratitude of the recipients of their services. As the number of their well-to-do legitimate clients diminishes during the inevitable exodus their attention to the poor remains unremitting. Day after day and night after night the familiar modest conveyance with its lonely occupant can be seen in the depopulated streets, wending its way to the hovels of the poor on its errands of mercy. The unselfish work of the doctor has never been properly appreciated. From the most ancient times, when battles were fought hand to hand with the most primitive weapons, medical men were on hand ready to dress the wounded and to heal the sick. None of them have ever attained the fame of the innumerable heroes who distinguished themselves on the battlefield and whose deeds have been immortalized in prose and poetry. In rank, pay and social position the military surgeon has always been at a disadvantage as compared with the leaders of troops. The one that knows how to kill and mutilate has reaped more credit for his work than the one bent on his sole mission to prevent and treat disease and to heal wounds. Fame, influence and public recognition are within easy reach of the successful military commander; they need not be looked for, much less expected, by the hard-working, faithful, skilful surgeon. His greatest reward, in military or civil practice, always has been and always will be the consciousness of having performed his duty to his fellow-men.

During the present war with Spain the medical profession has responded promptly and nobly to the call of the country. The medical officers now in the field can be classified as follows: Surgeons and assistant-surgeons United States Army; surgeons and assistant-surgeons United States Navy; surgeons and assistant-surgeons of Volunteers; acting assistant-surgeons United States Army; acting assistant-surgeons of United States Navy. The surgeons of the army and navy, after a long, comparative rest, have now found an opportunity to make good use of their special training. Many of these men have taken a course in the Army Medical School and most of them have enjoyed excellent clinical opportunities in the large cities. Surgeon-General Sternberg has taken special pains to stimulate the younger members of his department to improve themselves by stationing them for a year in medical centers, where they had an opportunity to attend lectures and clinics and to do laboratory work. The advantages of instruction of this kind will become obvious in this war. The professional military surgeon is well versed in the executive part of his duties, which is sadly lacking in the less favored volunteer surgeon. To the praise of the former it must be said that he is always ready to impart knowledge of this kind to his colleague from civil life. The volunteer surgeon represents that portion of the young men of our profession who possess not only a full measure of patriotism, but also a laudable degree of surgery and enthusiasm. Many of them now in the field have left a lucrative practice, and are now giving their services to the country for an insignificant salary. Many of our volunteer surgeons have had hospital experience either as internes or attending physicians, or both. Their practical experience has been such as to prepare them well for their work in the field. Without exception all are anxious to go to the front to assume the hardships of active military life. They are anxious and ready to learn and work. The only complaints I have heard were about the monotony and nothing-to-do of camp life. Every one that goes to the front is envied by those left behind. They have left their homes, their families, their practice, to sacrifice themselves, if need be, for the good cause. I am sure when the Medical and Surgical History of the American-Spanish War is written it will be brim full of the good work done by the volunteer surgeons. It will record at the same time many deeds of bravery and heroism on their part. The acting assistant-surgeons, both in the Army and the Navy. are so-called contract surgeons. They are appointed, without examination, by the respective Surgeon-Generals, for the duration of the war, and are given the rank and pay of a first lieutenant. They are mostly bright young men, recently from college or hospital, who will do their good share in preventing disease and in relieving the sufferings of the sick and wounded. The Association of Military Surgeons of the United States has done the most during its short existence of eight years in establishing the most friendly relations between the professional and civilian military surgeons, and in preparing the medical service for war. The interest in this association will be greatly enhanced by the present war, and the first meeting after the close of hostilities will be a large and enthusiastic one.

As I write, an order reaches me from Washington instructing me to be in readiness to leave this evening or tomorrow morning on the hospital ship *Relief*, which calls here on its way from New York to Santiago. Acting Assistant-Surgeon, Henry S. Greenleaf, son of the Chief Surgeon of the Army in the field, accompanies me, and will be associated with me in my future work.

FORTRESS MONROE, July 2, 1898.

HEADQUARTERS FIFTH ARMY CORPS,
BEFORE SANTIAGO, July 12, 1898.

As the hospital ship *Relief* came in sight of the seat of war every one of its passengers watched with interest and anxiety the indications of the present status of the conflict. When we sailed from Fortress Monroe, Sunday, July 3, fighting was in progress, and not having received information of any kind since that time we were impatient for news. On reaching Guantanamo we came in sight of a number of warships floating lazily on the placid ocean, like silent sentinels, some six to eight miles from the shore. The little bay was crowded with empty transports, all of which indicated that we were not as yet in possession of Santiago. The pilot of a patrol boat finally, in a voice like that of a fog horn, communicated to us the news that the greater part of the Spanish fleet had been destroyed and that the Spanish loss in dead, wounded and prisoners was great. Among the most important prizes of the naval battle was the heroic admiral of the Spanish fleet, who was then a prisoner on board of one of the men-of-war. The land forces were near the city making preparations for the final attack. A partial, if not a complete victory had been won, and we had the satisfaction of knowing that we had not come in vain. Our captain was directed to bring his ship to anchor near Siboney. When we came in sight of this little mining town we saw on shore rows of tents, over which floated the red cross flag, showing us that we had reached the place for which we had been intended. The little engine of a narrow-gauge mining railroad was puffing and screeching up and down along the coast conveying supplies from the landing to the camp. On the side of a hill were the shelter tents of a company of infantry on detail for guard duty. On the crest of a number of high hills which fringe the coast could be seen block-houses recently vacated by the Spaniards. A grove of palm trees in a near valley reminded us that we had reached the tropical climate. The steamer *Olivette*, floating the Red Cross, was anchored near the shore. Major Appel, surgeon in charge of this hospital ship was the first person to board our vessel, and gave us the first reliable account of the recent battle. His appearance was enough to give us an insight into his experience of the last few days. He was worn out by hard work and his anxiety for the many wounded under his charge. He spoke in the most flattering terms of the services of Acting Assistant-Surgeon Parker of New Orleans. Owing to the depth of the ocean, it was impossible to find anchorage for the *Relief* on the first day. The sea was quite rough and it was under difficulties that Majors Torney, Appel and the writer were landed on July 7. The first person I met on landing was Major Nancrede, professor of surgery in the University of Michigan. He reached Cuba at the right time to give his valuable services to his country. Hundreds of wounded had received the benefit of his skill. Slight in figure, and anything but robust, he persisted in working night and day, until he was worn out by fatigue and loss of sleep. I found him under a fly-tent, resting on the hot sand. He was making preparations for an early departure, in charge of 301 wounded, on the transport ship *City of Washington*. The country, and especially those who received his careful attention, owe a debt of gratitude to Major Nancrede that can never be paid.

On reaching the camp I met my friend of years ago, Major LaGarde, U. S. A., in charge of the hospital at Siboney, which had been made the base of operations of the troops in the field. It would have been difficult indeed to find a better man for this trying and responsible position. By nature and training a perfect gentleman, learned in his profession and experienced in warfare, he was in possession of all the qualities required of a medical officer in charge of such an important post. The difficulties he encountered often appeared insurmountable, but were met successfully by his cool and mature judgment and promptness of action. His kind but dignified conduct commanded the respect of his subordinates, who were only too willing to carry out his orders. Considering the limited supplies within his reach, and the many urgent demands for them from all sides, it is a source of astonishment that so much was accomplished in so short a time. Inadequate preparations had been made for casualties on such a large scale, but he made the best of the limited resources and used them where most needed, often regardless of prescribed military channels. In less than four days nearly 1000 wounded soldiers sought the shelter of his tents. During this trying time he worked incessantly, regardless of his own health and personal comforts. When the roll of honor is made out at the close of the war, the name of Major LaGarde deserves a well-merited place at the head of the list. In his arduous duties he was ably assisted by Major McCreary and Captains Ireland and Fountleroy of the United States Army, and a corps of acting assistant surgeons. The camp is on the shore, on a limited plateau at the base of the mountain rising behind the little mining village. The condition of the wounded men furnished satisfactory proof that good work had been done here, as well as at the front. On my arrival many of the wounded had already been placed on board a transport ship, but more than 400 remained in the general hospital. On the whole, the treatment to which the wounded men were subjected was characterized by conservatism. Only a very small number of primary amputations were performed. Bullets that were found lodged in the body were allowed to remain undisturbed, unless they could be removed readily and without additional risk. A number of cases of penetrating wounds of the abdomen and chest were doing well without operative interference. Penetrating gunshot wounds of the skull were treated by enlarging the wound of entrance, removal of detatched fragments of bone, and drainage. Several cases in which a bullet passed through the skull, injuring only the surface of the brain, were doing well. With few exceptions, wounds of the large joints were in a fair way to recovery under the most conservative treatment.

A study of the immense amount of material collected at this station satisfied the surgeons that the explosive effect of the small caliber bullet has been greatly overestimated. The subsequent employment of the X-ray in many of these cases will undoubtedly confirm the results of these observations. The battle of Santiago resulted in 157 killed and 1300 wounded. Nearly all wounds of the soft parts healed rapidly. Suppuration in these cases was the exception, primary healing the rule. The deceptive nature of wounds of the soft parts is best shown by a case of gunshot injury of the knee-joint that came under my care during the first afternoon. The knee-joint was distended to its utmost, painful and tender on pressure. A rise in temperature and corresponding general disturbances indicated the existence of infection. A small opening was found over the inner border of the patella on a level with the articulations. A careful search for the wound of exit proved negative. During the preparation of the limb for the operation another effort was made to find a second wound with the same result.

After the patient was under the influence of the anesthetic the limb was rendered bloodless by elastic constriction made at its base. The knee-joint was opened freely by an incision in line with the wound of entrance. A large quantity of liquid blood escaped. A furrow on the surface of the internal condyle of the femur led to a deep groove in the under surface of the patella, and taking these as a guide the wound of exit was finally discovered with the groove directly over the inner surface of the knee-joint in the form of a small slit. Through this slit-like opening a probe was inserted and advanced into the grooves in a straight line without any difficulty. There could remain no further doubt as to the existence of a wound of exit. The joint contained a large quantity of blood, but no detached fragments of bone. The joint was washed out with a 2 per cent. solution of carbolic acid, the capsule sewed with catgut and the external wounds with silk and, after dressing, the limb was immobilized by the use of a posterior splint, made of the sheath of the palm leaf. The patient was doing well when sent home on a transport, two days later.

AFTER THE BATTLE.

The day after my arrival I went to the front, about ten miles from Siboney. A colored orderly was my only companion; he rode at a respectful distance to the rear. The whole distance the road was crowded with mule teams, soldiers and refugees. The refugees made up a seething mass of humanity from start to finish. At a low estimate, I must have passed on that day two thousand souls, including men, women, children and naked infants. The day was hot, and the suffering of the fleeing inhabitants of Santiago, the besieged city, and adjacent villages can be better imagined than described. Indian fashion, the women walked while some of the men enjoyed the pleasure of a mule- or donkey-ride. Most of them were barefoot and dressed in rags; children and infants naked. Dudes with high collar, white necktie and straw hat were few and far between. An occasional old umbrella and a well-worn, recently-washed white dress marked the ladies of distinction. Their earthly possessions usually consisted of a small bundle carried on the heads of the women, or a worn-out basket meagerly loaded with mangoes or cocoanuts. The color of the skin of the passing crowd presented many tints, from white to jet-black. The women were noted for their ugliness, the men for their eagerness to get beyond the reach of guns. Little squads of Cuban soldiers were encountered from time to time, apparently anxious to get only as far as the rear of our advancing army. These men display an appearance of courage just now that is something marvellous. Before the blue-coats came here they infested the inaccessible jungles at a safe distance from the Spanish guns, making an occasional midnight raid to keep the Spaniards on the lookout; now they can be seen on the roads in small groups relating to each other how they cut down the Spanish marines with their national weapon on reaching the shore after their vessels were demolished by our navy. The ragged refugees, fleeing in all directions and mingling freely with our troops, as they do, carry with them the filth of many generations and a rich supply of yellow fever germs, which will ultimately kill more of our men than the Spanish soldiers. On the way to the front Chicago push and enterprise came in evidence by the appearance of a mule of the smallest species carrying a rider all out of proportion in size to the diminutive animal. Suspended from the neck and dangling over the breast of the animal, was a piece of pasteboard on which was inscribed, "The Chicago Record." To my question, "How is the Chicago Record?" the rider answered, "All sold out." On reaching General Shafter's headquarters, I reported to Lieut.-Colonel Pope, Chief Surgeon of the Fifth Army Corps. Colonel Pope has worked night and day since the troops landed here. He has done all in his power to make his limited supplies meet the enormous demands. At headquarters is the principal field hospital, in charge of Major Wood, a graduate of Rush Medical College, ably assisted by Major Johnson and a corps of acting assistant-surgeons. At the time of my arrival, 68 wounded officers and men were under treatment at this hospital. Major Wood kindly invited me to perform an amputation of the thigh, for gangrene caused by a gunshot injury, which had fractured the lower portion of the femur and cut the popliteal artery. The wound of entrance was over the inner margin of the patella and that of exit over the lower and outer aspect of the thigh. The knee-joint and thigh were enormously swollen and the gangrene had extended to within a few inches of the knee-joint. The pulse was rapid and the temperature over 105 degrees F. The amputation was made at the seat of fracture, above the condyles of the femur, by making a long oval anterior and a short oval posterior flap. The vessel was tied above the seat of injury. Notwithstanding the extensive edema of the tissues, the wound was in excellent condition three days later, and the temperature normal. Here I found many interesting cases on the way to recovery in which the nature of the injury would have been ample excuse for rendering a very grave prognosis—among them a number of cases of penetrating wounds of the chest and abdomen. Four laparotomies for gunshot wounds were made here by a volunteer surgeon, but as all the patients died it was deemed expedient to assign him for duty at a place where he could do more good than harm.

IN THE CAMP OF THE ENEMY.

In the afternoon I accompanied Acting Assistant-Surgeon Goodfellow to El Caney. The trip was made for the purpose of taking charge of sixteen wounded Spaniards we were to transfer to the Spanish Army. On the way to El Caney we found many recent graves and numerous dead horses covered only with a few inches of dirt. The stench from this source in some places was almost unbearable. The little village of El Caney is located on the summit of a hill with an old dilapidated church for its center. The public square and the few streets were thronged with refugees, from 8000 to 10,000 in number. Crowds of refugees were also seen in the woods around this village gathering mangoes and cocoanuts, about the only food supply at this time. In the vestry room of the church we found a representative of the Red Cross Association dealing out hardtack and flour to the hungry multitude. The wounded Spaniards were lying in a row on the floor of the church, one of them in a dying condition. All that could be transported were conveyed in four ambulances under a small detachment of troops to our fighting line. Here a flag of truce was received, which was carried by an orderly, the detachment was left behind and we passed our line. As soon as the Spanish intrenchments came in sight the signal was given and was promptly answered by the enemy. Two officers with a flag of truce advanced toward us and we were halted at a little bridge very near Santiago and below the first intrenchment. We were received very courteously by the officers and asked to a seat upon the grass in the shade of a clump of trees. Rum, beer and cigarettes were furnished for the entertainment of the callers. The object of the visit was explained, whereupon a hospital corps of about thirty men with sixteen litters, in charge of a captain of the line and a medical officer, made their appearance. The wounded men were unloaded from the ambulances and conveyed on litters to within the Spanish line. The visit was such a cordial and pleasant one that we found it very difficult to part from our newly made friends. After bidding the officers a hearty adieu and mounting my horse, I was urged to dismount and say another farewell, a request which was responded to with pleasure. The two little parties then separated and made their way in a slow and dignified manner in the direction of the respective breastworks.

ARTILLERY ATTACK.

The first armistice expired at noon, July 11. In the afternoon a heavy cannonading commenced and was kept up until late in the evening. Next morning it was resumed, however with less vigor. During this bombardment the Spaniards renewed their recently gained reputation as effective marksmen. One of our best cannons was hit and literally lifted into the air. An officer was killed and a number of men injured. During the afternoon, while cannonading was still going on, I went to the front, but on reaching our line bombardment was discontinued, and under a flag of truce the commanding generals met and held a conference. The result of this interview remains a secret to this hour.

GENERAL MILES ARRIVES.

Major-General Miles and staff reached Siboney, yesterday, on the steamer *Yale* and today he proceeded to headquarters.

The appearance of yellow fever at different places occupied by our army has made our troops more anxious than ever to complete their task. The frequent drenching rains and inadequate equipments have also done much to render the men restless and anxious to fight.

RECENT EXPERIENCES IN MILITARY SURGERY AFTER THE BATTLE OF SANTIAGO.

ON BOARD THE HOSPITAL SHIP "RELIEF,"
JULY 22, 1898.

WOUND INFECTIONS.

Military surgery is no more no less than emergency surgery in civil practice. The surgeon in daily practice has learned long ago that every accidental wound must practically be regarded and treated as an infected wound. In this respect the military surgeon of today has the advantage over his colleague in civil practice in knowing that the small caliber bullet inflicts wounds which *per se* are more often aseptic than septic. Our recent experience in Cuba has shown that the small jacketed bullet seldom carries with it into the tissues clothing or any other infectious substances. Most of the wounds of the soft tissues, uncomplicated by visceral lesions, which in themselves would become a source of infection, healed by primary intention in a remarkably short time. If infection followed it usually did so in the superficial portion of the wound in connection with the skin, and what is more than suggestive, the wound of exit was more frequently affected than the wound of entrance. This can be readily explained from the larger size of the wound and more extensive laceration and tearing of the tissues. In many of the cases ideal healing of the wound did not occur, owing to a subsequent limited superficial suppuration of the wound. The deep tissues were seldom implicated in such cases. I have reason to believe that some of the compound fractures which are now suppurating had such a source of infection, that is the extension of a superficial infection to the seat of fracture. Two weeks have now elapsed since the battle of Santiago was fought and we are now in a position to inquire more critically into the manner in which the wounds became infected. The many failures in protecting the more serious wounds against infection are attributable to three principal causes: 1. Inadequate supply of first dressing. 2. Faulty application of first dressing. 3. Unnecessary change of dressing. The medical officers with the regiments and in the field hospitals were hampered in their work by an insufficiency of proper material. The rapidity with which the invasion was planned and executed, the difficulties encountered in transporting the hospital supplies to the front and the unexpected large number of wounded readily explain the lack of dressing material when it was most needed. Many of the dressings were too small and not sufficiently secured to keep them in place in transporting the wounded from the front to the field hospitals. As a rule not enough attention was paid to the immobilization of the injured part, an important element in securing rest for the wound and in guarding against displacement of the dressings. It is a source of regret that plaster-of-Paris dressings were not more frequently employed in the treatment of gunshot fractures of the extremities. Another very palpable evil in causing infection was the too common practice of unnecessary change of dressing. The transfer of patients from one surgeon to another could not be avoided. Patients brought from the first dressing station to the Field Hospital usually were subjected to a change of dressing and, when a few days later they reached the General Hospital at Siboney, they had to undergo the same ordeal and often not only once, but as often as they came into the hands of another surgeon. Patients not thus treated were dissatisfied, as the laymen are still laboring under the erroneous impression that the oftener a wound is dressed the quicker it will heal. It is difficult to eradicate such a deep-rooted and time-honored belief, and patients will continue to clamor for a change of dressing, and the good-natured, hard-working surgeons only too often yield to such unreasonable requests. The evil of meddlesome surgery has become very apparent during our brief Cuban campaign and has taught us an important lesson that must be heeded in the future. Our military surgeons must learn to realize the value and importance of the first aid dressing. In all cases in which the first examination does not reveal the existence of complications which require subsequent operative treatment the diagnosis tag should convey this important instruction: *"Dressing not to be touched unless symptoms demand it.* Such instruction is significant and must be followed to the letter by all surgeons in subsequent charge of the patient.

I am satisfied more than ever of the necessity of including in the first aid dressing package an antiseptic powder. For years I have used for this purpose a combination of boracic acid and salicylic acid, 4 : 1, with the most satisfactory results. I am also partial to absorbent sterile cotton for this particular purpose, as it constitutes a more perfect filter than loose gauze. A teaspoonful of this powder dusted on the wound forms with the blood that escapes and the overlying cotton a firm crust, which seals the wound hermetically. Should the primary dressing become saturated with blood, the same powder should be dusted over the wet dressing, and an additional compress of cotton is added to the dressing. After the first dressing has been applied it should not be removed except for good and substantial reasons. Much can be done in the after-treatment in the way of readjusting the bandage and in immobilizing the injured part, but the first dressing must remain unless local or general symptoms set in which would warrant its removal. Malaria and yellow fever, that crept in upon us so insidiously, are responsible for many unnecessary changes of dressing. The appearance of fever in a wounded man naturally leads to the suspicion that there is something wrong in the wound. Many dressings were changed on this ground, nothing abnormal was found in the wounds, and a day or two later the nature of the fever was recognized and the patients were either given quinine or were sent to the yellow fever hospital, in accordance with the diagnosis made. *Every change of dressing, more especially in military practice, is attended by risk of infection and must be scrupulously avoided, unless local or general symptoms indicate the existence of complications which demand surgical intervention.* In writing the above it is not my intention to cast any reflection on the work of our surgeons; on the contrary, I willingly bear witness to the ability, faithfulness and unselfishness with which they have done their duty. A better and more conscientious group of medical officers it would be difficult to select anywhere. The results on the whole are excellent, but I am hopeful that they can be improved in the future by placing more stress and attention to the value and importance of the first dressing, and wish to repeat again and in a most forcible way the language of the late Professor von Nussbaum: "*The fate of the wounded rests in the hands of the one who applies the first dressing.*" If this is true in civil practice, its meaning can not be misinterpreted in military surgery.

EFFECTS OF BULLETS ON THE SOFT TISSUES.

In recent cases the small tubular wound made by the Mauser bullet was surrounded by a narrow zone of contused tissue, and the wound space itself filled either with liquid or coagulated blood. A few days later the wound itself was found surrounded with an area of suggillation, which varied in extent according to the nature of the tissues and the amount of extravasation. In cases in which the bullet passed through the tissues some distance, and not far from the surface of the skin the location and direction of the wound canal was indicated by discoloration of the skin a few days after the injury occurred. In a number of cases of aseptic wounds in which the bullet had lodged in the tissues and was removed a week or ten days later, I had an opportunity to study the remote effects of the injury on the tissues. In all cases the swelling of the tissues at this time had nearly or entirely obliterated the tubular wound, the location of which was indicated by a dark discoloration, parenchymatous extravasation, remains of fluid or coagulated blood, and a limited area of edema and infiltration. These conditions served as a useful guide in following the course of the bullet. The bullet itself was usually found loose in a small cavity filled with liquid blood or bloody serum, while a more extensive zone of infiltration indicated the early stage of encapsulation. I have no further doubt but what the new bullet will become encapsulated and remain harmless in the tissues, as readily or more so than the old-fashioned leaden bullet. In isolated cases late suppuration at the seat of the bullet resulted in the formation of a circumscribed abscess, a complication which aided the surgeons in locating, finding and removing the missile. It was a surprise to us all to find that in more than 10 per cent. of all the wounded, the bullet was found lodged in the tissues, a vastly greater number than we had any reason to expect. The reason for this became apparent when we began to study the condition of the bullets removed. A large proportion of the bullets removed were found deformed, showing that they were deflected bullets, which had struck a hard object or passed through a resisting medium before they reached the final object for which they were intended. The ground upon which the battle was fought is stony and covered with trees and thick underbrush, furnishing the most favorable conditions for deflection of the missiles. Some of the firing was done at a great

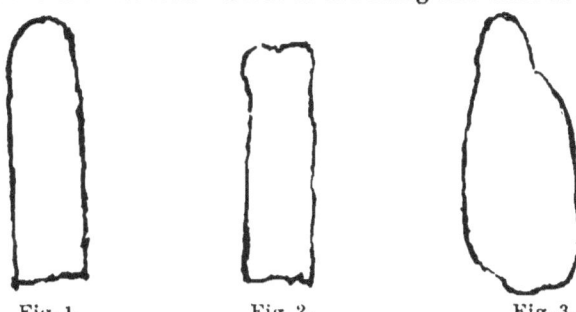

Fig. 1.   Fig. 2.   Fig. 3.

distance, so that occasionally a spent ball was found in the soft tissues without injury of the bones. Such a bullet is shown in Fig. 1. The bullet is a nickel encased Mauser projectile, natural size, the jacket perfect, and was removed from behind the tibia about four inches above the ankle joint. It entered the calf of the leg below the popliteal space and never touched

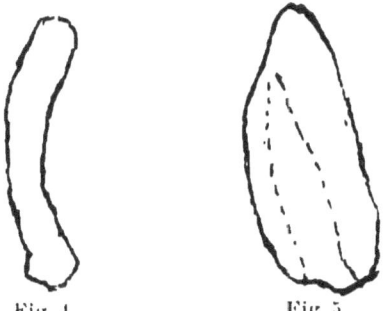

Fig. 4.   Fig. 5.

the bone. Fig. 2 represents the same kind of a bullet, the point flattened and mushroomed, removed from the head of the tibia. This bullet was probably fired from a great distance, and the deformity was produced by the bone. Figs. 3, 4, 5, represent a nickel-clad bullet very much deformed. It was found lodged in the deep tissues of the thigh about two inches from the wound of entrance, slightly overlapping the femur near the middle of the shaft. The bullet evidently struck a stone behind its point, and was deflected before it entered the tissues. It was much flattened and curved. Fig. 3 shows the convex side point of bullet and jacket perfect. Fig. 4 shows the edge and curve of the bullet. Fig. 5 represents the convex side, showing a wide rent in the jacket indicated by the dotted lines, the lead exposed between them. Figs. 6, 7, 8, illustrate the deformity of a large caliber brass-clad bullet. As the bullet was removed from the soft tissues from a wound without bone injury, the deformity must have been caused outside of the body. The bullet is flattened on one side from a point near the tip to near the base of the lead core. Fig. 6 shows the convex side; behind the last transverse groove the lead is ex-

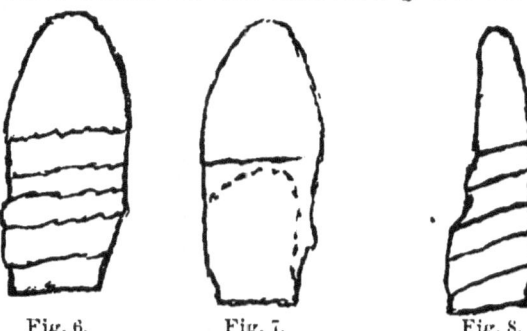

Fig. 6.   Fig. 7.   Fig. 8.

posed. Fig. 7 illustrates the flattened side of the dotted line, indicating a defect in the brass jacket. Fig. 8 shows the margin of the bullet, and the location and extent of flattening. As the Spanish army is armed exclusively with the Mauser rifle, the weapon from which this bullet was fired must have been in the hands of a volunteer, or possibly a Cuban.

THE VALUE OF THE X-RAY IN MILITARY PRACTICE.

The use of the probe as a diagnostic instrument in locating bullets in modern military service has been almost entirely superseded by dissection and the employment of the X-ray. If from the nature of the injury and the symptoms presented the bullet is located in a part of the body readily and safely accessible to the knife and it is deemed advisable and expedient to remove it, this can often be done more expeditiously and with a greater degree of certainty by enlarging the track made by the bullet than by relying on the probe in finding and on the forceps in extracting the bullet. If, as is often the case, the whereabouts of the bullet is not known, its presence and exact location can be determined without any pain or any additional risks to the patient by the use of the X-ray. All of the bullets removed on board the hospital ship *Relief* were located in this manner. Dr. Gray, an expert in skiagraphy, who has charge of the scientific work of the floating hospital, has been of the greatest service to the surgeons in enabling them to locate bullets and in guiding them as to the advisability of undertaking an operation for their removal. His large collection of skiagraph pictures will also furnish a flood of new light on the effects of the small caliber bullet on the different bones of the body. Dr. Gray's work will constitute an essential and enduring corner-stone of a much-needed modern work on military surgery. The skiagraph has enabled us to diagnosticate the existence or absence of fracture in a number of doubtful cases in which we had to depend exclusively on this diagnostic resource. In fractures in close proximity to large joints the X-ray has been of the greatest value in ascertaining whether or not the fracture extended into the joint. In one case of gunshot wound at the base of the thigh in which the bullet passed in the direction of the trochanteric portion of the femur, opinions were at variance concerning the extent of injury to the bone. Some of the surgeons made a diagnosis of fracture while others contended that there was no fracture but believed that the bullet had made a deep groove in the anterior portion of the bone and had possibly opened the capsule of the joint at the same time. The X-ray picture clearly demonstrated the absence of fracture and the existence of a deep furrow with numerous fragments on each side. The X-ray apparatus also proved of the greatest practical utility in showing the displacement of fragments in gunshot fractures of the long bones, which enabled the surgeons to resort to timely measures to prevent vicious union. The fluoroscope has greatly added to the practical value of skiagraphy. In the light of our recent experience the X-ray has become an indispensable diagnostic resource to the military surgeon in active service, and the suggestion that every chief surgeon of every army corps should be supplied with a portable apparatus and an expert to use it, must be considered a timely and urgent one.

THE WOUNDED OF THE BATTLE OF SANTIAGO.

It will be of interest to the profession to learn something defi-

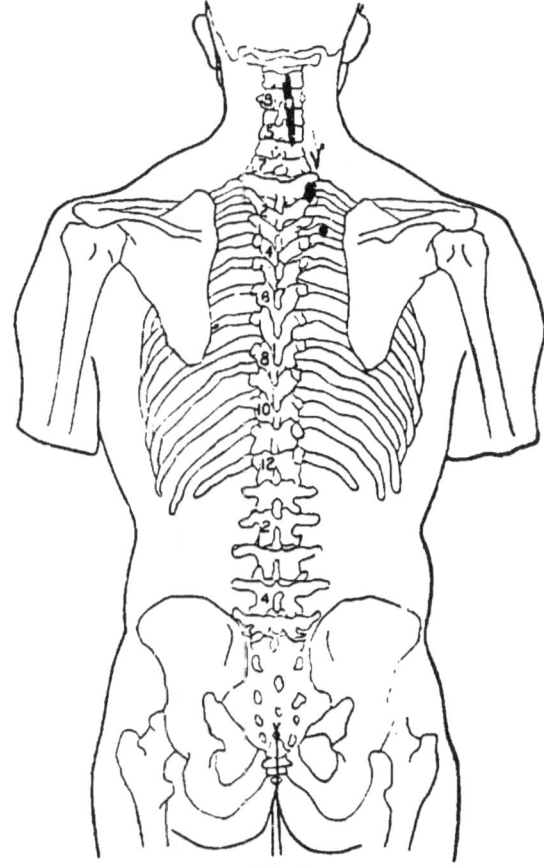

Fig. 9.

nite of the nature of the wounds and their more remote results on the victims of Spanish bullets in the battle of Santiago. Two weeks have passed away since the battle. A considerable number of the wounded have died since, and many have left for the United States on the *Olivette*, *Solace* and transport ships. Among the 130 wounded now on the way to their homes on the hospital ship, *Relief*, I have selected a number of cases of more than usual interest, for the purpose of studying the effects of the small caliber bullet, immediate and remote, on the different organs and regions of the body. It is my intention to give the course of the bullets by marking on the diagrams accompanying the report of each case, the wound of entrance and exit. A study of the diagrams will show that deflection of the bullet in the body is exceptional. As a rule, the wound canal was in a perfectly straight line from one wound to the other. By following the track of the bullet it is not difficult to determine the organ or organs implicated in the injury. I shall classify the cases so as to embrace gunshot wounds of 1. the head ; 2, the neck ; 3, the spine ; 4, the chest ; 5. the abdomen ; 6, the extremities.

GUNSHOT WOUNDS OF THE HEAD.

To my own knowledge, a number of gunshot wounds of the head that survived long enough to be transported to the general hospital at Siboney, died within twelve days after the receipt of the injury. In all of the cases intracranial infection was the immediate cause of death. Encephalitis and leptomeningitis constituted the fatal complications. The beginning of the intracranial inflammation was always announced by cerebral hernia, which in size was proportionate to the extent and intensity of the inflammatory process. The surgical treatment resorted to in most instances proved powerless in limiting the infection. If these cases had been studied with a little more care during life, and if postmortem examinations had been made more frequently, valuable material could have been obtained for the advancement of the as yet imperfectly developed science of cerebral localization.

Case 1.— Fred Shockley, Company D, Tenth Cavalry, wounded July 2. When injury was received the patient was lying on his abdomen with chest and head extended at the base of the ridge occupied by the enemy, which position readily explains the unusual course of the bullet. The bullet struck the occipital base at a tangent, producing a comminuted fracture with depression ; it then made a deep groove in the back of the neck and then re-entered the body on a level with the first rib to the left of the seventh cervical vertebra, passed through the chest and escaped in front through the second intercostal space, a little to the left of the mammary line (Fig. 9). Soon after the injury was received he coughed up a small quantity of blood; no hemorrhage since or any indications of pneumothorax, pneumonia or pleuritis. The chest wounds healed by primary intention. At first had convulsions for a few moments; no loss of consciousness, but clonic spasms of both arms. At present intellect is unimpaired; has some headache and a sensation of throbbing in the head; some impairment of motion and sensation of right leg and complete loss of motion of toes of right foot; has some pain in eyes and slight dimness of vision.

Case 2.—Patrick Ward, Company I, Third Cavalry, admit-

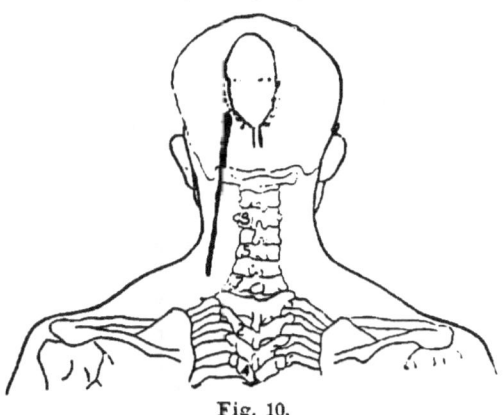

Fig. 10.

ted from hospital at Siboney to hospital ship, *Relief*, July 11. Injury probably received in the same manner as in Case 1. A large defect in the occipital bone marked the wound of entrance and exit in the skull, the opening enlarged by operation. The linear wound below, and extending as far as the last cervical vertebra, was undoubtedly made in following and removing the bullet. The cranial defect and course of bullet are outlined in Figure 10.

A cerebral hernia projects from the opening, and a deep-seated cerebral abscess was recently discovered, opened and drained. In part the hernia is covered by skin. Both parietal bones are the seat of a comminuted fracture. Mental faculties not impaired; no focal symptoms. The patient is losing strength rapidly and will soon succumb to the intra-cranial lesion.

Case 3.—Jerome Russel, Company A, Thirteenth Infantry, was wounded July 1. When brought on board the *Relief* a cerebral hernia about the size of a hen's egg was found over the sagittal suture, an inch in front of the occipital protuberance. The wound was suppurating, and digital exploration revealed a small circular opening directly in front of the occipital protuberance. This opening was evidently the wound of entrance, and by operation, had been connected with the wound of exit by a channel an inch in length and half as wide. The

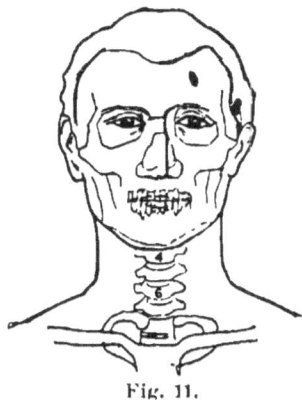

Fig. 11.

hernia occcupied the wound of exit. A number of loose fragments of bone have been removed at different times. There is marked hemiplegia on the left side, the forearm is strongly flexed and in close contact with the chest. Sensation is not diminished; speech clear, but ideas confused; pupils react to light; incontinence of urine; extensive decubitus over sacrum; temperature 100.5 degrees F.; pulse and respiration normal.

Case 4.—B. C. Parker, Company C, Fourth Infantry, was wounded July 1. The bullet entered the left temporal region, comminuting the bone in that region extensively, and escaped over the left frontal eminence (Fig. 11). The cranial defect was increased by the removal of a number of loose fragments. There had been quite a profuse sero-purulent discharge from the wound. The only focal symptom consists in a pricking sensation in the right foot or chest when the wound is being dressed. His mind is clear most of the time, occasionally slight confusion and wandering. The absence of cerebral hernia in this case is the surest indication that the infection is local.

GUNSHOT WOUNDS OF THE NECK.

Case 5. — Lieut. Albert Scott, Company C, Thirteenth Infantry, on July 1, while standing with his company at the foot of a hill, during the advance on Santiago, received a wound in the neck. The bullet entered the neck on the right side just below the inferior maxillary bone, one inch in front of the angle of the jaw. The wound of entrance is a clean cut hole about the size of a lead pencil. The course of the bullet

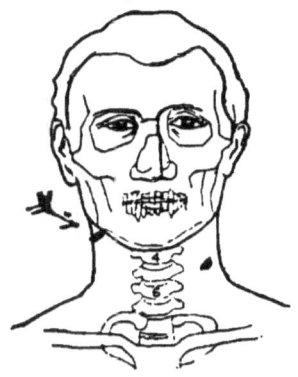

Fig. 12.

was backward and slightly downward, emerging at the back of the neck on a level with and to the left of the fifth cervical vertebra (Fig. 12).

At the moment the injury was inflicted he felt no pain in the wound, but he experienced a sensation as if he had been grasped by the wrists and thrown violently to the ground. The wound of exit is of the same size and appearance as the wound of entrance. Very slight hemorrhage. A few minutes after receiving the injury he was carried from the firing line by members of his company, and was soon transported to the First Division Hospital, where he remained for ten days, after which he was removed in an ambulance to the hospital at Siboney, a distance of seven miles over a very rough road, and a day later was transferred to the *Relief.*

He first became aware of the existence of the wound on the way from the field to the hospital. At the time he came on board the hospital ship he was voiceless, and made constant efforts to clear his bronchial tubes of mucus. Complete paralysis of right arm and leg, and partial loss of power in left arm and leg. Respiration normal, but an almost constant spasmodic cough, no control over sphincters, involuntary passages from both bladder and bowels, great debility and profuse sweating; complains of pain all over the body. Morphia and atropin given to subdue pain. A radiograph taken by Dr. Gray shows an injury of one of the cervical vertebræ, probably the fifth. Injury seems to be to the left of the body of the bone. Has received no treatment other than complete rest

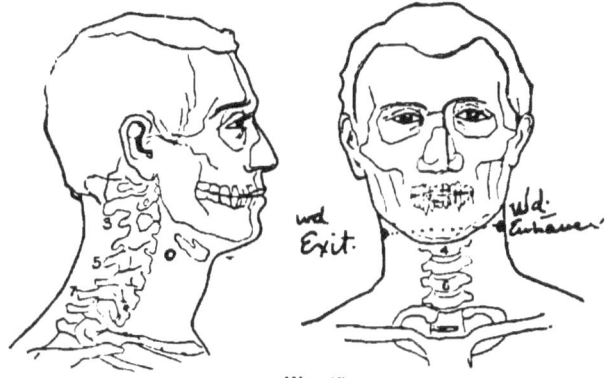

Fig. 13.

and a nightly anodyne as noted above, which secures a good night's sleep, and markedly diminishes the sweating. Has regained control of the sphincters, and is able to use bed pan and urinal.

July 19.—During the past six days there has been a decided improvement in the general condition of the patient. He is brighter in appearance, he can articulate more distinctly, and there is a decided return of power in the right leg. The right hand is still absolutely powerless, but the grip of the left hand is decidedly stronger. Appetite and circulation good.

July 21.—Improvement in general condition still continues. The external wounds healed by primary intention, and the scars can only be seen on making a very careful inspection.

Trional and sulphonal have been substituted for the morphia.

Case 6.—Oscar C. Buck, Company F, Second Infantry, was shot by a sharpshooter hiding in a tree, July 11. The bullet passed through the neck from side to side. The first and only evidence the patient had that he was injured was bleeding from the throat, the hemorrhage at first being quite profuse. Stiffness of the neck and pain on movement have been the only symptoms complained of since. The bullet entered over the sterno-cleido-mastoid muscle on the left side, about two and one-half inches from the mastoid process. The wound of entrance was circular and very small; the wound of exit on the same level but about half an inch nearer the spine (Fig. 13). Three days later a small superficial abscess formed in the wound of exit, which was evacuated by dilating the wound. Both wounds were perfectly healed July 20. Judging from the course of the bullet it is difficult to understand how the principal nerves and large vessels of the neck escaped injury. This is one of those cases that require careful watching, as a traumatic aneurysm may develop later in the throat if the bullet injured the external tunics of either of the carotid arteries.

Case 7.—Charles F. Flickinger, Company C, Fourth Infantry, was wounded July 1, while lying down. The bullet entered the left posterior cervical triangle on a level with the spinous process of the fifth cervical vertebra, midway between the spine and the posterior border of the sterno-cleido-mastoid muscle, and emerged opposite the spinous process of the seventh dorsal vertebra, and equidistant from that point and the posterior border of the scapula (Fig. 14a). The patient complains of severe pain in shoulders on attempting to move, but is free from any symptoms that would indicate any injury to the spinal cord. He was within 100 yards of the enemy when he was wounded.

GUNSHOT WOUNDS OF THE SPINE.

All cases of gunshot wounds of the spine in which the cord was seriously damaged have died, or will die in the near future. The immediate cause of death in such cases is either a septic leptomeningitis or sepsis and exhaustion from decubitus. Death from the first named cause takes place early as the result of infection of the wound and extension of the inflammation at the seat of the visceral injury along the meninges and surface of the spinal cord. The first case of this kind I saw was at El Caney a few days after the battle of Santiago. The patient was a Spanish prisoner. I found him lying on the bare stone floor of the village church. The bullet had entered over the center of the spine at the junction of the dorsal with the lumbar vertebræ, its course apparently being directly forward. Complete paraplegia below the seat of injury. The bladder was distended, nearly reaching the level of the umbilicus; incontinence of urine. The neck, trunk above the wound, and upper extremities rigid; fever; pulse rapid and small, countenance extremely pale. The wound was protected by a small

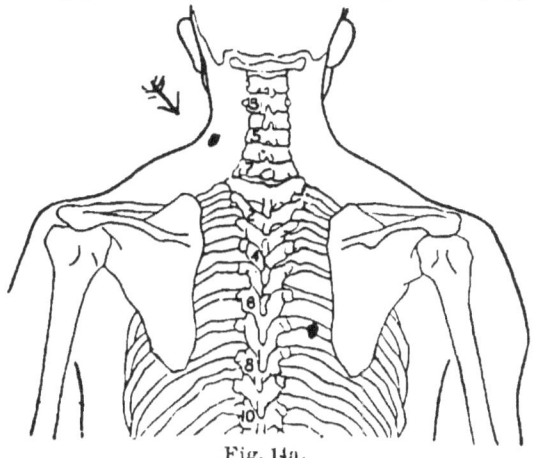

Fig. 14a.

dirty dressing, and was suppurating. I doubt not that the patient died in less than twenty-four hours after I saw him. Wounds of the spine without injury to cord were frequently attended by temporary paralysis varying greatly in degree and duration.

Case 8.—George Kelly, Company C, Seventeenth Infantry, was shot July 1, while lying in a prone position. The bullet, which was fired from a blockhouse on the summit of a hill, at a distance of about 600 yards, entered the body at a point a little below and at the middle of the right ilium, and emerged from the opposite side about three inches below the crest of the left ilium (Fig. 14b). The patient asserts that he suffered intense pain immediately after he was shot, and that he is now free from pain except when he attempts to walk. The pain thus caused he refers to the sacro-coccygeal articulation. The wounds are healed, and the absence of paralysis is the best evidence that the contents of the spinal canal escaped injury,

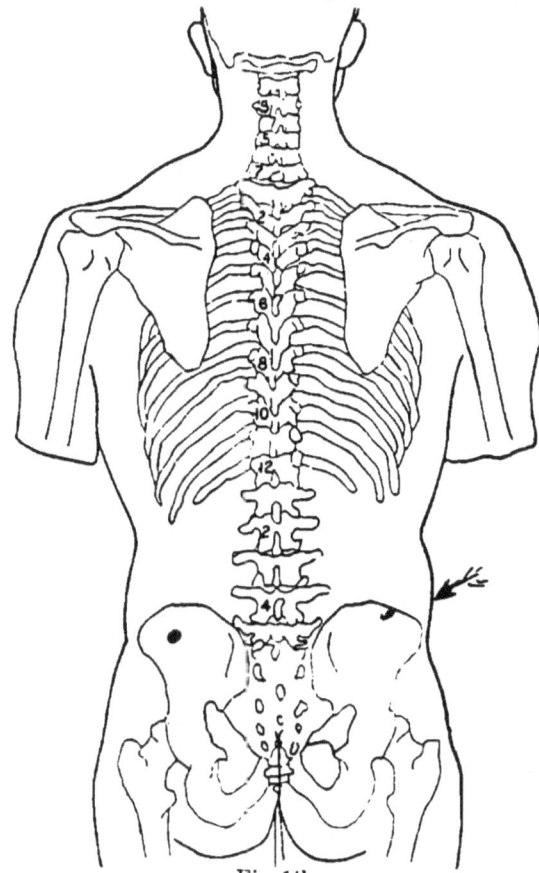

Fig. 14b.

although the bullet must have passed transversely through the first sacral vertebra.

Case 9.—John Robinson, Company C, Twenty-fourth Infantry. The bullet entered the supraspinous fossa of left scapual and escaped from the right lumbar region, having perforated in its long course the lung, spinal cord, diaphragm and liver

(Fig. 15). Wounds healed in ten days. Expectoration bloody, complete paraplegia. Beginning extensive decubitus over sacrum and spinous processes.

Case 10.—Otto Derr, Company A, Twenty-first Infantry, was

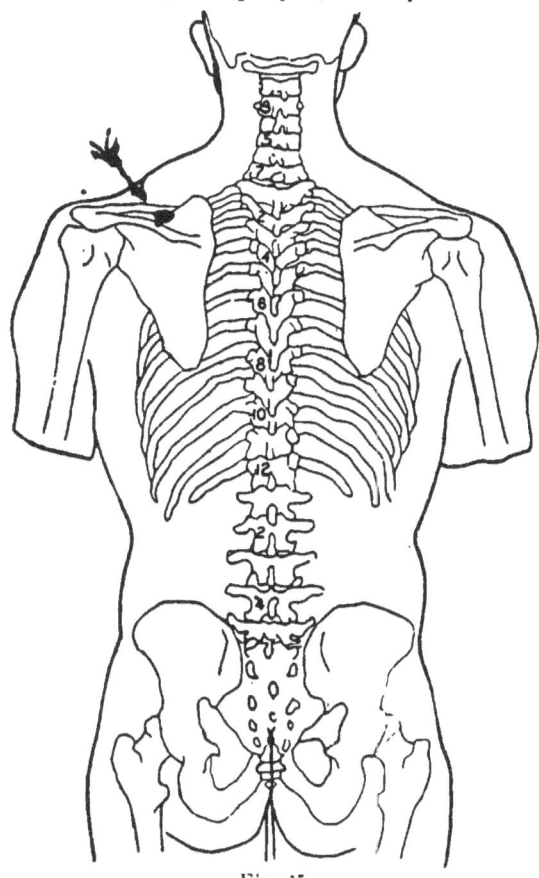

Fig. 15.

wounded July 2. Bullet passed through the chest from side to side from the post-axillary line on the right side to a corresponding point on the opposite side, on a level with the seventh intercostal space. Complete paralysis of motion and sensation below the seat of spinal injury. The wounds healed, but life was threatened at the time from a commencing septic decubitus.

Case 11.—Lewis W. Carlisle, Company K, Seventy-first New York Volunteers, was hit by a shrapnel in the back, on a level with the third lumbar vertebra, shattering the spinous and left lateral processes of the same. The missile was removed as soon as the patient reached the Division Hospital. As profuse suppuration set in and continued, the patient was anesthetized July 18, and a number of fragments of bone removed. A large abscess cavity in the right lumbar region communicated with the wound. The cavity was drained by making a counter-opening in line with Simon's incision. Impaired sensation in the right leg was the most important local symptom in this case.

Case 12.—Charles J. Reardon, Company C, Sixteenth Infantry, was wounded by a fragment of shrapnel which struck him as he lay on his back with his shoulders raised ready to fire. The wound was directly over the spine, on a level with the fourth dorsal vertebra, the missile evidently opening the spinal canal and injuring its contents. The foreign body remains imbedded in the tissues; its location so far has not been determined. Paraplegia is complete below the level of the umbilicus. On July 18 the patient was still alive, but an extensive moist decubitus became the direct cause of death in the course of a few days.

GUNSHOT WOUNDS OF THE CHEST.

It is well known that during the Civil War men had a better chance for life when the bullet passed through the chest than when the chest was opened and the ball removed. The same remains true now, although not to the same extent, as the small caliber bullet is less likely to carry with it into the chest clothing or other infective material. The number of cases of chest wounds that lived long enough to reach the hospital on the coast is still more astonishing, and what is surprising is the fact that unless the hemorrhage was severe the symptoms were mild, some of the patients being confined to bed only for a few days. All of these cases were treated on the expectant plan, i.e., by dressing the external wound or wounds in the usual manner. In no instance was the pleural cavity opened for the purpose of arresting the hemorrhage.

Case 13.—Wm. A. Cooper, Company A, Tenth Cavalry, was wounded July 1. The bullet entered an inch below the left nipple, and escaped from the body an inch below the costal arch in the mammary line (Fig. 16). It is questionable whether the bullet opened either the pleural or peritoneal cavity, as the

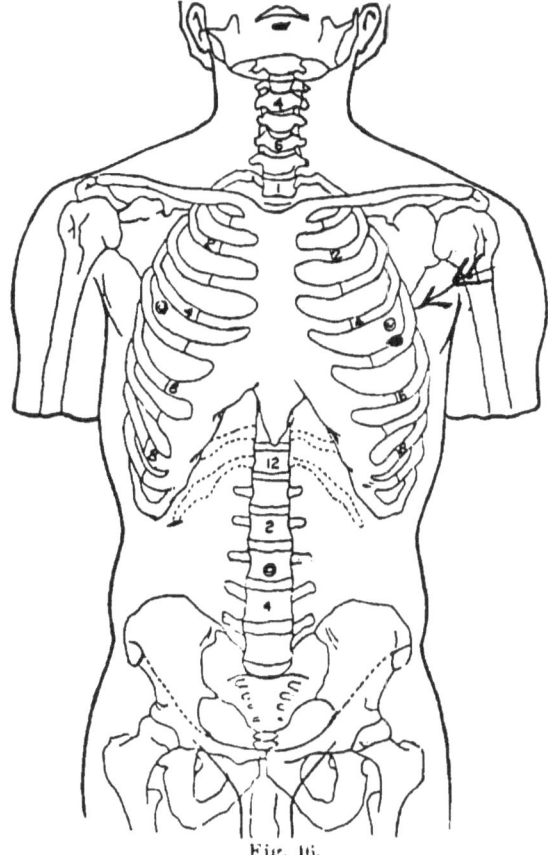

Fig. 16.

injury was not followed by any symptoms referable to visceral wounds of the chest or abdomen, although the course of the bullet was such as to give rise to the suspicion that either or both of these cavities might have been invaded.

Case 14.—Edward O'Flaherty, Company C, Sixteenth Infantry, was wounded July 2 by a 45-caliber ball from a bursting shrapnel. The projectile entered below the angle of the right scapula, passed through the lung, diaphragm and liver, lodging beneath the skin in front, between the seventh and eighth ribs (Fig. 17). Bloody expectoration for some time and slight rise in temperature.

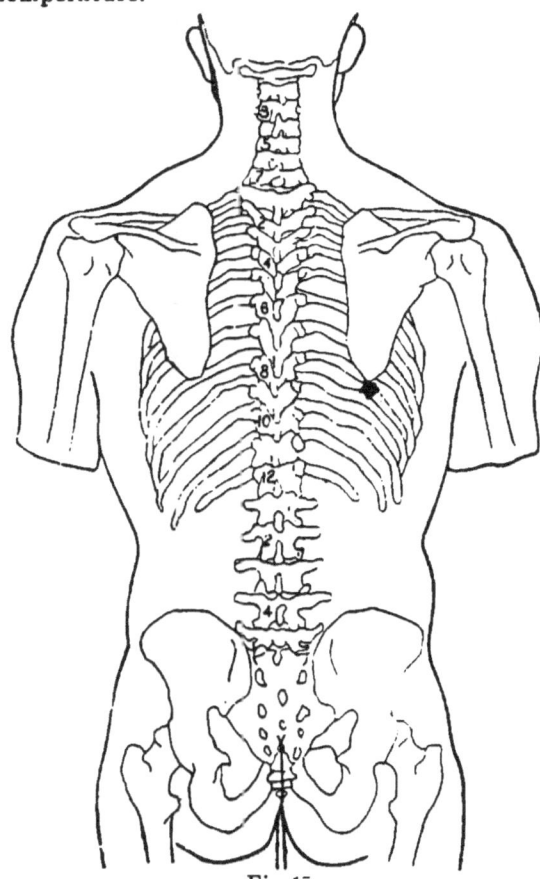

Fig. 17.

July 12.—Temperature normal.
July 21.—Patient suffers but little inconvenience from his wound. No peritoneal or pleural effusion. General condition promises an early and complete recovery.

Case 15.—John B. Semca, Company G, Twenty-second Infantry, was wounded July 1, by a bullet which entered his back just below the angle of the left scapula, passed upward through the lung, neck and jaw and emerged through the

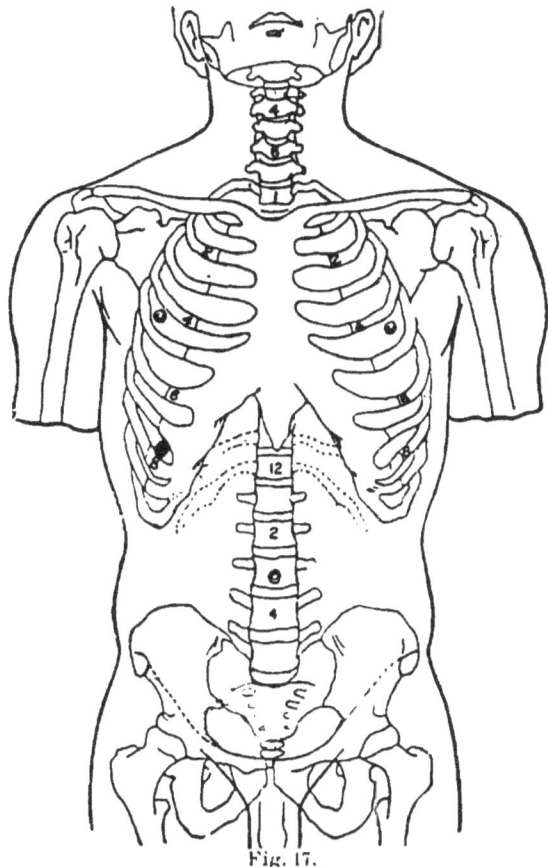

Fig. 17.

alveolar process of the right bicuspid tooth, cutting the tongue slightly (Fig. 18). All wounds healed in a short time by primary intention. Hemoptysis profuse immediately after he was shot, and slight for the following few days. Left arm at first nearly powerless, with desquamation of skin of the hand. Function of the arm is returning gradually. In three weeks the patient was able to sit up for a short time each day. Physical examination of the chest at this time revealed nothing abnormal.

Case 16.—Winslow Clark, Company G, First Volunteer Cavalry, was wounded July 1, by a bullet which entered the chest

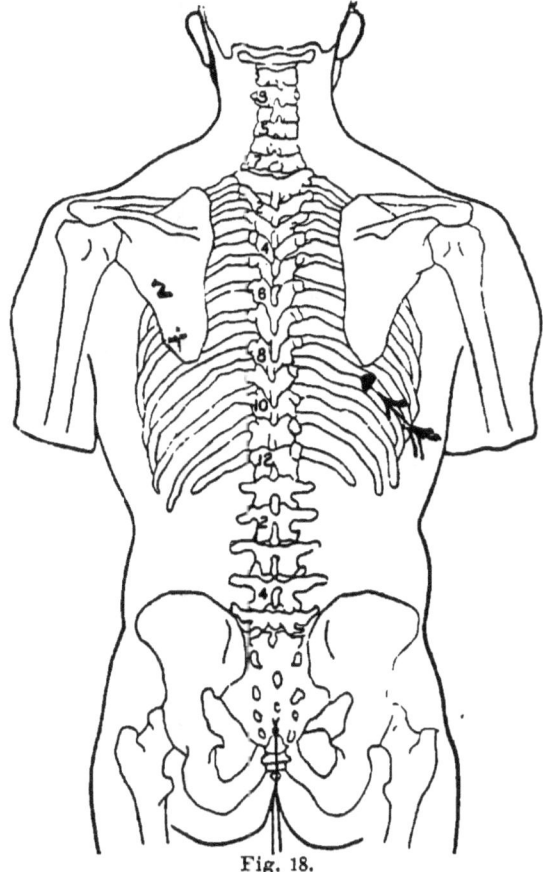

Fig. 18.

by first perforating the left scapula through the infraspinous fossa, three inches above the angle and a inch from the spinal border (Fig. 19). No wound of exit. The probable course of the bullet was downward and forward. Some hemoptysis and fever. No vomiting of blood. The hemothorax was quite extensive and was relieved by tapping, a week after the injury. He is now (July 22) convalescing rapidly.

Case 17.—Arthur Fairbrother, Company C, Third Cavalry, sustained a perforating gunshot wound of the chest July 1.

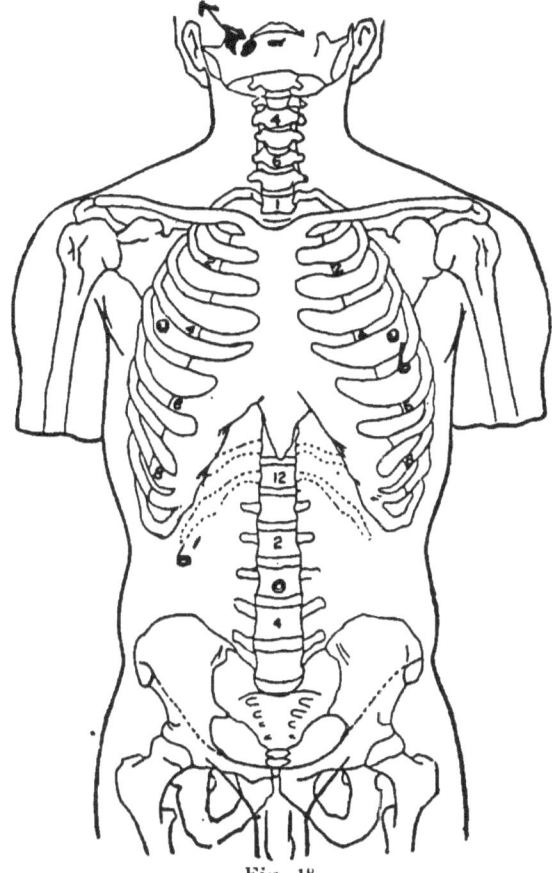

Fig. 18.

The bullet entered the chest just below the middle of the right clavicle (Fig. 20). No wound of exit. Hemoptysis rather profuse, followed by hemothorax. Has had fever, off and on, probably malarial. Patient was admitted to the *Relief* July 15. Wound not completely closed. On coughing, dark fluid blood escapes. Nearly the entire pleural cavity filled with blood. Two days later three pints of dark fluid blood were removed by tapping and siphonage. Sputum at this time still bloody.

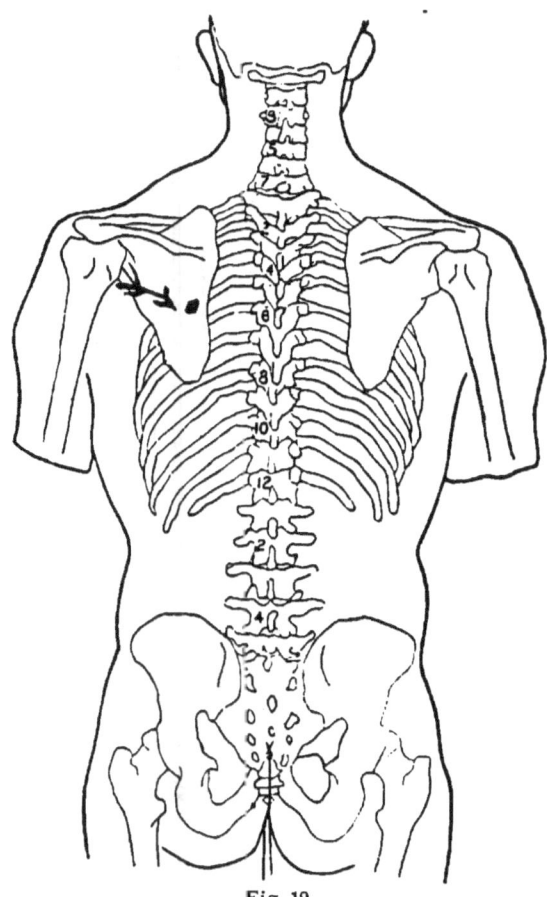

Fig. 19.

July 22.—Patient much improved. No signs of empyema. Hemothorax diminished, but may require a second tapping.

Case 18.—Scanlon, Company K, Third Cavalry, was wounded on the second day of the battle of Santiago. The ball entered the chest through the third rib midclavicular line on the right side, passed downward and backward and escaped in the gluteal region on the same side, after perforating the ilium (Fig. 21). The ball must have passed through the lung, diaphragm and liver. Hemoptysis slight, but distressing nausea, vomiting and pain. Admitted to the hospital ship *Relief* July 15. At that time he had a constant temperature ranging between 100 and 102 degrees F., vomiting, diarrhea and rapid emaciation. Great pain over the liver and ascending colon. Hemothorax and marked swelling in the region of the liver and abdominal cavity

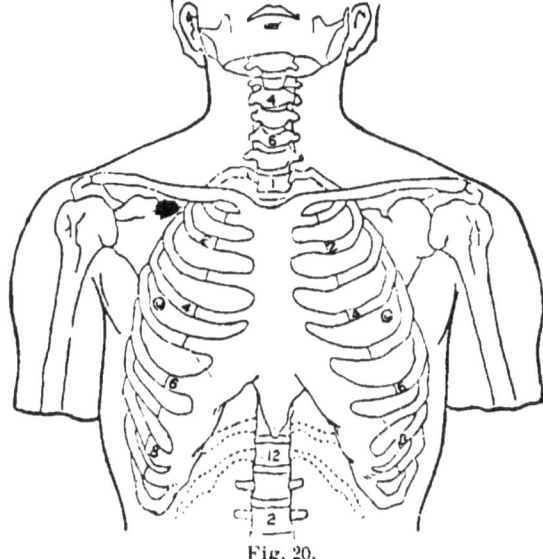

Fig. 20.

on the right side. Examination of urine negative. Owing to the great debility and pronounced anemia it was not deemed advisable to resort to laparotomy.

Case 19.—Harry Mitchell, Company C, Seventh Infantry, was wounded July 1. The bullet entered over the right acromion process, passed through the apices of both lungs and escaped through the second intercostal space above the right nipple (Fig. 22). No hemoptysis at any time, dry cough and a moderate hemothorax on the right side. Has suffered from quotidian form of malarial fever, which is yielding to quinin. A speedy and complete recovery is expected.

Case 20.—Lieut. John Robertson, Company G, Sixth Infantry, received a gunshot wound of the upper third of right thigh about 10 o'clock July 1. The profuse hemorrhage was partly controlled by an improvised tourniquet applied by an officer of the line. He was carried to the rear by the men of his com-

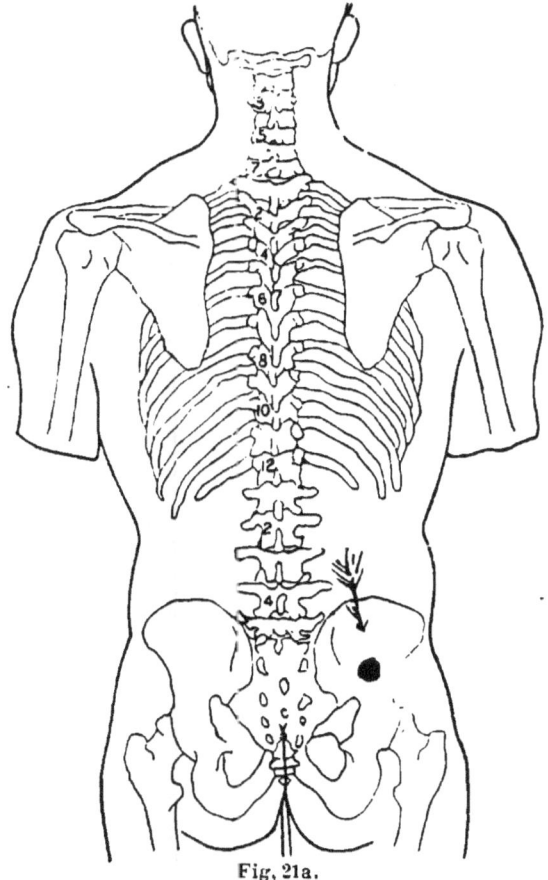

Fig. 21a.

pany, and while thus conveyed he was shot in the left breast, the bullet entering just below the left nipple and passing through the chest in an antero-posterior direction (Fig. 23). He was wounded a third time, the bullet grazing the inner side of the left knee. The first dressing was applied in the First

Division Hospital. The fracture of the thigh was dressed by the use of a long splint. From here he was sent, on July 9, to the Third Division Hospital, and two days later was brought on board the *Relief*. At this time both chest wounds were healed. The thigh wounds remained aseptic. A radiograph

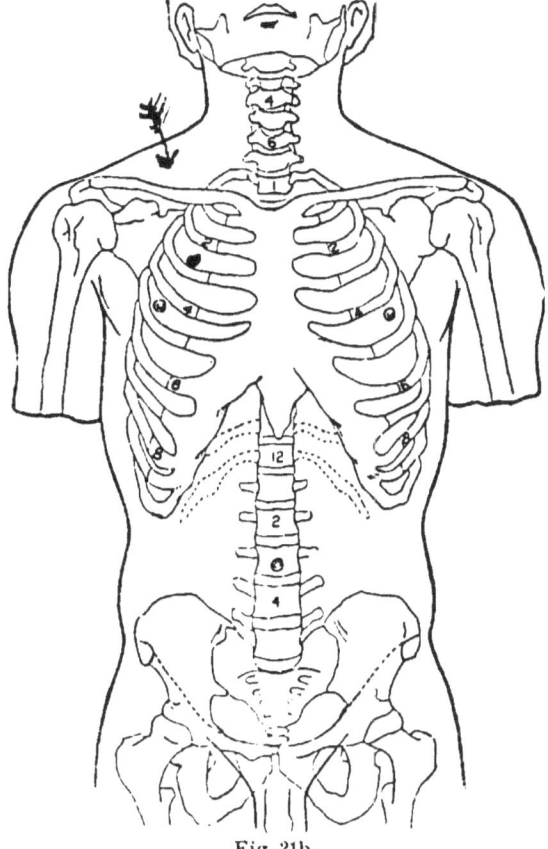

Fig. 21b.

showed great displacement of the fragments by overlapping. The fracture was then treated by confining the limb upon a double-inclined plane, consisting of a hollow posterior splint made of the sheath of the leaf of the cocoa palm, to which was added an anterior thigh splint of wire gauze. After dressing, the limb was placed in a sling. No pulmonary or pleuritic complications.

Case 21.—Henry T. Darby, Company D, Thirteenth Infantry, received a perforating gunshot wound of the chest July 1. The ball entered on the right side, above the angle and at the outer

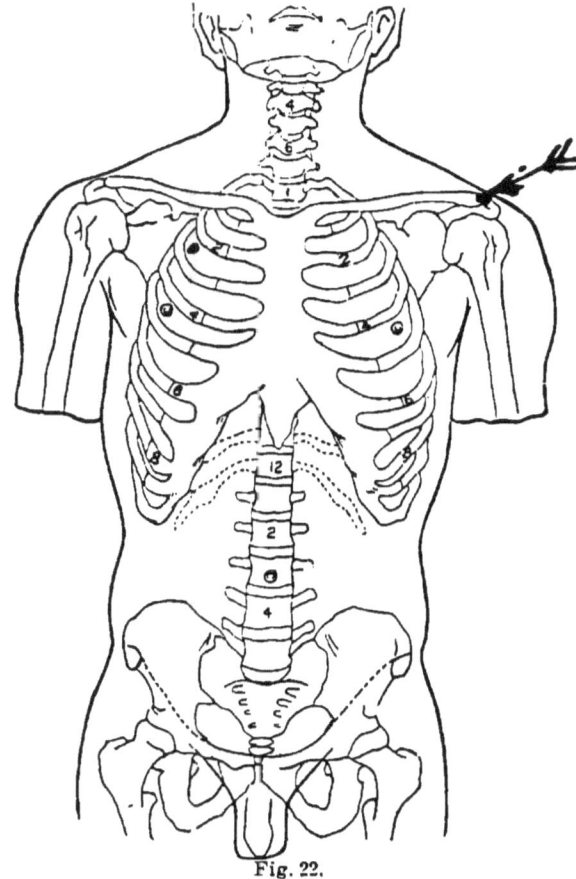
Fig. 22.

border of the right scapula, passed through the chest and escaped through the fourth intercostal space in front, on the opposite side, two inches outside of the mammary line (Fig. 24.) When the patient came on board the *Relief*, July 9, he complained of great difficulty in breathing; he was pale and greatly prostrated; temperature 102 degrees F. The physical signs indicated the presence of a copious pleuritic effusion on the left side. The chest was opened by an incision through the sixth intercostal space, in the axillary line, July 11. About three

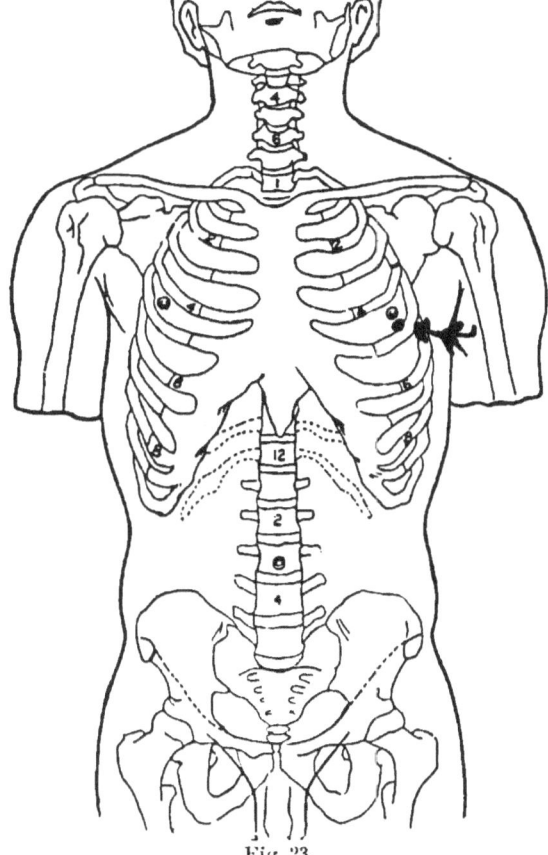
Fig. 23.

pints of fluid blood escaped. Gauze drainage. The lung expanded rapidly and the patient commenced to improve.

No further doubt can remain in regard to the difference in the mortality of gunshot wounds inflicted with the large and small caliber bullets. The cases related above appear to prove that the danger incident to gunshot wounds of the chest made by the small projectile, consists in complicating injuries involving the heart and large blood-vessels, and that in the absence of such injuries the prognosis is favorable. It seems that empyema is a rare remote result of such injuries. Rib resection and free incision and drainage of the chest in such instances must be reserved for cases in which a positive diagnosis of empyema can be made. The safest and best treatment for hemothorax requiring operative interference is tapping and evacuation by siphonage.

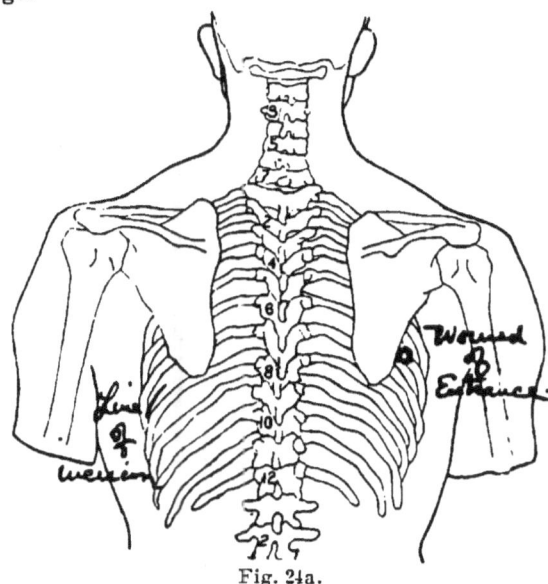

Fig. 24a.

GUNSHOT WOUNDS OF THE ABDOMEN.

Our recent experience in Cuba has more than ever confirmed my conviction that not infrequently cases of penetrating gunshot wounds of the abdomen will recover without active surgical interference. For years I have maintained, as the result of clinical experience and experiments on the cadaver, that a bullet may pass through the abdomen on a level and above the umbilicus in an antero-posterior direction without producing visceral injuries demanding operative intervention. Elsewhere the results of my experience and experimentation concerning such injuries have been published. If the bullet traverses the small intestine area it is more than probable that from one to fourteen perforations will be found.

Four laparotomies for perforating gunshot wounds of the abdomen were performed in the First Division Hospital, the only ones, to my knowledge, during the Cuban Campaign. All of the patients died. This unfavorable experience should not deter surgeons from performing the operation in the future in cases in which from the course of the bullet it is reasonable to assume that the bullet has made visceral injuries which would be sure to destroy life without surgical interference.

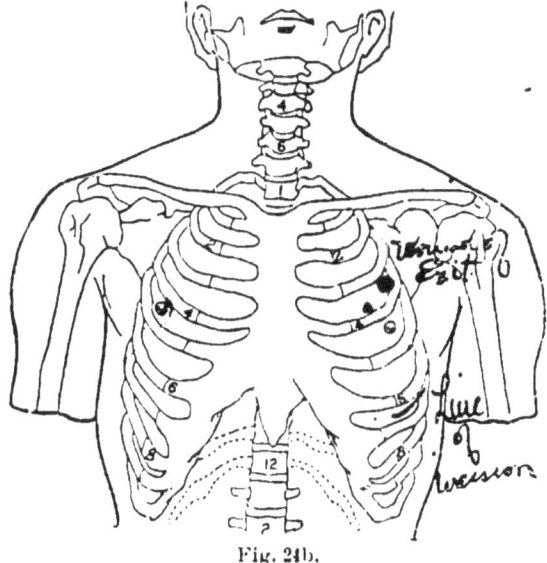

Fig. 24b.

In other cases the employment of diagnostic tests for the purpose of demonstrating the existence or absence of intestinal perforations will enable the surgeon to decide what course to pursue. Abdominal section is always justifiable in cases of internal hemorrhage sufficient in amount to threaten life.

A number of cases of gunshot wounds of the abdomen have been related in connection with gunshot injuries of the neck and chest, in which the cavity of the chest and abdomen and their contents were implicated at the same time, and which are on the way to recovery without laparotomy having been performed. I have seen a number of cases of perforating wounds of the abdomen in the First and Third Division Hos-

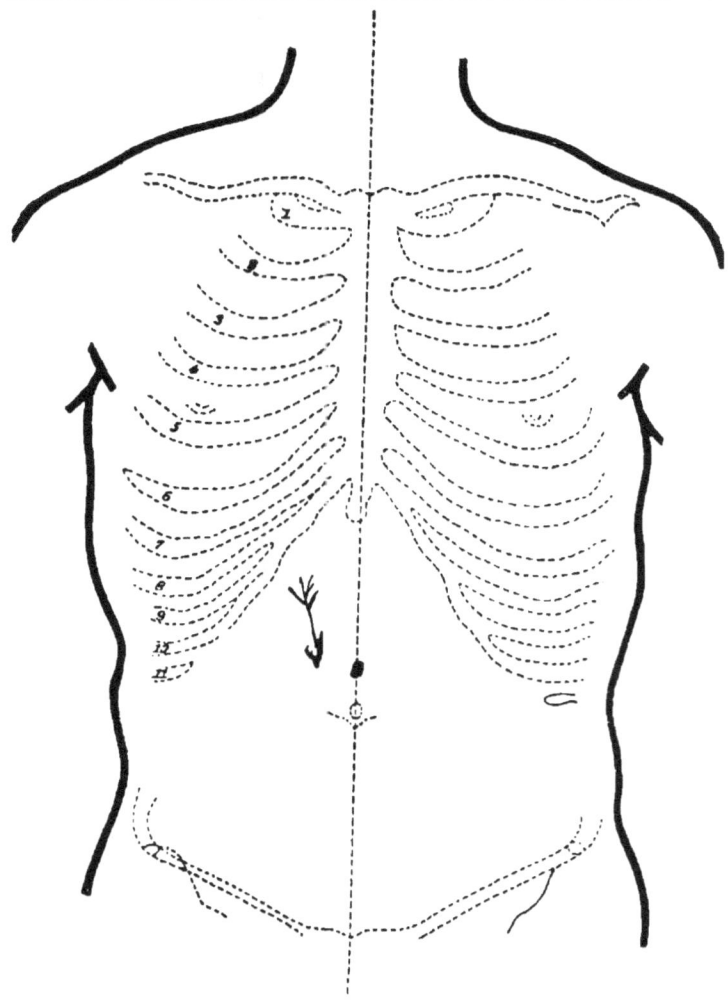

Fig. 25a.

pitals that were on a fair way to recovery without operation before they were sent home on transport ships. In most of these instances the bullet wounds were either in the umbilical region or one of the iliac fossæ. The following case presents features of more than usual clinical and surgical interest:

Case 22.—J. F. Taylor, Company D, Tenth Cavalry, was wounded July 2. At the time the injury was received he was

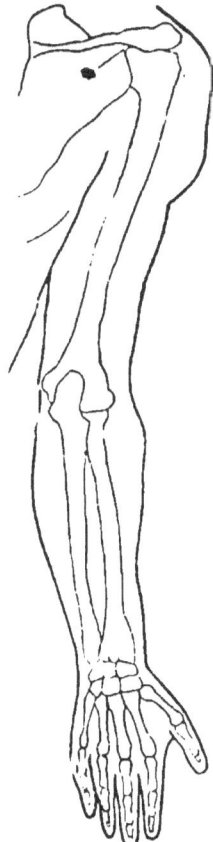

Fig. 25b.

in the ventral prone position. The bullet entered the left shoulder in the infraspinatus fossa one inch below the spinous process of the scapula, and passed downward and inward and lodged under the skin in the median line, two inches above the umbilicus (Fig. 25). Hemoptysis considerable during the first day, when it gradually subsided. He complained of great pain and tenderness in the right side of the abdomen. No vomiting or symptoms of more than a circumscribed peritonitis. An abscess formed in the abdominal wall, which was opened July 20, and the bullet was removed. From this time on the patient improved rapidly.

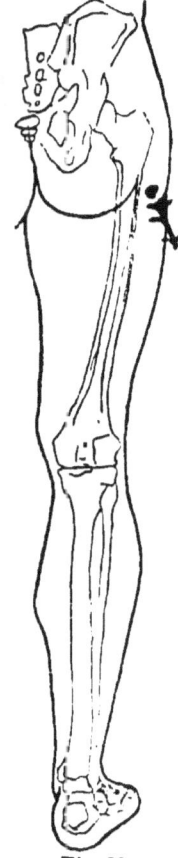

Fig. 26a.

GUNSHOT WOUNDS OF THE EXTREMITIES.

It is a source of gratification to know that very few primary amputations were made for gunshot injury of the extremities. All of the surgeons realized the importance of conservative measures in the treatment of such injuries, and limited amputation to cases in which the condition of the soft tissues precluded such a course. A number of secondary amputations became necessary to save life in cases of infected compound fractures, usually complicated with injury and infection of the adjacent joint. Two cases of traumatic aneurysm are now on

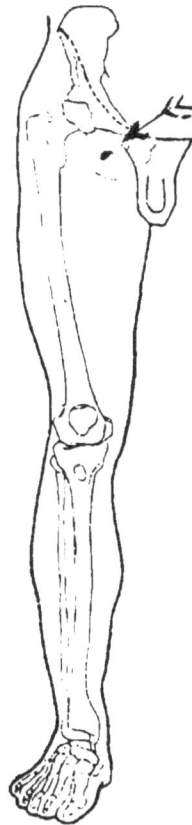

Fig. 26b.

board the *Relief*, one an aneurysmal varix, the other an aneurysm of the femoral artery.

Case 23. — Captain Mosher, Company G, Twenty-second Infantry, received a bullet wound July 1, during the advance on Santiago. Those who saw the patient first assert that the hemorrhage was severe, and that the patient lost consciousness. He was removed to the First Division Hospital and transferred July 10 to the Third Division Hospital, and the following day he was brought on board the *Relief*. I examined the patient at the front five days after the injury and confirmed the diagnosis made by the attending surgeons, who had recognized the anatomic nature of the aneurysm.

The wounds healed by primary intention in less than two weeks. One wound is in the middle of Scarpa's triangle and the other at the level of, and one inch posterior to the great trochanter on the same side. From the fact that there is, as shown by the radiograph, a piece of the jacket of a bullet in the right popliteal space, it is probable that he was wounded by a plunging fire and that the bullet inflicted the latter wound after emerging from the wound in Scarpa's triangle. The wound in the popliteal space is suppurating. Patient is very anemic and weak. In the triangle directly under the wound there is a pulsating swelling in the direction of the femoral vein, which extends to Poupart's ligament. Fremitus and the characteristic bruit extend a considerable distance above and below the communicating opening between the artery and vein. The treatment consists in rest and tonics. General health of the patient is improving, but there is no change in the local condition. The mental condition much impaired since the injury is gradually improving.

Case 24.—John J. Welch, Company M, Second Massachusetts Volunteers, was wounded July 1. The bullet entered the middle and back of Scarpa's triangle, three inches below Poupart's ligament, directly over the femoral artery, and escaped at a point corresponding with the gluteal crease and to the outside of the femur on the same side (Figure 26). Not much hemorrhage. A well-marked aneurysm developed, presenting all the physical signs characteristic of such a pathologic condition. The swelling is somewhat elongated, a little larger than a hen's egg, and has not increased in size since the patient came on board the hospital ship. The leg is somewhat edematous and painful. A number of gunshot fractures of the thigh and leg have become infected and are now being treated by establishing free tubular drainage and resorting to frequent or continuous antiseptic irrigation. Owing to the want of reliable plaster of Paris, we had to resort to various kinds of splints, single and double inclined plane, in effecting immobilization. The sheath of the leaf of the cocoa palm has served as an excellent material for this purpose. There is every prospect that most of these cases will utimately recover with useful limbs.

In conclusion I desire to thank Acting Assistant-Surgeons Metcalfe, Torney, Greenleaf, Hartsock, Morrow and Schultze for valuable assistance in preparing this communication.

Insert

Foldout

THE SURGERY OF CAMP WIKOFF.

The great national Camp Wikoff has been made the recipient of the returning army of Cuba. Three months ago the invasion of Cuba was ordered. Our troops left the different camps in excellent condition and good cheer to meet the Spanish army in the neighboring island, fully informed and impressed with the events that awaited them. The army of invasion considered it a privilege to be called to the front to represent the military prowess and power of this country. The outside world had no conception of what our army could accomplish at such short notice in a distant tropical country. The authorities, and particularly the medical department, were fully aware of the fact that the invasion of Cuba meant more a battle with climate and disease than the weakened, sickly, half starved Spanish forces. The invasion was planned on the spur of the moment, and the corps were rushed to the front with a haste that appeared all out of proportion to the conditions of things as they presented themselves at the seat of war. It was decided that our flag should float over the city of Santiago on the Fourth of July regardless of consequences. The army of invasion was packed on transports days before the final order was given to sail. Here was one of the many causes that impaired the health of our troops. The lack of harbor facilities on the coast of Cuba, where our army landed, made disembarkment and the landing of supplies exceedingly difficult. Most of the barges intended for this purpose were wrecked during the voyage, a serious loss which could not be remedied in time. Much suffering was caused by the lack of efficient landing and transportation facilities. Our troops were supplied with rations calculated for our climate, but not adapted for a tropical country. Our soldiers were exposed at once to malarial infection in all of the camps. Occupation of the buildings in which yellow fever had full sway for years, and the free intermingling of the filthy Cuban refugees and soldiers with our troops could not fail in starting and disseminating this disease among our soldiers soon after landing on Cuban soil. Typhoid fever, which prevailed in all of our large camps before the army sailed for Cuba, soon gained a firm foothold at the seat of war and did its share in increasing the mortality and in shattering the efficiency of the service. Amebic dysentery and diarrhea, the two greatest enemies of the Spanish army, thinned out our ranks and crowded our imperfectly equipped hospitals. It was fortunate that the enemy yielded to our arms so early, and made it possible for our troops to return so soon to the invigorating climate of the North for proper care and speedy recuperation. Those who saw the different regiments leave our State and national camps would find it difficult to recognize and identify the soldiers of the Cuban campaign. The men left in excellent spirits. Most of them return as mere shadows of their former selves. The pale faces, the sunken eyes, the staggering gait and the emaciated forms show only too plainly the effects of climate and disease. Many of them are wrecks for life, others are candidates for a premature grave, and hundreds will require the most careful attention and treatment before they regain the vigor they lost in Cuba. The surgery of Camp Wikoff represents cases and pathologic conditions which we would expect to occur in men suffering from the effects of disease, exposure and the debilitating effects of a tropical climate. Our work has consisted largely in the treatment of abscesses and operations for fistula ani and hemorrhoids. I was ordered to Camp Wikoff on my return from Porto Rico, and reported for duty August 22. The field operating tent and surgical wards, already in construction, were completed in two days. I have been assisted in my surgical work by Major Charles Adams, U. S. V., and Acting Assistant-Surgeon Henry Greenleaf. The Sisters of Charity have charge of the surgical wards, and two of them make the necessary preparations for operation and assist in the operating tent.

SURGICAL HOSPITAL.

The surgical hospital at Camp Wikoff is a part of the general hospital. It consists of nine wall tents, placed end-to-end and supported by a substantial wooden frame and floored throughout, constituting a pavilion of 126 x 14 feet in extent. The front tent, No. 1, facing southeast, boarded at the sides, with a broad table shelf on either hand, is used as an operating tent. It is equipped with a regulation operating table, iron frame and top. Sterilized dressings, gauze sponges, ligatures, etc., are kept in sterilized towels in readiness for use at

MAJOR HEITZMANN, SURGEON U.S.A.

any moment. The shelves and tables are covered with white rubber cloth, which is kept scrupulously clean. The instruments, after sterilization, are kept in trays containing a 2 per cent. solution of carbolic acid. Saline and antiseptic solutions are kept ready for use in four-gallon bottles. All surgical paraphernalia not in use are covered by clean white sheets. The second tent, open at the sides for free ventilation and coolness. is used for the office of the surgeon in charge. It is supplied with a field desk, table and chairs. Section No. 3 is the preparation room. The instruments are kept here under lock and key. Two sterilizers, basins, buckets, pitchers and a table constitute the equipment of this room. A glass irrigator and a number of fountain syringes furnish the facilities for irrigation. A field operating case, a Paquelin cautery, a full set of dental forceps, a complete set of urethral instruments, a case of eye and ear instruments and aspirator have furnished all the instruments required. The instruments are sterilized by boiling, the dressings by dry heat.

Hand disinfection consists in scrubbing for at least five minutes in hot water and potash soap, washing in absolute alcohol followed by prolonged immersion in a 1 1000 solution of bichlorid. Just before the operation is commenced the hands are washed once more in alcohol. The field of operation is disinfected in the same manner as the hands. Section 5 answers the purpose of a pantry and kitchen for special diet. From here the distribution of food takes place as it is received from the main kitchen of the hospital. Between the supply tent and the pantry is an open passage-way four feet wide, through which the patients and nurses enter and leave the hospital. The four tents remaining are used for wards, having a capacity of 32 beds. This hospital in the course of a few days was filled, when ward A, adjacent. occupied by medical cases, was evacuated to make room for surgical cases. The present arrangements affords room for seventy-five surgical patients. At the present time, September 10, every bed is occupied. The six Sisters of Charity in charge are assisted by three orderlies from the Hospital corps. Patients are prepared for operations with proper antiseptic precautions, and no pains are spared to give them the benefit of modern surgical methods in every detail, during their stay in the hospital. The nursing and care of the sick are faultless, and the diet is not only ample in quantity and quality, but often luxurious, far exceeding what is served on the table of the officers mess tent. The patients much re-

Major Brown, Surgeon U.S.V., in his Office, General Hospital, Camp Wikoff.

duced in flesh and strength by fever or suppurative affections, are furnished with a liberal supply of stimulants including champagne and port wine. With very few exceptions indeed, prompt improvement has followed the operative interventions, more especially in the cases of large phlegmonous and ischio-rectal abscesses. It is my intention in writing this paper to give the profession a general idea of the surgical work done in Camp Wikoff since I took charge of this branch of the hospital work August 22. Nothing had been done up to that time in caring for the surgical cases. The hospital was overcrowded, and the available physicians were extremely busy in looking after the welfare and accommodation of the fever patients. In two days I had the surgical ward in a condition to receive patients, and on the third day the first operations were performed. At first a pocket case did sole duty in the operating room. The hospital outfit and supplies were picked up here and there, and in a few days we were ready to begin systematic, efficient work. Many of the patients were so weak and anemic that the administration of an anesthetic was deemed dangerous. In such cases the patients were given strychnia subcutaneously and a liberal dose of whisky by the mouth. Patients considerably enfeebled by disease were given ether in preference to chloroform. Chloroform by the drop method was the anesthetic of choice in all cases where the general conditions of the patient did not contraindicate its use. Operations were performed during the forenoon, beginning at 9 o'clock.

TOOTHACHE.

Of the organs frequently affected among the returning soldiers were the teeth. Patients suffering from carious aching teeth were numerous. In most instances they presented evidences of serious malnutrition following disease and exposure : suppurative alveolitis was less frequent. Infection of many oral cavities showed that teeth had been sadly neglected during the campaign. In Cuba and Porto Rico I saw occasionally a soldier with a tooth brush under the hat band, but I have reason to believe that most of the tooth brushes were either left at home or thrown away on the march, as unnecessary articles of the limited toilet outfit. I did all I could in the way of conservative dentistry by cleaning out cavities and packing

with cotton saturated with carbolic acid, but in the majority
of cases the patients returned and insisted on having the painful tooth extracted. Tooth extraction was a conspicuous and
grateful part of the surgery of Camp Wikoff. Hardly a day
passed without two or three such operations. A very complete
set of tooth forceps furnished by the government did good service in relieving the victims of toothache of their agonizing suffering. Much has been said in favor of attaching a dentist to
each regiment to look after the teeth of the men, and the observations made in Camp Wykoff tend to support the propriety
of such a much-needed addition to the medical service. It is
interesting to know that among these patients there was not a
single officer, undoubtedly because the officers were more particular in the care of their teeth than the privates.

HERNIA.

The number of hernias that presented themselves in Camp
Wikoff astonished us all. In every case the statements of the
patients were to the effect that the hernia appeared since the
enlistment. It might be surmised that at least in some of the
cases this physical defect was overlooked during the examination. This might have been so in isolated instances, in the
case of volunteers, but such a view would not hold good in men
belonging to the regular army. I saw more cases of hernia in
men belonging to the latter, than the former branch of the
military service. Our army in Cuba was not subjected for any
length of time to hard marching or violent exertions of any
kind, consequently the causes which led to hernia must be
sought outside of such mechanical influences. Careful examination appeared to prove that in most, if not in all cases, the
hernia was of recent origin. I attribute the hernia-formation
principally to the relaxation of tissue, caused by disease and
its effects, aided undoubtedly by the prevalence of intestinal
affections which must have often resulted in increased abnormal intra abdominal tension. The uncertainty of the duration
of the encampment induced me to advise against operative interference, and in most cases the general condition of the patients was such as to constitute in itself a strong contraindica-
tion to the performance of a radical operation. The patients
were fitted with a truss and advised to have a radical operation

performed after their general health was restored, after leaving the service or obtaining a furlough.

VARICOCELE.

The frequency with which varicocele is met with in men from 18 to 45 years was shown in the examination of 9901 volunteers in Camp Tanner, Illinois. As a member of the board of examiners, I was very anxious to obtain accurate information regarding this subject, and accurate notes were kept at the time. We found varicocele, slight, 992; medium, 692; large, 295. Of the slight cases 10 were double, 7 of the right side only; of the medium cases, 7 were double, and 4 of the right side only; of the large cases 4 were of the right side only. The percentage of varicoceles to total number examined was 21.17. Only six were regarded as physical disabilities, and those on account of size and pain. At that time I wrote a paper calling attention to the great frequency of varicocele in men of the age for military service, and claimed that ordinary varicocele was no valid objection to the enlistment of men for military duty. Of the more than 15000 men who returned from Cuba and were landed at Montauk, only five cases of variococele applied for treatment at the surgical ward. In all of these cases the local symptoms were such as to warrant an operation. The operation was performed by excising through a straight incision, directly over the cord, the enlarged veins between double ligatures. The veins were carefully isolated by dissection from the spermatic cord and the accompanying artery. After excision the two stumps were brought together by a single catgut suture, and by tying over this a thread of one of the ligatures left long from each side. The stumps were buried by several fine catgut sutures with which the deep layers of the tissues were united. The external wound was always closed with horsehair sutures. Elongation of the scrotum sufficient in degree to require attention was corrected by transverse suturing of the external wound. The wound was sealed with collodium, a few narrow strips of iodoform gauze, and a pledget of absorbent cotton over which the usual dressing and bandage were applied.

Case 1.—John D. Deboer, aged 24, colored; Troop B, First Cavalry; has had varicocele for the last eighteen months. Enlisted five weeks ago. Marked ectasia of the spermatic veins on the left side with corresponding elongation of scrotum on same side. He has had no pain, but much discomfort in hot weather from relaxation and dragging sensation. Operation under chloroform narcosis August 31. General health not much impaired.

Case 2.—William Cantwell, age 31, Company B, Sixteenth Infantry; has been in the service fourteen years. Varicocele appeared eighteen months ago. Since he entered the active service the swelling has often been painful, especially during forced marches and in hot weather. He is much concerned about his condition, and submitted willingly to the operation, which was performed under ether anesthesia September 3. On exposing the varicose veins it was found that the tunica vaginalis had remained patent from the external inguinal ring to the testicle, but contained no fluid. The veins were isolated with some difficulty from the cord and the spermatic artery. After disposing of the vein stumps in the usual way the tunica vaginalis was closed with fine catgut sutures over the cord. The scrotum was shortened by transverse suturing of the wound.

Case 3.—Wm. Reed, age 23, colored; Troop H, Ninth Cavalry. Made its appearance soon after his enlistment two months ago. The varicocele is of large size and gives rise to much pain on riding or walking any distance. Operation under chloroform narcosis September 3.

Case 4.—Robert Duseman, age 21, Second Volunteer Engineers. Entered the service two months ago. Six weeks ago, during drill, he bruised the left side of the scrotum, and attributes the varicocele to this cause. He complains of a dragging sensation in the testicle on the left side, the seat of the varicocele of medium size. Usual operation under ether, September 11.

In all of these cases the general health of the patients was not much impaired, and the wounds healed rapidly by primary intention.

HYDROCELE.

Hydrocele from puberty to the age of 45 occurs much less frequently than varicocele. Of the 9901 cases examined in Camp Tanner, we found only 49 cases of hydrocele of the tunica vaginalis and 18 of the cord. Only one case of hydrocele of the tunica vaginalis came for treatment to the surgical ward of Camp Wikoff.

Case 5.—John Craigie, Company E, First Artillery, a young soldier whose health had become greatly undermined by malaria, was sent from the medical to the surgical ward. for a painful affection of the left testicle of a few days' duration. Patient very anemic and emaciated. A few days ago, on recovering from his illness for which he had been sent to the hospital, the left testicle became painful and tender, accompanied by a gradually increasing swelling. He came under surgical treatment August 27. Careful examination revealed an acute hydrocele of the tunica vaginalis on the left side, without any palpable visceral lesions of the testicle or epidydimis. The fluid, straw colored, was evacuated by tapping with a small trocar. One dram of equal parts of alcohol and carbolic acid was injected. The reaction was moderate and the patient left a few days later, the swelling gradually diminishing in size.

BONES AND JOINTS.

Only a few cases of injury and disease of bones and joints came under observation in the surgical department of the general hospital, but these isolated cases present features of interest sufficient to justify mention in connection with the subject of this communication.

Case 6.- Gunshot fracture of femur. S. M. Wetmore, age 25, trumpeter, Troop D, First Volunteer Cavalry, was shot through the right thigh at the junction of the lower with the middle third, the bullet passing in the antero posterior direction, the wound of exit being on a higher level than the wound of entrance. The wounds were dressed with idoform and healed by primary intention. Just before he was transferred from the hospital at Siboney to the *Relief* he became very much debilitated and manifested other and more characteristic symptoms of iodoform intoxication. A plaster cast was applied, and he was sent to the fever camp as a case of yellow fever—a diagnosis which was never confirmed by the physicians in charge of the hospital. He suffered from malaria, and his present condition indicates to what extent the malarial intoxication has advanced. He is extremely anemic, and emaciated to a skeleton. The spleen is much enlarged. The fractured limb is shortened two inches and a half; marked overlapping of fragments; union fibrous. Plaster of Paris bandage reapplied. Tonic and stimulating treatment.

Case 7.--R. Whitington, aged 25, First Volunteer Cavalry, on August 14 was riding bareback, when his horse made a quick turn and in tumbling over an embankment the horse fell upon his left leg, producing an oblique fracture of the tibia about two inches above the base of the malleolus, and of the fibula about four inches higher. For some days the limb was placed in a fracture box, but it was found impossible to immobilize the fragments properly. During this time the patient suffered from pain and loss of sleep. August 27 he was placed under the influence of chloroform, the fragments were properly adjusted and the limb immobilized in a plaster of Paris splint extending from the base of the toes to the knee. Since that time he has been free from pain and has slept without the use of anodynes.

Case 8.—Maj. Gen. S. B. M. Young injured his ankylosed elbow-joint, September 2, and received first aid at the surgical ward the next morning. During the War of the Rebellion he received two gunshot wounds of the right arm. One shattered the lower third of the humerus, the other perforated the elbow joint. After a prolonged siege of suppuration he finally recovered with ankylosis of the elbow-joint, in flexion at an angle of about 110 degrees, and in a position of marked pronation. September 1 he stumbled and fell, striking upon the hand and elbow. He complains of severe pain in and about the joint. The elbow-joint is swollen and very painful on pressure and manipulation. Ecchymosis over both condyles. There is some motion but no crepitation, indicating the existence of ruptured intra and periarticular adhesions. The patient states that this is the fourth time since the ankylosis occurred that it has been broken by injury of some sort. The limb was padded with a thick layer of cotton from the base of the fingers to the shoulder-joint, over which a light plaster of Paris bandage was applied. The patient was placed in charge of Major Nancrede, his attending physician, who a few days later substituted for the plaster dressing an angular wire splint. In less than a week he reported for duty at Camp Meade.

Case 9.—Thomas A. McDonald, age 24, Second Infantry. While in action before Santiago the stock of his gun was struck by the fragment of a shell, the arm was violently twisted and the radius fractured. The forearm now presents the characteristic "silver fork" deformity of an imperfectly reduced Colles' fracture. There is swelling of the wrist, inability to use fingers, and pain on attempted pronation and supination. Massage, manipulation and electricity advised.

Case 10.—Preston Guthrie, aged 34, Company F, Twentieth Infantry, re-enlisted three and one-half months ago. States that he cut his left arm two years ago. The wound was slow in healing and left a scar adherent to the underlying ulna. Nothing in the clinical history would indicate that the bone was affected at that time. A contusion of same region occured while loading a transport in Cuba, which was followed by a complexus of symptoms pointing to the existence of a central osteomyelitis. An abscess which formed later ruptured through the old scar, an occurrence which was followed by prompt relief. A moderate discharge has continued since. Examination made August 26 disclosed two fistulous openings over the posterior surface and center of the ulna, leading into a central osteomyelitic cavity. Ulna at the seat of disease considerably enlarged. Through a straight incision the fistulous openings in the involucrum were exposed and the cavity freely laid open by chiselling. A sequestrum lying loosely in the bone cavity was removed and the granulations lining the cavity scraped out by a vigorous use of the sharp spoon. After thorough disinfection of the cavity the periosteum was sutured carefully, over which the wound was closed in the usual manner, leaving only a small space for gauze drainage. The wound remained aseptic and healed rapidly by primary intention.

Case 11.—George Oppel, aged 21, enlisted in the Second Infantry one month ago. He was admitted to the surgical ward with a fluctuating swelling over the inner aspect and a little above the left knee-joint. Ten years ago he was struck in this region with a brick and suffered from an acute bursitis. The bursa has been enlarged ever since, but has not been painful until recently. There is no tubercular history in his family. The swelling is flat and in circumference is as large as a medium sized orange. On palpation no fluctuations can be felt, the sensation imparted being of a semi-elastic nature. The swelling is somewhat tender to touch and is painful when he attempts to walk. August 31, the patient being under the influence of a general anesthetic, the bursa was punctured with a small trocar in three different directions through the same opening in the skin and was thoroughly injected with a 5 per cent. solution of carbolic acid. Pressure was applied over the bursa and the limb immobilized upon a posterior splint. In the course of a week the swelling had almost entirely disappeared and the patient returned to his command for duty.

REMOVAL OF FOREIGN BODIES.

Two interesting cases of removal of a foreign body lodged in the tissues presented themselves for operative treatment.

Case 12.—Benjamin Nelson, age 23, Company F, Third Infantry. Came under observation and treatment September 6. Three years ago he fell backward against a window and sustained several cuts of the scalp by fragments of broken glass. The wounds healed rapidly without suppuration. After his recovery he was aware of the presence of a piece of glass which had remained encysted in the pericranial tissues ever since, without giving rise to any inconvenience until recently. A few weeks ago the scalp over the embedded foreign body was bruised, and since that time it has caused irritation and pain. The piece of glass could be readily outlined by palpation. On the day mentioned, without anesthesia, a straight incision parallel to the long axis of the foreign body was made. No suppuration within or outside of the capsule. The piece of glass was found surrounded by a firm capsule of fibrous tissue and measured two centimeters in length and two tenths of a centimeter square at the end. The broken surface was irregular in outline. The wound was sutured with horsehair and union was found complete at the time of his discharge, September 11.

Case 13. Sergt. Oscar F. Winter, age 52, Company F. Ninth Infantry, seventeen years in service. On July 2, while in the act of rising just behind the trenches, he was wounded by the bursting of a shell near him. He was confident at the time, from the sensation experienced, that he had received a blow from a large fragment of shell on the crest of the left ilium. He says a large ecchymosis formed at once and he could see no evidence of penetration. He was assured by a medical officer that he had suffered a contusion only, that there had been no penetration. He says, however, on being questioned, that a small rent existed in the clothing over the supposed contusion, but is very positive that he must have been struck by the convex side of a large piece of the bursting shell. An abscess developed soon after the injury was received and has discharged at a point near the anterior superior spine of the ilium and the resulting sinus has remained since. The patient has done duty without missing a day since he received the wound, until reaching Camp Wikoff. The existence of an abscess cavity and the history of an opening in the clothing led to exploration for a foreign body. The existing opening was slightly enlarged, under chloroform anesthesia, and exploration of the cavity with the finger located a shrapnell ball at about $3\frac{1}{2}$ inches downward from the opening of the sinus. Counter-opening was made at this point and the ball extracted. Tubular drainage, irrigation with peroxid of hydrogen and $2\frac{1}{2}$ per cent. carbolic solutions and moist carbolic dressing. Speedy healing of the wounds.

ABSCESSES.

We would naturally take it for granted that among the returning soldiers from Cuba, owing to their greatly debilitated condition, suppurative affections in different forms, and affecting various tissues and organs, would furnish a rich and interesting material for the surgical ward of the General Hospital. The sources of infection were many, and the resistance of the tissues to pathogenic microbes in most of the men who returned was at low ebb. A good share of the surgical work consisted in incising and draining abscesses, some of them of enormous size. In the treatment of all of these cases, owing to the pronounced anemia and great weakness, special precautions were resorted to to prevent the loss of even as much as a teaspoonful of blood in performing the operations. In abscesses in the anal region the Paquelin cautery was usually used in preference to the knife, in laying open the abscess cavity. In other regions the abscess was opened by making an incision through the skin and underlying fascia large enough to admit the tip of the little finger, when the remaining tissues were tunneled with a pair of curved, rather sharp pointed forceps, and the tubular wound enlarged to the requisite extent by expanding the blades of the forceps during the withdrawal of the instrument. In most instances a counter-opening was made by plunging the forceps into the abscess cavity, inserted into the first opening, through the tissues from within outward until the tip of the instrument made a cone of the skin which was then incised, not over, but on the side of the instrument, sufficiently to permit the easy escape of the instrument when the canal was enlarged by expanding the blades, after which the end of the drain was grasped transversly and by withdrawing the instrument through drainage was established. The drains used were freely fenestrated, the openings being numerous, but never larger than to correspond in size to one-fourth of the circumference of the tube. The opening and counter-opening were made in places where drainage and irrigation would prove most efficient. In several cases in which the counter-opening could not be made by the use of the forceps, the abscess was opened in the usual way, and after evacuation of its contents peroxid of hydrogen was injected until the cavity was well distended, when the second opening was made in the same way as the first. After opening and draining the abscess, irrigation with a $2\frac{1}{2}$ per cent. solution of carbolic acid, followed by peroxid of hydrogen, and finally again with the carbolized solution. In all abscess cases the dressing consisted of a compress of gauze wrung out of a $2\frac{1}{2}$ per cent. solution of carbolic acid, over which oiled silk was applied with absorbent cotton around its edges, to act as a filter, and the whole confined in place by a well-applied bandage. In the more serious cases the dressing was removed, the abscess cavity flushed, and a new compress applied twice daily. Whenever it was deemed necessary, the affected limb was immobilized. This treatment proved uniformly successful in preventing profuse suppuration and was always followed by rapid improvement in the general condition of the patient.

In the medical treatment of these cases quinin was used freely, as well as alcoholic stimulants. Iron preparations and a nutritious diet proved most effectual in improving the condition of the impoverished blood and in restoring normal nutrition.

CONNECTIVE TISSUE ABSCESSES.

The connective tissue was the tissue most frequently the primary or secondary seat of infection. The phlegmonous inflammation which led to connective tissue abscesses occurred almost exclusively in men whose general health was shattered. As a rule the patients suffering from this affection presented an anemic, almost waxy appearance and were greatly emaciated. The deterioration of health was due to antecedent causes, malaria, yellow fever, dysentery, diarrhea, exposure and improper or insufficient food. The phlegmonous inflammation in most instances pursued a rather insidious process and was clinically not characterized by the complexus of symptoms which ordinarily accompany the inflammation preceding an acute abscess. The pain was often slight, tenderness moderate, and the skin seldom showed the inflammatory blush which so constantly is seen during the development of an acute subcutaneous abscess. A tendency to burrowing was manifest in most cases. The induration of the abscess wall, so common in acute abscess, was lacking in most of our cases. There seemed to be a total absence of a tendency to the limitation of the area of abscess formation. The cases that came under our observation resembled in their symptomatology, pathology and clinical course very closely abscess formation as seen during the latter course of any prolonged acute infective disease, or during convalescence from such. In opening these abscesses I was always careful to make the openings some distance from the center of the abscess cavity, in preference at its margins, and the same location was selected in case a counter-opening was made. By following this method of incising and draining the abscess the skin over the center of the abscess, damaged to the greatest extent by the underlying phlegmonous process was avoided, and complete evacuation and free drainage secured. The same careful preparations were made for the operation as in cases requiring surgical intervention for aseptic conditions. with a view of guarding against secondary infection.

Under this treatment, the general and local conditions of the patients improved very rapidly. In abscesses of very large dimensions from two to four incisions were made and as many points of drainage established. As suppuration ceased and the abscess cavity commenced to shrink, the drains were shortened from time to time to enable the process of healing to proceed without hindrance from mechanical causes.

Case 14.—Robert Bloedel, age 25, Third Infantry Band, enlisted fifteen months ago. Had chills and fever in Cuba for about a month, followed by dysentery. Is still suffering from the diarrhea which followed the dysentery and the patient is much emaciated and very anemic. Before going to Cuba he noticed a small pimple on his neck. Just before leaving Santiago, swelling of the neck began in the connective tissue, at the site of the pimple, and has progressed steadily. Examination of the cavity of the mouth does not reveal a source of infection. There can be but little doubt that the minute furuncle, which proved harmless as long as the patient remained in good health, became the focus of infection of the underlying connective tissue which was made more susceptible to infection by the effects of disease. A large fluctuating swelling in the neck, just below the angle of the jaw, marks the location and extent of the connective tissue abscess. Pain has never been severe. Edema, but no redness of skin. All of the local symptoms indicate a slow, subacute inflammation of the deep connective tissue. The patient was etherized and through drainage was established, the drainage tube being placed in an oblique direction from the floor of the abscess to a point opposite and behind. A large quantity of creamy pus was evacuated and the cavity thoroughly washed out with carbolized solution and peroxid of hydrogen. A large moist antiseptic compress covered with oiled silk was applied and held in place by a bandage. Very little suppuration after operation, speedy healing of the abscess cavity accompanied by a marked improvement in the appearance of the patient.

Case 15.—P. P. Sprague, age 29, Seventh Infantry, Company 1, entered the regular service seven months ago. He landed in Cuba July 10. Contracted malaria, lost flesh and strength, but continued to perform his usual duties. About three weeks ago he experienced a sense of soreness in the calf of his right leg in the region of a scar from an injury received during childhood. The soreness increased slowly in severity, and for a number of days he has suffered from a throbbing pain sufficiently severe to prevent sleep. The patient is much enfeebled from the effects of the previous disease, aggravated by the recent attack of phlegmonous inflammation. No local source of infection could be found on the most careful search. It is very probable that the scar tissue furnished the *locus minoris resistentiæ* which determined localization of pus microbes floating in the general circulation sufficient in number and virulence to give rise to a subacute phlegmonous process. The whole leg is swollen from the ankle to the knee, tense and edematous, a circumscribed inflammatory blush over the lower portion of the gastrocnemius muscle. Fluctuation deep-seated, somewhat obscure and diffuse.

The diagnosis made at the time, was deep-seated phlegmonous abscess, involving the connective tissues between the deep-seated muscles of the leg. August 29, under ether unesthesia the abscess was opened by an incision over the posterior aspect of the leg in the median line, at a point where the muscle terminates in tendon ; a large quantity of thin bloody pus escaped. As it was found impossible to make a counter-opening in the upper recess of the abscess cavity by the use of forceps, peroxid of hydrogen was injected through the opening to distend the abscess cavity sufficiently to facilitate incision from without. The second incision was made in the usual way over the upper third of the fibula and a counter-opening established on the tibial side, effecting in this manner efficient through drainage below and from side to side. Digital exploration through the three openings located the abscess correctly anatomically. In exploring the interior of the abscess the tibia and fibula could be distinctly felt. The abscess cavity was disinfected in the usual way and after applying the wet antiseptic compress, the patient was returned to his cot and the limb placed in an elevated position. The final recovery of the patient was retarded by several severe attacks of malaria during one of which the mercury reached 106 F. The chills and fever yielded to large doses of quinin.

Case 16.—Henry H. Mix, age 21, Third Infantry, Company F, enlisted three months ago. On June 6 last, while on parade had an attack of heat exhaustion followed by diarrhea for several days. At Tampa, June 8, two days later, he was put on sick list for two furuncles behind the left knee. These healed promply. July 10 on reaching Cuba, he suffered from furuncles on buttocks, also malarial fever and diarrhea. At this time an abscess formed in the right popliteal space, which pursued an insidious, chronic course. At the time the patient reached Montauk, he was very anemic and almost reduced to a skeleton, and the abscess had opened at different points. The subcutaneous tissue was extensively undermined, and through the openings the fungous lining of the cavity could be distinctly seen. Ths abscess cavity discharged profusely and extended from the middle of the thigh to the upper portion of the calf of the leg. August 29, the sinuses were enlarged, a number of counter-openings made and free tubular drainage established. The abscess cavity was thoroughly disinfected and a large moist. antiseptic compress applied. As there was some tendency to contraction of the knee joint, the limb was placed in a straight. position and immobilized by the use of a well padded anterior wire splint so applied that the abscess could be exposed and treated without disturbing the limb. Malarial fever, which developed on the second day after the operation, retarded the healing process, and for a few days threatened the life of the patient. After the fever was under control by the administration of large doses of quinin, a satisfactory process of repair set in, which soon effected healing of the abscess and restoration of tisssues lost by the extensive destructive process.

Case 17.—Joseph McGuire, Ninth Massachusetts Volunteers, Company C, had some febrile attack in Cuba, the nature of which is not known. He was admitted to the surgical department of the General Hospital, September 7, suffering from a superficial connective tissue abscess over left triceps about two inches below the shoulder joint. He has at the same time an alveolar abscess which is discharging through a carious tooth. The infection in this case evidently took place from the blood, as there are no traces of the existence of a local infection atrium to which the phlegmonous process could be attributed. Through drainage and moist carbolized dressing.

Case 18.—James F. Dite, age 21, First Illinois Infantry, Company H, received a severe contusion of anterior surface of right thigh from falling log near Santiago. He was treated by a Cuban doctor for rheumatism, and then sent to the Division Hospital where a swelling which had formed at the site of injury was incised, but no pus escaped. The swelling remained, and gradually increased in size. When admitted to the surgical ward his general health was precarious. Marked anemia and emaciation. The anterior aspect of the affected thigh from near the knee to the inguinal fold was the seat of a fluctuating swelling. The center of the swelling was occupied by a small granulating area marking the place where the incision was made. The abscess was underneath the quadriceps femoris muscle, and evidently the incision had not been made deep enough to reach the pus. As the skin was not broken by the injury, infection was determined by microbes floating in the circulation and their localization and growth in the contused deep connective tissue. Under anesthesia the abscess was opened at the most dependent point and a counter opening made on the opposite side with the aid of distension of the cavity by peroxid of hydrogen injection. Through drainage and thorough disinfection of the interior of the abscess cavity completed the operation. Prompt relief and improvement followed the operative intervention.

Case 19.—Dennis Riley, age 21, First District of Columbia Infantry, Company E, after passing through a rather severe attack of typhoid fever was admitted to the surgical ward suffering from multiple abscesses, varying in size from that of a pea to a walnut, involving the face and the neck. The largest abscess was above the left eyelid. All of these abscesses had their primary starting point in the subcutaneous connective tissue. Treatment by incision and drainage. Convalescence progressed without any further interruption. The location of these abscesses on the exposed part of the body would indicate that the infection had a local source, probably slight abrasions inflicted by the patient himself during the course of the fever.

Case 20.—Edwin Stockwell, aged 28, Second Infantry, Company I, was well until the day before leaving Cuba, August 10; on that day felt very weak and sick. On boarding transport had to lie down, vomited, then felt better for a time, then weak and sick and nausea and vomiting again. He was feverish all the time and slightly jaundiced, but continued on duty with the sick. Some doubt remains as to whether this attack was a mild form of yellow fever or malaria. Since his arrival here he has done duty as a nurse. Five or six days ago a furuncle developed on the middle of the posterior aspect of the right thigh, below the gluteal fold. This opened and discharged slightly, but the swelling has continued to increase in size. On examination, a crater-like defect in the skin marks the site of the primary focus of infection. From this point a red zone of inflammation extends in all directions equally to a distance of two inches. The phlegmonous progressive connective tissue inflammation had its origin from the furuncle. Such a complication would probably not have occurred if the patient's general health and power of resistance to general infection had not been impaired by the antecedent attack of fever. The skin around the furuncle was extensively undermined. The cavity was freely laid open by a vertical incision and the necrosed tissue and infectived granulations scraped out with a sharp spoon, and after thorough disinfection was lightly packed with a strip of iodoform gauze, and a large moist compress applied.

Case 21.—John A. Johnson, aged 24, Third Infantry, Company H, enlisted eight months ago. Phlegmonous inflammation of middle finger of left hand. Three weeks ago had an attack of malarial fever in Cuba, which was complicated by diarrhea. He was treated four days in one of the hospitals, when he returned to his command for duty. The fever left him in a weakened condition. Ten days ago on leaving Santiago, he noticed a soreness over the dorsal side of the middle finger of the left hand directly over the middle joint. Cause of infection not known. An acute superficial abscess formed, attended by great pain until it ruptured. A considerable portion of the overlying skin sloughed, leaving a ragged surface with edematous red margins. On August 27, the patient was placed under an anesthetic, when a thorough examination showed that the infective process did not extend to the joint or the extensor tendon. With sharp spoon, scissors and forceps the infected tissues were removed, the resulting surface disinfected and packed with iodoform gauze and the finger immobilized on a palmar splint. The wound healed promptly and the prospects are that the finger will regain its normal functions.

Case 22.—Richter, aged 23, First Illinois Infantry, Company

D, contracted typhoid fever in Cuba five weeks ago. During the fever a copious herpetic eruption made its appearance on the upper lip and about the nasal orifices. The fever left him in a greatly emaciated condition. A swelling formed in the left cheek during the last three or four days and increased rapidly in size. Pain and tenderness not well marked. The patient sought medical treatment at the surgical ward Sunday, September 11. The left cheek was the seat of a large fluctuating swelling. Diagnosis made at the time—abscess of cheek. The abscess was incised from the mouth and a large quantity of very offensive pus was evacuated. The patient was directed to resort to frequent rinsings of the mouth with a saturated solution of boracic acid and was given a furlough to enable him to return as quickly as possible to his home. Infection in this case undoubtedly occurred through the skin defects left by the herpetic eruption.

GLANDULAR ABSCESS.

In the discussion of phlegmonous abscess, infection was traced either to a *portio invasionis* or local conditions, which determined localization from local causes, in cases in which it was reasonable to suppose that the essential cause of infection existed in the general circulation. Without calling attention to the fact, it is reasonable to suppose that in the first class of patients the essential microbic cause reached the tissues through the connective tissue spaces, that is, that a direct anatomic connection existed between the primary essential infection-atrium and the seat of secondary phlegmonous manifestations. In the consideration of glandular infection it is essential to connect the infection-atrium anatomically and physiologically, with the secondary glandular suppurative conditions. We are able from the clinical history and the pathologic conditions presented in most of the cases to establish such a direct connection between the primary source of infection and the secondary glandular manifestations. I have reason to believe that in most of these cases the essential cause of infection was the streptococcus pyogenes, because it is well known that this pyogenic agent usually follows either the connective tissue spaces or the lymphatic channels in giving rise to a distant infective suppurative process.

Case 23.—Patrick Collins, age 28, Company C, Eighth Infantry, enlisted one year ago. About the middle of July, while in Cuba, had a malarial chill followed by fever. Has had fever and diarrhea, and has been on the sick list ever since. While returning on transport from Cuba he experienced soreness in the region of the left parotid gland ; this symptom has been followed by the usual clinical evidences indicative of the existence of an abscess in that locality. On August 29 he presented himself at the surgical ward, and at that time it was not difficult to diagnosticate the existence of a large abscess in the region of the parotid gland. At that time, under ether anesthesia, it was easy to recognize a diffuse abscess in the parotid region. It was more difficult to decide whether this abscess was of malarial or typhoid origin. Two incisions were made, an extensive purulent product was evacuated, and efficient through tubular drainage was established. In this instance the whole gland seemed to be surrounded by the suppurative products and the through drain was passed underneath the gland that was the primary seat of the secondary field of infection. The patient improved rapidly after the operation.

Case 24.—John Williams, age 25, Ninth Cavalry, Troop F., colored, enlisted four months ago. Following a strain in lifting and exposure in rough weather, while on duty in the Camp at Tampa, Fla., he became aware of the enlargement of the inguinal glands on the right side. The glands were very painful when he was on active duty. There are no evidences of general infection of any kind and the most scrutinizing examination failed to detect any tangible source of infection in the distal side of the lymphatic circulation. On palpating, three or four inguinal glands were found distinctly enlarged with plain evidences of beginning perilymphadenitis, but no distinct abscess formation. On August 22 chloroform was administered and a curved incision made, with the convexity directed upward in such a manner as to expose the infected glands freely. The glands, three in number, honeycombed with pus were enucleated. A place for drainage was established, the wound thoroughly disinfected with iodoform, when the external incision was closed with sutures of horsehair. The wound healed promptly by primary intention.

Case 25.—George A. Roberts, Sixteenth Infantry, Company H., colored, was ill eight days with malaria in Cuba, was after that on duty until his arrival in Montauk, when he again had malarial fever. During this attack a furuncle developed on calf of the right leg and opened spontaneously. From this point a lymphadenitis started, which extends to the deep lymphatic glands in Scarpa's triangle and terminated in a lymphadenitis and perilymphadenitis. The lymphatic glands in this region, being in a state of inflammation, resulted in the formation of a tender and painful swelling four inches in length and about three inches in width. No fluctuation and no inflammatory discoloration of the skin. The patient was confined to his cot with the affected limb in an elevated position. A large compress saturated with $2\frac{1}{2}$ per cent. hot solution of carbolic acid. Applied Credé's silver ointment to be rubbed into the skin over the swelling once a day. Under this treatment the inflammatory process subsided and the prospects are, that the swelling will disappear without pus formation.

Case 26.—Frederick Warner, age 37, colored, Ninth Cavalry, Troop L, contracted chancroid about six weeks ago, while on duty at Tampa. The lymphatic glands in the inguinal region became infected and the suppurative lymphadenitis terminated in the formation of three glandular abscesses, which opened spontaneously. At the time the patient was operated upon, September 1, three fistulous openings were found, and the connective tissue was extensively infiltrated. No scars or other evidences of the primary lesion can be detected. It was plainly a case of suppurative lymphadenitis, caused by invasion with pus microbes from the external genitals. Under chloroform anesthesia the sinuses were enlarged, and the remaining broken down gland tissue and infected granulations removed by a vigorous use of the sharp spoon. The resulting wound was thoroughly disinfected, iodoformized and packed with iodoform gauze and covered with a large moist antiseptic compress of gauze, over which was placed an overlapping piece of oiled silk, and the whole dressing held in place by a bandage embracing the pelvis and upper part of thigh. The patient left the hospital a week after the operation, at which time the abscess cavities were much diminished in size and lined by vigorous healthy granulations.

Case 27.—John H. Butler, age 21, Ninth Cavalry, Troop L, colored. Tubercular lymphadenitis of submaxillary gland. Family history negative. Mother and father living; two children died in infancy; rest living and in good health. About two months ago began to have pain in right side of neck and submaxillary region, and then noticed a small, hard swelling below the angle of the jaw. Additional glands in the same region became involved. At the time he entered the surgical ward a large glandular mass, composed of several enlarged lymphatic glands, was found in the right submaxillary region. On palpation the swelling was painful, but no distinct fluctuation could be felt. Inspection of the mouth failed to reveal anything which could be regarded as an infection-atrium. The tubercular nature of the glandular affection was recognized, and a radical operation for the removal of the glands was performed September 6, the patient being under the influence of chloroform. The glandular mass was freely exposed by a semilunar incision with the convexity downward and by reflection of the cutaneous flap in an upward direction. The whole mass was dissected out in one piece, which included not only the tubercular glands, but likewise the infiltrated connective tissue surrounding them. The submaxillary gland was exposed, and during the latter part of the operation it became necessary to cut and ligate the facial artery. The gland tissue throughout had undergone coagulation necrosis; each gland contained several foci of caseation. The wound was iodoformized and sutured throughout with horse-hair, provision for gauze drainage having been made by making a button-hole near the margin and center of the flap. Healing by primary intention.

Case 28.—Schuyler C. Black, age 31, Ninth Cavalry, Troop I, colored, enlisted four months ago. Chronic balanitis and bilateral plastic lymphadenitis of inguinal glands. In June last noticed enlargement of inguinal glands on both sides, following a small sore on the glans penis near the corona. He was treated for primary syphilis, and was given large doses of potassic iodid. At no time was there any induration at the base of the sore, which always presented the appearance of an abrasion rather than an ulcer. At no time have there been any indications of secondary syphilis. The lymphatic glands in other regions of the body are normal. The patient states that the sore has healed repeatedly, reappearing at varying intervals in the same place. Examination of the penis reveals slight phimosis, chronic balanitis which has resulted in great thickening of the mucosa lining the prepuce. The sore, which has been a source of great mental distress to the patient, appears in the form of a very superficial abrasion not larger than a split pea with ill-defined margins and no induration whatever at its base. Recently the preputial margin became the seat of a herpetic eruption. The lymphatic glands in both groins are hard, not very tender to the touch and vary in size from that of a pea to a hazelnut. September 13, typical circumcision was performed under chloroform narcosis. It is expected that the removal of the direct cause of the lymphadenitis will be followed by a speedy reduction in the size of the glands. The essential cause is to be attributed to the entrance of pus microbes into the lymph channels from the local lesions of the glans penis and prepuce which became arrested in the lymphatic filters, producing an inflammation which came to a standstill short of suppuration.

Case 29.—Robert V. Smith, age 21, Tenth Cavalry, Troop E, colored, enlisted June 20. A month ago while in camp in Florida, he noticed a number of small pimples on the scalp on the right side. These small furuncles still exist, and a week ago gave rise to a deep-seated lymphadenitis affecting the lymphatic glands in the superior posterior triangle on the corresponding side of the neck. When the patient came under observation, September 13, a large and somewhat diffuse swelling marked the location of the infected glands; evidently the connective tissue around and between the glands is secondarily implicated in the inflammatory process. The swelling is hard and tender on pressure. No signs of central softening. Evening temperature 102 F., morning temperature 100 F. Directions were given to clip the hair short, and to disinfect the entire scalp. Credé's silver ointment to be rubbed into the skin over the swelling and to apply a hot, moist antiseptic compress. The patient is anemic, for which condition Gude's pepto mangan was prescribed. There is some prospect that the removal of the source of infection and the local applications will succeed in arresting the process and in effecting resorption of the inflammatory product.

This hope was not realized, as a few days later, September 23, distinct fluctuation was felt and the abscess was incised and drained, the patient being under the influence of chloroform. Rapid improvement followed the operation.

ABSCESS FOLLOWING TYPHOID FEVER.

It is somewhat singular that among the hundreds of cases of typhoid fever, that I had an opportunity to see and examine in Porto Rico and in this great national camp, no cases of perforation have come to my notice. I kept myself in readiness to perform laparotomy at a moment's notice, but my services were never requested for this particular purpose. I have no doubt but that some of the deaths from typhoid fever were due to this cause, and that this fatal complication was either overlooked or the general condition of the patient was so grave when it occurred, that the attending physicians did not deem it advisable to send for the surgeon. In this camp we had all the necessary facilities for abdominal operations, and I was hopeful that I should have an opportunity to give surgery a fair trial in such cases, but in this I have been disappointed. The most important, and most frequent complications of our typhoid fever patients have been bedsores and abscesses. The careful and attentive nursing our patients here have received, has done much in reducing the mortality and suffering from decubitus. Frequent washing with alcohol of the parts exposed to decubitus and the use of rubber pillows, and in the worst cases, of water or air beds, have contributed much in the prevention and successful treatment of this complication. We have had however, an excellent opportunity to study the etiology and pathology of abscesses as a complication of typhoid fever. The material was abundant and interesting. It is a source of regret to me that we did not have at our disposal a well-equipped bacteriologic laboratory to enable us to study in a more satisfactory manner the contents of those abscesses. Acting Assistant-Surgeon Ewing brought his own microscopic outfit, including the different stains, and did good work in the microscopic examination of pus and other pathologic products, but we had no facilities for making cultures. He examined the contents of three abscesses in as many patients, and found as the essential bacteriologic cause the bacillus of typhoid in one and the ordinary pus microbes in the remaining two cases.

The typhoid or so-called metastatic abscesses are caused by the bacillus of typhoid fever or by pus microbes which find their way into the circulation through some infection-atrium, especially the intestinal ulcers, as the result of a mixed infection. I have no doubt that in some cases the colon bacillus finds its way into the general circulation and produces the same results. The only case of bone and joint infection that came under my observation, and that could be brought in connection with the typhoid infection occurred in the case of a young soldier recovering from a severe attack of typhoid fever.

Case 30.—William Fairweather, age 22, Company A, Twelfth Infantry, about one week after the surrender of Santiago, was attacked with fever which continued for three weeks. He reached this camp with his regiment, emaciated to a skeleton, and extremely anemic. A week ago, while moving about, he was attacked rather suddenly with a severe pain in the right sacro-iliac synchondrosis and extending to the leg on the same side. The pain in the leg subsided after a few days but increased in severity at the point where it first commenced. The pain is of a dull, aching, throbbing character. Slight swelling over and in the line of the joint. Evening temperature one degree above normal. No redness or edema of the skin. September 6, the joint was punctured with the largest needle of an exploring syringe and a 5 per cent. solution of carbolic acid was injected in different directions, so as to reach the infected tissues as far as possible. No difficulty was met with in injecting three drachms of the solution. The needle puncture was sealed with collodium and a pledget of cotton. Marked improvement followed the intra articular and parenchymatous injection. The pain and tenderness had nearly disappeared on the third day. Under tonics and stimulants the general condition of the patient improved from day to day. There is no reason to fear at this time that suppuration will take place.

This case represents one of those rare complications of typhoid fever in which a joint becomes the seat of secondary infection during the latter stages of typhoid fever or during convalescence, in which the inflammatory process often results in great destruction of tissue without pus formation. Whether or not the injection should be credited with having brought about the speedy cessation of active symptoms can not be decided, either way with any degree of positiveness. I have learned to value the therapeutic effect of parenchymatous injections of carbolic acid in the treatment of chronic or subacute inflammation of a non-tubercular inflammation, and I am inclined to attribute to it in this particular and similar cases positive curative properties, the evidence of which in this case appeared so shortly after it was made.

Case 31.—C. H. Baker, aged 22, Company F, Second Massachusetts Infantry, was sick two months in Cuba with fever, malaria, headache, anorexia, diarrhea, in consequence of which he became very weak. Shortly after boarding the transport, he became delirious and has been sick with typhoid fever for three weeks. A week ago, while convalescent, he was attacked suddenly with violent pain in the right testicle which rapidly increased in size, reaching the dimensions of a small orange in the course of two days. At that time, the temperature increased two degrees above normal. On the third day after the attack, the swelling was hard, very sensitive to the touch, the skin red and glossy. No chills. Under applications of lead water and opium the pain has been somewhat mitigated and the swelling slightly diminished in size. September 10, a week after the complication had set in, the patient was transferred to the surgical ward. At this time deep-seated fluctuation could be distinctly felt over the center of the swelling. Less discoloration of the skin than a few days ago. Swelling only about twice the size of the normal testicle. The abscess appears to occupy the center of the testicle. Under ether anesthesia the abscess cavity was opened at the most dependent point, and a counter-opening two inches higher up made by tunnelling the tissues from within outward with a curved hemostatic forceps, and through drainage established. The pus was of the consistence of cream and whitish in color. No transudation into the tunica vaginalis. The conditions revealed at the time of operation left no doubt regarding the parenchymatous central origin of the abscess. Microscopic examination of the pus removed showed typhoid bacilli in great abundance as the exclusive bacteriologic cause of the suppurative orchitis. The patient improved very rapidly after the operation, and was transferred in less than a week to one of the Boston city hospitals.

Case 32.— L. Gardner, age 38, Company A, Sixth Infantry, went through the Cuban campaign with two days' slight illness. He lost flesh, but felt well until he came on the transport four weeks ago, when he was attacked with fever which proved to be typhoid complicated by malaria as shown by the erratic temperature curves. Convalescence was preceded by inflammation of the left parotid gland. Emaciation marked. Spleen much enlarged. The liver dulness extends from the sixth rib to an inch below the costal arch. Lungs normal. Heart sounds clear and distinct. Pulse strong and regular. Tongue red and glazed. A week after the beginning of the attack, a large abscess had formed and fluctuation could be distinctly felt, extending from a level with the external meatus to near the angle of the jaw. At that time, September 7, the patient was etherized, the abscess opened at the lowest and highest points, and through drainage established, a large quantity of thick purulent, curdy pus escaped. The cavity was washed out with a 2.5 per cent. carbolic solution and peroxid of hydrogen, and a large, moist, hot antiseptic compress applied. Improvement followed at once and ended in a slow recovery without any interruptions.

Case 33.—Patrick Collins, age 26, Eighth Infantry, Company C, has been in the service one year. About two weeks after the fight in Cuba was attacked with malaria, which was followed by typhoid. The fever has persisted since. attended by diarrhea and other symptoms indicating its nature. While on the transport on his return he complained of a sense of soreness in the left parotid region, followed by swelling and redness. Patient much emaciated and very feeble. At the time the operation was performed, August 29, the swelling extended from the external ear to near the angle of the jaw, and deepseated fluctuation was distinct. Incision, drainage, disinfection and after-treatment the same as in the preceding case. Owing to the marked weakness of the heart's action, the patient was given two ounces of whisky before he was placed under the influence of ether. Alcoholic stimulants were administered in large and frequently repeated doses and acted very promptly in increasing the tone of the circulation and in building up the impaired nutrition. The discharge from the abscess in this, as well as the other cases of abscess of the parotid following typhoid fever, was very slight after the evacuation of the abscess contents.

Case 34.—Harold Robinson, age 28, Third Infantry, Company D, contracted typhoid fever in Cuba. He is now in the third week of the fever and has been delirious most of the time. The disease pursued almost from the beginning a very malignant course. About five days ago a swelling was detected in the region of the right parotid gland, which increased very rapidly in size, involving the skin after two or three days. The abscess ruptured on the fourth day into the external meatus, but evacuation was incomplete on account of the existence of several separate compartments in the abscess cavity, which were discovered at the time the operation was performed. The abdomen is intensely tympanitic, the skin of feet, legs and abdomen spotted with dark points of ecchymosis. The condition of the patient was critical when the operation was performed, September 10. The operation had to be performed without an anesthetic and in his ward, as he was too feeble to justify his transfer to the surgical ward. The impoverished condition of the blood made it necessary to make the incision only through the skin, completing the opening with hemostatic forceps. Free tubular drainage was established and the abscess cavity was treated in the usual way. Strychnia and alcoholic stimulants were administered freely, but the heart failed to respond and the patient died the next day. Notwithstanding that the openings were made largely by the use of blunt instruments, free oozing of blood followed the operation, which may have contributed in hastening the fatal termination.

Case 35.—Giles Potter, age 33, Second Massachusetts Infantry, had chills and fever while in Cuba, but was on duty continuously. Was still weak and ill when he came on board the transport. The parotid abscess began on transport. He is very weak and emaciated, at times delirious; temperature indicates typhoid fever. Conjunctivæ slightly jaundiced. Pulse small and thready. Spleen slightly enlarged. The abscess was incised and drained without the use of an anesthetic, in its stead a large dose of whisky was given. The pus in this case was of a green color. Patient improved rapidly after the operation and is now on the way to convalescence.

Case 36.—John Simpson, age 28, Troop K, First Cavalry, was admitted to the general hospital August 25, suffering from typhoid fever, with a temperature gradually declining until September 4, when it rose suddenly from 99.4 to 102 and 103, dropping on the 8th to 99. On admission patient had very marked roseolar eruption on abdomen and limbs. During the course of the fever numerous furuncles appeared on the forehead and back. Delirium has been a prominent feature in the case almost from the beginning. Directly following the sudden rise of temperature on September 4, soreness and swelling of the right submaxillary gland were noticed. Today, September 10, a fluctuating swelling, the size of a small apple, marks the location and size of the abscess. Operation without anesthetic. Incision, counteropening, tubular drainage, irrigation with peroxid and carbolic solution, wet carbolic dressing. Rapid improvement followed the operation and the patient is now, September 13, fairly convalescent; abscess nearly healed.

The parotid gland, of all glandular organs, is the most frequent seat of secondary infection in typhoid fever. For reasons that remain unexplained the submaxillary is seldom involved, and the sublingual is still more rarely affected. The infective process begins in the parenchyma of the salivary gland but extends rapidly to the capsule and the surrounding connective tissue, leading to a phlegmonous process which in four or five days, as a rule, terminates in a well-marked abscess with the gland as a central point. The physician must be on the alert in such cases, and resort to the use of the knife in a most cautious manner as soon as fluctuation can be detected. It is advisable to establish through drainage for the purpose of securing free evacuation and thorough disinfection of the interior of the abscess cavity. The openings should be made by cutting only the skin and underlying fascia with the knife, completing them by tunnelling the remaining tissues with a curved hemostatic forceps. Dry dressings should not be employed in such cases; nothing is more grateful to the patient and more efficient in the after-treatment than the application of a moist, hot, antiseptic compress covered with oiled silk to retain heat and moisture. The safest and most efficient solution for this purpose is a saturated solution of acetate of aluminium, but when this can not be secured, a 2.5 per cent. solution of carbolic acid or a saturated solution of boracic acid answer as excellent substitutes.

In the next case the clinical history is very defective, and it is impossible to say with any degree of certainty whether or not the parotid abscesses followed in the course of typhoid fever, or whether they were external manifestations of a general septic process that developed independently of that disease.

Case 37.—Austin Dunlap, age 19, Company H, Third Infantry, was taken suddenly ill in Tampa, about July 1, with pain in the back and joints and nausea. The disease was diagnosticated at the time as malaria. He was sent to quarters, and after four days returned to duty. On arrival at this camp, August 14, had three severe chills during the first twenty-four hours and has been very sick since. When admitted to the surgical ward with bilateral suppurative parotitis and large bedsores, he was reduced to a skeleton. Extensive herpes labialis which near the left angle of the mouth have caused ulceration; abscess over elbow joint. Pulse rapid and very small, temperature irregular. When first admitted the case was regarded as a forlorn one and whiskey was given in ounce doses hourly. The swelling in the parotid region, on both sides, was hard and very sensitive to the touch. Credé's silver ointment and hot antiseptic compresses constituted the local treatment. Five days later distinct fluctuation could be detected and one of the parotid abscesses was incised and free tubular drainage effected. Owing to his critical condition the operations had to be performed without an anesthetic. The next day, September 10, the opposite abscess was treated in the same manner. The patient has been placed on a water-bed and was restless and most of the time delirious. No evidences of metastasis in any of the internal organs. Under the stimulating treatment he rallied promptly and at the present time, September 13, his mind is clear and the temperature normal. Discharge from abscess cavities slight. The drains are shortened from time to time to permit early definitive healing of the abscesses.

I am confident that early operative treatment and the heroic employment of alcoholic stimulants have been the principal means in saving the life of this patient.

Case 39.—Corporal George F. Shilling, age 18, Company G, First D. C. Volunteers. Enormous typhoid abscess of arm. Family history negative. Health excellent before he went to Cuba. On August 15 reported sick at the hospital. Had been feeling ill for some days. He has been delirious most of the time since admission to the General Hospital here. The temperature has been on an average 103 degrees F., with daily variation of a degree and a half from August 19 to September 4. Since latter date the temperature at no time has been over 101 degrees F. The pulse is small, rapid and weak, tongue dry, brown and fissured. On arriving here on transport there were five large bedsores on back and numerous small abscesses of the skin. He was placed at once upon a water-bed, but the bedsores continued to still further undermine the skin. Two days ago when the nurse was dressing the bedsores, she discovered a swelling of the right arm on the outer edge of the biceps muscle. This has rapidly increased in size and now presents itself as an enormous abscess extending from the shoulder to the tendon of the biceps muscle. Fluctuation is most distinct over the outer aspect of the arm. On palpation a crackling sensation is felt, and on percussion the swelling was distinctly tympanitic. The presence of gas in the abscess cavity could not be doubted. September 12 the patient was almost pulseless, lips cyanotic, respiration shallow, and marked twitching of the muscles of the upper extremities. In the afternoon the abscess was cautiously opened above and below and a rubber drainage tube drawn through. A large quantity of an offensive gas and creamy pus was evacuated. The abscess cavity was freely irrigated with peroxid of hydrogen and 2.5 per cent. of carbolic solution and the moist, hot antiseptic compress applied. In place of an anesthetic the patient was given an ounce of whiskey, which was to be repeated hourly. Hot water bags were applied to relieve the embarrassed peripheral circulation. Contrary to our expectations, the patient rallied under this treatment and presented a much more encouraging condition the next morning, when it was reported that the temperature was nearly normal, mind clear and the pulse full and strong. Microscopic examination of the pus by Dr. Ewing revealed: 1, many cocci resembling staphyloccus pyogenes; 2, a few large capsulated cocci; 3, a few fine slender bacilli staining faintly with methylene blue. There is nothing that resembles the bacillus aerogenes capsulatus. The patient is in a fair way to recovery (September 17).

Case 40.—Fred Angier, age 23, First Cavalry, Troop I, is under treatment for typhoid fever probably during the third week of his illness. Patient is delirious and it is impossible to obtain reliable information as to duration of his sickness. Very recently the right eye became affected by an acute inflammatory process which appears to involve all of the tissues of the organ. The eyelids are swollen, red and somewhat edematous. The edema extends over the whole malar region. Exophthalmus well marked. Pupil contracted and immovable. Conjunctiva in a state of catarrhal inflammation. Hypopion. Sent to the New York Hospital, August 30, for treatment by specialist of the eye complication. This is the only case of secondary infection of eye of a typhoid character that was observed in the camp. It was a well-marked case of panophtalmitis and if the patient recovers it will be with the loss of the affected organ.

ERYSIPELOID.

Erysipeloid, an acute inflammatory affection of the skin, described by J. Rosenbach, is a disease of the skin not often recognized. It is usually mistaken for erysipelas. The parasite was described by Rosenbach more than ten years ago, but it has never been classified. Attempts to cultivate it have failed so far. This disease is met with usually among persons engaged in the handling of fish and meat, that is, cooks and butchers. It is attended by very slight constitutional disturbances and its local progression is slow as compared with erysipelas. The starting point is generally a finger, where infection takes place through slight surface defects or a puncture. It consists, pathologically speaking, of a subacute inflammation of the lymphatic channels of the skin. The affected skin presents a bluish color instead of the bright red seen in erysipelas. Another and perhaps more important characteristic sign in the differentiation between erysipeloid and erysipelas is the appearance of the margin of the inflamed area. In erysipeloid the shading from diseased into healthy skin is gradual, the line straight, in erysipelas abrupt and the margin presents well-marked fan-shaped projections instead of a straight line. The thickening of the skin by infiltration in erpsipeloid is slight and the only thing the patient complains of is a sensation of burning or smarting. The disease travels in the direction and against the lymph-current, so that when the point of infection is some distance from the tip of the finger, this is reached in time by extension of the inflammation downward from the point of infection. The disease travels slowly, it usually takes a week or more before the inflammation reaches the base of the finger when infection takes place anywhere near its tip. The lymphangitis seldom if ever extends beyond the elbow joint. The infection may extend from one finger to another when the inflammation travels in a distal direction. The skin soon returns to its normal condition behind the zone of infection. A case of this kind came to the surgical ward for treatment.

Case 41.—Patrick J. M. McGeoch, age 24, kitchen employe, presented himself September 9, complaining of a burning, smarting pain in the right index finger, which commenced four days ago. Over the radial side of the affected finger, opposite the middle joint, is a small abrasion covered by a thin adherent crust. The skin half as far as the tip of the finger and an inch above this point is slightly swollen and presents a bluish-red color. The discoloration is most marked on the dorsal side. At the proximal margin of the zone of inflammation the diseased gradually shades into the healthy skin, both in regard to color and swelling. Patient is able to follow his occupation. The case presents all the characteristic signs of Rosenbach's erysipeloid. An alcohol compress with oiled silk over it was applied. In three days the inflammation had extended to the base of the finger while the distal portion, the seat of the disease when the patient first came under observation, presented a normal appearance, the skin being somewhat shrivelled by the action of the alcohol application.

AFFECTIONS OF THE RECTUM, ANUS AND ADJACENT TISSUES.

Rectal affections in some form were very common among the returning troops from Cuba. It is fair to presume that some of the soldiers were the subjects of a mild form of hemorrhoids when they entered the service, but it is equally certain that none of them were affected with fistula or abscess. To show the disproportion of rectal disease between the recruits who applied for enlistment and the soldiers returning from the field, I will state that of 10,000 applicants examined in Camp Tanner last spring the following rectal affections were noted: Hemorrhoids, internal, 2; external, 219; inflamed, 1; fistula, 1; prolapsus, 2. I attribute the prevalence of rectal diseases among our patients in this camp to the following causes: 1, intestinal affections contracted in the camps and Cuba; 2, improper food; 3, the relaxing effect of a tropical climate; 4 frequent exposure. Few of our soldiers escaped diarrhea or dysentery. The irritation of the rectal mucous membrane could not fail in many instances to produce a catarrhal proctitis. The inflamed mucous membrane became .permeable to the passage of pathogenic microbes, which so constantly infest even the healthy rectum. The loose pararectal connective tissue, under the influence of general causes, became more susceptible to infection, it is therefore not astonishing that we should have found so many cases of perianal, perirectal and ischiorectal abscesses and their consequences, fistulæ. Inflammatory affections of the rectum play also an important etiologic rôle in the development of hemorrhoids. We found in a number of cases a direct connection between an antecedent rectal inflammatory affection and the subsequent appearance of hemorrhoids. The intense tenesmus which attends catarrhal proctitis and dysentery causes muscular changes and lesions of the mucous membrane which often become the principal cause of pararectal inflammation and hemorrhoids.

PARARECTAL ABSCESS.

Under this head I will report all cases of suppurative inflammation in the vicinity of the anus and outside of the rectal wall that have been operated on in Camp Wikoff. In all cases the suppurative inflammation pursued a very rapid course, The pain, as a rule, was intense, and fluctuation could be felt distinctly in the course of four or five days. In high-seated paraproctitis the general symptoms were usually severe, a high temperature and a rapid bounding pulse. It was in these cases that the affection assumed the most progressive form. The abscess contents were always fetid, otherwise presented the usual appearance of pus as found in acute abscesses in other localities.

Case 42.—Robert F. Stanley, age 22, Troop G, Ninth Cavalry, colored. Perianal and ischio-rectal abscess. While in Cuba had diarrhea for eighteen days—August 27 to September 1—had chills and fever. Reached Camp Wikoff September 3, on which day he had pain about the rectum before and during defecation and on sitting down. He was admitted to surgical ward September 8. By careful palpation a small area of circumscribed induration as large as a pea could be felt on the right side of the sphincter muscle and about one-third of an inch from the surface. This swelling could not be detected from the rectum. Pain was greatly increased under pressure. A small incision was made and about half a dram of pus escaped. The little cavity was washed out with peroxid of hydrogen and carbolized water and loosely packed with a strip of iodoform gauze. As an external dressing a hot moist antiseptic compress was used and held in place by a T bandage. Immediate and almost complete relief followed the operation. On the ninth, the temperature rose to 100 degrees F., on the tenth to 101. The pain was intense and referred to the opposite side of the rectum. September 10, a fluctuating swelling could be felt from the perineum and the rectum. The abscess bulged externally as well as on the rectal side. The patient was again anesthetized and the abscess incised through the perineum to the left of the median line. A large quantity of extremely fetid pus escaped. As the undermining was extensive two counter-openings were made, one below and one above the first opening. Two fenestrated rubber tubes were employed in draining the large cavity. The abscess was washed out with carbolized solution and peroxid of hydrogen, and the moist antiseptic compress applied. The pain was relieved at once and the discharge after the operation slight. No tendency to further undermining, on the other hand all indications point to an early and permanent healing of the abscess cavity.

It is in cases like these that practitioners so frequently make a serious mistake by postponing from day to day opening and draining of the abscess. If we had deferred the operation for another day or two the abscess would have ruptured into the rectum and would have led almost inevitably to the formation of an internal or complete fistula. The horseshoe fistulæ following cases of ischio-rectal abscess, so frequently found in any of the large surgical clinics are the best proof of the necesity for early operative interference. The rule should be to open such abscesses early, from the external surface, and if fluctuation can not be felt from this direction but from the rectum, the tissues on the side of the rectum can be tunnelled with forceps after making a superficial incision, until the abscess cavity is reached. The surgeon must so conduct the treatment that the formation of a fistula can be avoided, and this can be done in nearly all, if not all, cases in which the abscess is opened before it ruptures into the rectum.

Case 43.—Alva J. Vananken, age 27, Troop K, First Cavalry. Perirectal abscess. On his last day in Cuba the patient had a mild fever and diarrhea; the latter persisted fifteen or sixteen days. For the last ten days has had a throbbing pain in the post anal region. An abscess found and opened in the median line, between the anus and coccyx. Under ether anesthesia the abscess cavity behind the rectum was freely opened with the Paquelin cautery, taking the fistulous opening in the median line as a guide for the incision. The cavity was thoroughly disinfected and packed with iodoform gauze, over which the usual moist dressing was applied. Rapid healing of the cavity by granulation.

Case 44.—Robert Sylvester, age 24, Company G, Fourth Artillery. Has been ill with typhoid malarial fever while in Cuba. Returned from Cuba on the steamer *Leona*, and reached Camp Wikoff about September 1. Soon after his arrival he noticed pain on the left side of the rectum. The pain and tenderness increased rapidly in intensity. September 7, he was admitted to the surgical ward and the operation was performed without anesthesia three days later. At this time the abscess was prominent on the side of the anus and the overlying skin presented an inflammatory blush. Fluctuation very distinct from the rectum as well as from the surface. The abscess was opened by a single incision and tubular drainage established, as the incision was large enough to serve for drainage. After disinfection of the cavity and packing it lightly with iodoform gauze, a moist antiseptic compress was applied. The patient was very weak at the time the operation was performed, but gained sufficiently in strength in a week to warrant his transfer to a hospital in Philadelphia.

Case 45.—Joseph Barret, age 28, Third Infantry, Company G. Ischio-rectal abscess. About the time of the surrender of Santiago had general malaise, fever, vomiting and diarrhea for which he has since been on the sick list. Several days ago he began to experience pain in the rectum which has increased steadily since, and at the time he was admitted to the surgical ward the ischiorectal abscess had opened spontaneously on the right side just within the anal margin. General health much improved. On August 31, under chloroform anesthesia the abscess cavity was distended with peroxid of hydrogen for the purpose of ascertaining its exact size and location. A grooved director was inserted into the fistulous opening and used as a guide in laying open the abscess cavity freely with the knife point of the Paquelin cautery. The abscess cavity was disinfected and packed loosely with iodoform gauze over which the moist compress was applied. He improved rapidly after the operation and a few days later was transferred to a hospital in Boston.

Case 46.—William Head, age 20, Eighth Ohio Infantry, Company G, enlisted two and a half months ago. Admitted to the surgical ward with a history of malarial fever and dysentery in Cuba, followed by ischiorectal abscess which discharged itself near the anal orifice on the right side. Discharge continues profuse. The peroxid of hydrogen test was applied to ascertain the extent of the abscess cavity which was found to extend high up into the ischiorectal fossa. Owing to the marked anemia and general debility a counter-opening was made lower down and thorough drainage secured, in place of opening the abscess cavity freely with the Paquelin cautery. Chloroform was used as an anesthetic. The general and local conditions improved promptly after the operation.

FISTULA.

The spontaneous rupture of a pararectal or ischiorectal abscess into the rectum is generally followed by the formation of a fistula. If the abscess communicates with the rectum its existence can be surmised from the intermittent discharge of pus and local symptoms which refer to the rectal lesion. An internal fistula of such an origin is often made complete by the abscess finding eventually an external outlet somewhere in the anal region. An external fistula caused by the opening of a pararectal abscess not infrequently becomes complete by the destructive process penetrating the rectal wall. I have long ago abandoned the probe in differentiating between an external fistula and a complete one. Injection of peroxid of hydrogen into the cavity under pressure makes a positive diagnosis at once. If the fistula is external the abscess cavity becomes tense, if complete the peroxid foam enters the rectum and will escape from the anus. The probe is only used after the test has made the diagnosis and then only as an aid in performing the necessary operation. In diagnosticating the existence and location of an internal fistula the rectal speculum is of the greatest importance. Rectal fistula will be less frequently met with when the profession as a whole recognizes the importance of early operative interference in cases of pararectal abscess. In my surgical work in Camp Wykoff only two cases of rectal fistula presented themselves for operative treatment.

Case 17.—Lieut. G. W. Goode, Troop I, Ninth Cavalry. Hemorrhoids and fistula. He was admitted to the surgical ward August 24. He has been almost habitually constipated, and has been much in the saddle. He knows of no definite preceding illness to account for present condition. He has had much pain and bleeding on defecation, pain persisting for an hour or two after. Examination reveals large internal and external hemorrhoids and an incomplete internal fistula following the rupture of a post rectal abscess, into the rectum through the middle of the sphincter muscle, posterior side. The abscess cavity, the size of a walnut, was freely laid open upon a grooved director with the knife point of the Paquelin cautery. The incision was carried directly backward through the median line. The hemorrhoids, two in number, affecting the posterior segment of the anal ring were removed by clamp and cautery. The abscess cavity was loosely packed with a strip of iodoform gauze. The rectal tampon remained for two days, The patient made a rapid recovery and was able to leave the hospital September 13. The agonizing pain attending and following each bowel movement disappeared immediately after the operation.

Case 48.—John M. Boyd, age 29, Troop G, Third Cavalry, enlisted four months ago. Admitted to the surgical department of the General Hospital August 27. His health was good until he went to Tampa, June 8. At that time he suffered from diarrhea which was persistent, but did not prevent his doing duty in the saddle. For the past five weeks and following a severe pain in the rectum which continued several days, he has noticed a discharge of pus from the rectum. The pain did not disappear entirely after the abscess ruptured into the rectum and was always aggravated during defecation. August 28, under chloroform anesthesia the sphincter ani was dilated, the internal opening was found, the cavity distended with peroxid of hydrogen, external counter-opening made by the aid of the grooved director and the intervening tissues divided with the Paquelin cautery. Iodoform gauze packing and dry dressing. The internal opening in this case was just above the sphincter muscle, the abscess on the right side of the rectum. Rapid healing of the abscess cavity.

HEMORRHOIDS.

A large number of hemorrhoid cases came to the surgical ward with the desire and expectation of receiving the benefits of a radical operation. I am satisfied that only a small percentage of those affected were willing or prepared to be subjected to an operation. Some of the cases examined peremptorily declined to receive treatment knowing well that the results would put one claim for pension beyond their reach. In my capacity as operating surgeon of the camp I was very anxious to curtail the list of pensioners of this war by performing operations for surgical affections which, if left alone, would furnish a just claim upon the Government. On the whole, I found the colored soldiers much more willing than their white comrades to be benefited by surgery. They proved themselves worthy of their hire in the hospital as well as on the battlefield. Too much can not be said in praise of our colored soldiers. They showed a staunch faith in their doctors as well as their commanders, and were ready at all times to follow their advice as well as the commands of their officers. Nearly all of the hemorrhoids operated on showed pathologic appearances which demonstrated their recent origin. In a very large percentage of cases the first manifestation of hemorrhoidal condition was preceded by intestinal disturbances, diarrhea or dysentery. Fortunately, I had two Paquelin cauteries at my disposal as soon as the operating tent was opened. As I said in the beginning of this paper, my instrumentarium at first was a very scanty one. Instruments, however, began to come, day after day, and finally I had an excellent supply, including a number of cases for special work. The absence of a proper pile clamp from the outfit of the surgical ward at the outset, necessitated the use of something as a substitute. This was found in a curved hemostatic forceps. Except for its lightness, and therefore comparatively inefficient grasping power, this answered the purpose admirably. In fact, the facility and accuracy with which the hemorrhoidal swelling could be clamped and isolated, the small space required for its use, and its general convenience and ease of handling as compared with heavy clamps, now in the market, led to the devising by Major Adams of Chicago, of a hemorrhoid clamp similar to the forceps used, but so constructed as to obviate the defects of weakness and imperfect grasp found in that instrument. The use of the forceps as a clamp has demonstrated that the amount of pressure and crushing exerted by the old-fashioned instruments are unnecessary and uncalled for; also that there is no need of ivory plates to prevent the transmission of heat through the metal of the forceps to the underlying mucous membrane, as in no instance was any ill effect observed from this cause. Another advantage of the narrow blade forceps has been demonstrated in the absence of any hemorrhage whatever after operation. The new clamp has blades with a serrated grasping surface 5 cm. long, curved on the flat, the width of the blades closed is 9 mm., their thickness 6 mm., beveled away from the upper to the outer edge for 1 mm. The object of the bevel is to allow of the operation of the cautery with the least possible contact with the metal of the clamp, to avoid heating. The blades come into contact at the point first, so that uniform pressure is exerted the whole length of the blades when closed, and the hemorrhoid can not escape its grasp at the point, as often happens with the ordinary clamp.

The handles are arranged like those of a needle forceps. With one exception the hemorrhoids were removed with the knife point of the Paquelin at a dull red heat, after clamping the swelling at its base. The hemorrhoid was first grasped with a dissecting or hemostatic forceps, when the base of the cone elevated to the desired extent was grasped and clamped with the forceps and the mass outside of the grasp of the instrument shaved away with the cautery. The operation of

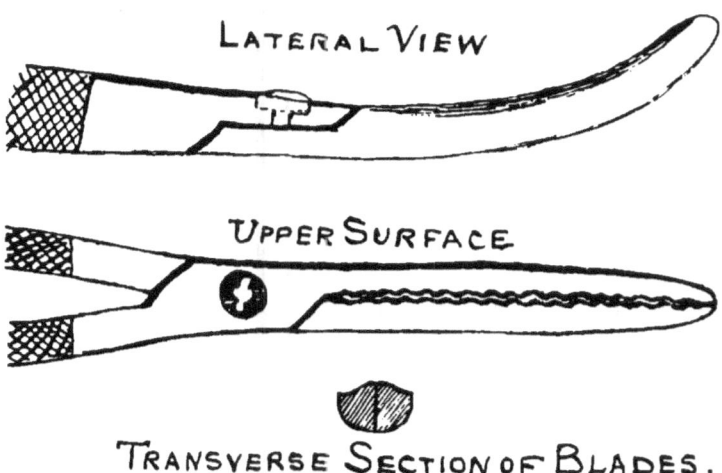

Hemorrhoid clamp, devised by Major Adams.

removal was always preceded by dilatation of the sphincter. The patients were always properly prepared for the operation the day before. The rectum was thoroughly cleared out by the administration of a cathartic and irrigation. The last enema was given on the morning of the operation. As a rule, two or three seizures were made. After dilatation of the sphincter the hemorrhoidal swellings were located and grasped with forceps so that the work of clamping and cauterization could proceed without interruption. Care was exercised in every case not to remove too much tissue; due allowance was given for subsequent contraction. The anal region was shaved and prepared in the same manner as for operations in other localities. One of the principal sources of pain after operations for hemorrhoids has been the protrusion and swelling of the cauterized surfaces. For many years I have succeeded in preventing this very painful post-operative complication by resorting to drainage and rectal tamponade. This method of dressing rectal wounds after this operation is not sufficiently known and practiced. Those who have not tried it might entertain a fear that it is a source of distress rather than comfort. Quite an extensive experience with this method of after-treatment enables me to make the unqualified statement that the rectal tampon, properly applied, is well borne by the patients and makes the use of anodynes superfluous. I never administer opiates after operation for hemorrhoids. The rectal tampon not only obviates unnecessary pain, but it also is almost an absolute protection against secondary hemorrhage and more than this, it provides for free rectal drainage and constitutes the best possible dressing for the cauterized surfaces.

When I first used this tampon, I was under the impression that it was something new, but I learned later that Mitchell Banks had used a very similar contrivance before. The tampon is made by taking a piece of rubber tubing eight inches in length and inserting into it a glass cylinder three-fourths of an inch in diameter and about 2 inches in length. The glass tube is placed where the gauze tent is tied over the rubber tubing for the purpose of furnishing a support to the string with which the gauze tent is tied upon the tube and to insure patency of the tubular drain. The rubber tube should project well over the glass cylinder on the rectal side. The gauze tent is made of one or two layers of iodoform gauze. After completion of the operation the tent is carefully folded and the upper portion covered with vaseline. The tube is then inserted into the rectum to the depth of three or four inches and the space between the tent and tube packed with strips of iodoform or plain sterile gauze. After the required amount of packing is inserted the tampon is pushed in the direction of the rectum sufficiently to bring the pressure above the grasp of the sphincter muscle. In doing this the projecting mucous membrane and what may remain of the external hemorrhoids are completely reduced. The gauze

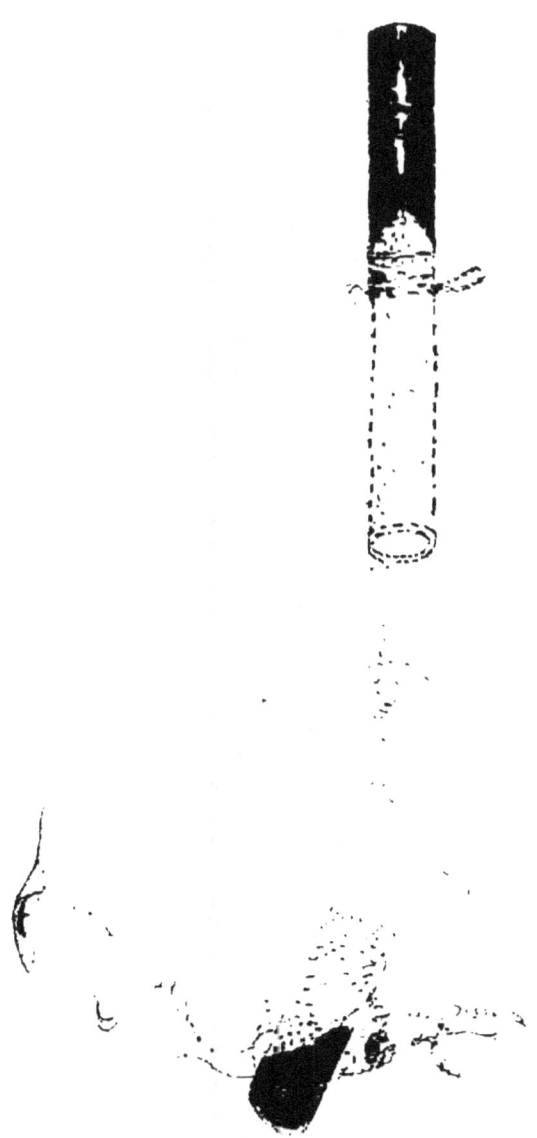

Rectal tampon. Rubber tube 20 cm., glass tube 8 cm.

outside of the anal orifice is then wound around the tube and forms a part of the external dressing. Over the gauze a wide ring of absorbent cotton is applied and the whole retained in place by a T bandage. The tampon should remain for 24 to 48 hours.

In removing it traction is made on the gauze tent sufficiently to bring the packing within easy reach when it is removed before an attempt is made to extract the tube. After the removal of the tampon the patient should be given a laxative and after this has acted the cauterized surfaces now minus the eschar are protected by applying carbolated vaseline or some other antiseptic non irritating ointment. I have made it a rule to keep the patient confined to bed for at least a week, still better two weeks. The cases of hemorrhoids operated upon in this camp with very few exceptions have been men whose general health was much impaired, yet in every case the wounds healed quickly and in the most satisfactory manner under the treatment outlined above.

Case 49.—M. J. McNulty, age 31, Company D, Sixteenth Infantry, enlisted six months ago. Has had small hemorrhoids for two years, causing inconvenience only after heavy drinking. In June, while in Florida, bleeding at stool occurred for the first time. Since he suffered from malarial fever and diarrhea during the Cuban campaign, he has suffered from profuse bleeding on defecation. September 3, under chloroform anesthesia, three hemorrhoidal swellings were removed.

Case 50.—George Morton, age 47, sergeant Ninth Cavalry, Troop A, colored, has been in the service ten years and seven months. Had dysentery two months ago, since then has suffered from pain in the rectum and bleeding with each evacuation of the bowels. August 26, under chloroform anesthesia, three hemorrhoids, partly external and partly internal, were removed by clamp and cautery.

Case 51.—Jesse Donaldson, age 30, Troop M, Ninth Cavalry, colored, enlisted three months ago. While in Tampa, patient suffered from malarial fever and diarrhea, the latter continued for three or four days. Has not been well since that time. Since August 1, he has been much inconvenienced by a hemorrhoidal affection which developed recently. Operation performed under chloroform narcosis, September 2. Three internal hemorrhoids, two posteriorly, one at upper right quadrant, were removed in the usual way by clamp and cautery.

Case 52. Claude F. Hall, age 23, Company G, Sixteenth Infantry, had hemorrhoids about four years ago, but not so severe an attack as the present. Recovered without operation.

Has been in the service since the 17th of September, a year ago. Following an attack of malaria and diarrhea in Cuba, he has been suffering from hemorrhoids for the past six weeks. He has no bleeding, but the hemorrhoids have been protruding constantly and are very painful. September 7, under chloroform anesthesia, three internal hemorrhoids were removed in the usual manner by clamp and cautery. They were located respectively in the posterior right and left quadrant.

Case 52.—James Jervis, age 19, Company K, Thirty fourth Michigan Infantry, enlisted three and a half months ago. Had diarrhea two weeks, before leaving Cuba. Has had much pain and bleeding with movements of bowels since. Never had rectal trouble of any kind before. August 31, under ether anesthesia, two internal hemorrhoids were removed.

Case 53.—Ora Keithley, age 23, Troop M, First Vol. Cavalry, first suffered severe pain from hemorrhoids in July, when on duty in Cuba. He had had previously an attack of rheumatism from exposure to rough and wet weather and sleeping on wet ground. On September 7, three hemorrhoids, partly external and partly internal, were removed.

Case 54.—Horace Carden, age 24, Troop M, First Vol. Cavalry, has suffered off and on for three years from hemorrhoids, the present attack was not preceded by any bowel complaint or other illness. Has had no bleeding, but much pain and itching. Operation under chloroform anesthesia, September 8, when three internal hemorrhoids were removed.

Case 55.—Silas McGovern, age 28, Troop A, Ninth Cavalry, colored, has been in the service three years. Patient was admitted to the surgical ward September 3. One week ago, directly following an attack of diarrhea, he noticed pain in the rectum on defecation. The mucous membrane of the rectum protruded with each stool. Day after admission the patient was chloroformed and three internal hemorrhoids were removed. The appearance of the swellings indicated their recent origin. The mucous membrane was in a state of catarrhal inflammation. The posterior half of the anal ring was principally affected by the hemorrhoids as well as by the catarrhal inflammation.

Case 56.—Joseph Etter, aged 19, Troop I, Ninth Cavalry, colored, has suffered for the past two months from hemorrhoids which he believes were brought on by heavy lifting. Since the supposed "strain" he has experienced severe burning pain with each movement of bowels and profuse bleeding. Pain has been persistent after stools for several hours. September 8, under chloroform, three large, dark-blue hemorrhoids were found, one on right and left side posteriorly, and one on anterior left quadrant. The swellings were removed as usual by the use of clamp and Paquelin cautery.

Case 57.—Lee Shanks, age 26, Troop A, First Vol. Cavalry, has been in the service three months. He has been suffering from hemorrhoids for the past month with no illness preceding. He has had much pain after defecation, but no bleeding. Under chloroform three external hemorrhoids were removed, September 2. One of the swellings occupied the posterior wall of the rectum to the right of the median line, one to the left of the median line posteriorly, and the third in the anterior left quadrant. The hemorrhoids were disposed of in the usual manner.

Case 58.—Corporal Samuel H. Edwards, Troop C, First Cavalry, began to suffer from profuse bleeding on defecation the latter part of July, following an attack of diarrhea while on duty in Cuba. Pain has not been severe at any time. September 10, under chloroform anesthesia, four very large internal hemorrhoids were removed by clamp and cautery, two from either side of the median line anteriorly. The hemorrhoids in this case were distinctly venous, the swellings being composed of ectatic veins almost exclusively.

Case 59.—Henri Meuronval, age 43, Company F, Second Volunteer Engineers, has suffered from hemorrhoids since puberty, with exacerbations at varying intervals. Recently much pain and bleeding. Examination under chloroform, September 11, revealed a large internal venous hemorrhoid on the right side, which, owing to the fact that the Paquelin cautery did not work that day, was treated by ligature. Before the silk ligature was applied, the mucous membrane at the base of the swelling was incised. An ulcer as large as a dime was detected directly over the sphincter muscle in the median line and posterior surface. This ulcer was evidently the remote result of a retroanal abscess which occurred a year ago. Since that time the pain during and after defecation has been much more severe. Besides stretching the sphincter, preliminary to ligation of the hemorrhoid the superficial fibers of the sphincter muscle were divided, carrying the incision through the center of the anal ulcer. Rectal tamponade as usual. The pain was relieved promptly by the operation.

Case 60.—Capt. Nat Phister, age 44, Company G, First Infantry, has had attacks of hemorrhoidal distress in 1888 and 1893 but not so severe as at the present time. He has suffered severely with present attack since August 19, the exciting cause being constipation. The suffering was much aggravated by a long ride in the saddle which he was compelled to take while the hemorrhoids were prolapsed. Since that time has had severe pain and constant muco sanguinolent discharge, necessitating the wearing of a diaper. Under chloroform a medical operation was performed September 8, consisting in the removal of two large hemorrhoids, largely external, and affected by extensive excoriations. The operation afforded the desired prompt relief.

Case 61.—John M. Dixon, age 40, Company B, First Infantry, had an operation seven years ago and had no trouble after that until about the first of August, when after a prolonged attack of dysentery he began to suffer with prolapse of the rectum. He has been in the service seventeen years and when last attack occurred he was in Cuba. He reached Camp Wikoff September 13. He has been greatly debilitated by the dysentery, and the prolapse occurs whenever he assumes the erect position or attempts to walk. Has much constant distress with pain, smarting, itching and occasionally bleeding. Under anesthesia operation was performed September 14. A large hemorrhoid was removed from the posterior aspect of the rectal wall and a vertical strip of mucous membrane by clamp and cautery. A smaller swelling and strip of mucous membrane were removed from the left quadrant in a similar manner. Rectal tamponade. Strict directions were given that the patient should be kept in the recumbent position for at least a week.

Case 62. James Skinner, age 28, Troop H, Ninth Cavalry, colored, was sick in Cuba with dengue fever, about twenty days, beginning about July 14. Recovered only partially from this before (beginning August 14) he had an attack of malarial fever lasting fifteen days. During both attacks he had poignant diarrhea. During the early stage of malaria the hemorrhoids appeared, with much pain, prolapses and bleeding. On September 13, under ether narcosis, two internal hemorrhoids were removed from the posterior wall of the rectum middle line, and the right posterior quadrant. Patient's health much impaired, anemia marked.

Case 63.—John Holloman, age 22, Troop B, Ninth Cavalry, colored, has always been in good health until the latter part of July, when he had diarrhea for three days while on duty in Georgia. Since then he has had pain on defecation, prolapse of the bowel and sensation of incomplete evacuation, but no bleeding. September 15, the patient was etherized and four internal hemorrhoidal masses removed by clamp and cautery.

Case 64.—Abraham Hill, Company C, Twenty-fourth Infantry, colored, has been in the service twelve years. About eight years ago he had hemorrhoids, which were operated on successfully. For the past three months, while on duty in Cuba, he has been suffering great pain on defecation and slight bleeding. Rectal prolapse at stool, always easily reduced. Has enjoyed fair health and attributes the attack to the heat and dampness of the Cuban climate. Operation under chloroform anesthesia performed September 16. Three very large internal hemorrhoids, located posteriorly and laterally, were removed in the usual way by the clamp and cautery.

The cases related above are instructive in showing what kind of surgery may be expected among soldiers who have participated in a campaign in a tropical country, subject to its indigenous diseases and debilitated by its climate, improper food and exposures. The results obtained must also counsel the military surgeons to practice their art not only on the battlefield, but also for surgical lesions caused independently of wounds and so often overlooked in the field hospitals. I have to record only two deaths, and both patients were operated on in the wards of the general hospital, being too weak to be transferred to the surgical ward. Both of them were low with typhoid fever complicated by large metastatic abscess, in one the parotid, in the other the submaxillary being involved. One died the next day after incision and drainage, the other on the third day. I am satisfied that many of our cases of phlegmonous and typhoid abscesses would have died without timely and thorough surgical interference. In many of the other cases, more especially hemorrhoids and fistula, the operations performed will restore the men, with the aid of proper general treatment, to their usual condition, and cut them off from the pension list. In all aseptic cases the wounds healed by primary intention, the best possible proof that good surgical work can be done in an operating tent in the field, and with very limited facilities for carrying out aseptic precautions. Since writing the above paper, a number of interesting surgical cases have been operated on in the surgical ward, which I will now report under the head of

MISCELLANEOUS CASES.

Case 65.—Edward J. Hill, aged 23, Troop I, Ninth Cavalry, colored, enlisted three months ago. Painful tetanoid spasm following gunshot wound of heel. About two months ago, while in Tampa, accidentally shot himself through the left heel with a Krag-Jorgensen carbine (30 cal.). The bullet passed transversely in an oblique direction through the os calcis. There is no evidence of comminution of the bone, the contour being well preserved and the surfaces smooth. While under treatment for the wound, he thinks he contracted "rheumatism in both loins." He has suffered twice from painful tetanoid spasm of the gastrocnemius, the attacks lasting about three hours, then subsiding as suddenly as they came on and leaving the leg painless and useful. He entered the hospital August 28, suffering from a third attack which lasted more than twenty-four hours, subsiding suddenly during the night after his admission. The gastrocnemius is firmly contracted, the heel raised, and any attempt to extend the foot aggravated the pain. No tenderness of heel or scars.

Case 66.—Wade H. Bell, age 21, Company A, Sixteenth Infantry, enlisted May 23. He has been troubled with varicocele for the past two months. It causes soreness and pain on walking any distance, incapacitating him for guard duty, and he believes the difficulty is gradually increasing. He first noticed the varicocele when he was sick first with malarial fever for five days. Had three such attacks. Veins nearly the entire length of the cord much dilated and tender on pressure. Operation by excision under chloroform anesthesia, September 5. Transverse suturing of the external wound to shorten the elongated scrotum.

Case 67.—James H. Hebel, age 21. Battery 3. Fourth Artillery, enlisted three and a half months ago. Purulent ophthalmia and perforative keratitis. On Saturday, August 27, he felt sensation of a foreign body in the right eye. The next day profuse purulent discharge. On examination August 31, the conjunctiva was found intensely swollen and vascular, discharge of pus profuse, eyelids swollen and edematous, pupil contracted; beginning of ulceration near the center of the cornea; beginning pannus, intense photophobia. There is no trace of gonorrheal infection. The treatment consisted of frequent cleansing with boracic acid solution and application of ice. Atropin could not be secured for three days. After that time it was used in sufficient strength to dilate the contracted pupil. In spite of all that could be done, the corneal ulcer perforated and the anterior chamber of the eye was partially evacuated. At this time the patient obtained a furlough and, on his own responsibility, undertook the journey to his home in Chicago. He was advised to place himself on his arrival under the care of Professor Hotz.

Case 68.—George Slate, age 24, civilian. Habitual dislocation of the left shoulder joint. This is the sixth time during the last two years the accident occurred. Patient probably under the influence of liquor when injured, as he does not know how it happened. Became aware of the dislocation on waking up in the morning. Several contusions on other parts of the body were discovered. Dislocation of head of humerus downward and forward underneath coracoid process of the scapula. On request of the patient chloroform was administered, and the luxation reduced very easily by extension and rotation. The arm was immobilized by a Velpeau bandage. Accident September 15, reduction the following forenoon.

Case 69.—Peter Hansen, age 32, farrier, Troop L, First Cavalry, fell from stumbling horse September 15, in such a way that he struck the ground with his left shoulder. He has been unable to raise his arm since. Carries affected shoulder lower than the opposite one. Pain and circumscribed tenderness over the clavicle about an inch from the acromio-clavicular articulation. Patient somewhat obese, so that the distal side of the clavicle can not be readily traced. Fracture of the clavicle near the accromion process was diagnosticated, although no distinct displacement could be made out or crepitus elicited. Arm supported in a mitella.

Case 70.—Edward Consan, age 24, Troop I, Ninth Cavalry, colored. Enlisted four months ago. Admitted to the surgical ward September 7, with swelling and extreme tenderness of anterior surface of the left tibia. Previous diagnosis of osteomyelitis had been made. No history of injury. The swelling is most marked over the central portion of the shaft of the bone. The onset of the disease, the location and character of the swelling and the nocturnal exacerbations of the pain left no doubt as to the syphilitic nature of the periostitis. Inquiry develops a history of primary syphilis four years ago. Has had secondary eruptions and mucous plaques, etc., and at the present time there is hyperplasia of the lymphatic glands in all the principal accessible regions.

Rest in bed, elevation of limb, hot, moist, antiseptic compress and the internal use of potassic iodid in 15 grain doses, four times a day constituted the treatment that was directed. Under the iodid the pain and tenderness diminished, as well as the swelling. A few days after his admission a small fluctuating swelling could be felt in the center of the inflamed area, but as no pus was expected the use of the knife was refrained from. This superficial central softening is often seen in gummatous swellings and will disappear under the treatment the patient is receiving now. If absorption of the liquid contents of the fluctuating swelling does not take place, tapping and washing out with a 5 per cent. solution of carbolic acid will be resorted to.

Case 71.—L. J. Torney, age 24, Troop D, Sixth Cavalry, has been in the service two years and four months. Pressure paralysis of radial nerve. While in Cuba was in the hospital three days for chills and fever. He joined his command after his discharge from the hospital and was quite well for three weeks, when suddenly he became unconscious and was afterward wildly delirious and had to be tied to a litter for safe transportation. During this trip he lost the use of the extensor muscles of the right hand. The paralysis remains complete, otherwise the patient is in fair condition, although occasionally the temperature rises to 102 F. The patient is not confined to bed. The paralysis of the musculo spinal nerve was undoubtedly caused by pressure during the transportation on the litter. Massage and electricity were advised.

Case 72.—Thomas Clemens, age 21, recruit, Twenty fourth Infantry, enlisted two months ago. Hydrocele of the cord. Came to the surgical ward for diagnosis September 16. Six months ago, while in the act of lifting a heavy box, was taken rather suddenly with pain in the right side of the scrotum. In a few days a swelling developed, the size of a hazelnut, which has remained. The swelling is tender to the touch and is connected with the cord about an inch above the epididymis. The swelling is circumscribed and fluctuates distinctly. It was diagnosticated as a hydrocele of the cord.

APPENDICITIS.

It is somewhat astonishing that, in these days of appendicitis rage, of the many thousand soldiers who have landed at Montauk, not one case of appendicitis came under my notice that would have justified an operation. We would naturally expect that among such a large body of men, almost all of them at some time during the last five months the victim of intestinal affections, the appendix should have claimed its good share of disease. The climate, the diet, the previous intestinal affections contracted in Cuba, should have, according to our ideas of the nature of appendicitis, combined in exciting the disease. But such was not the case. The profession is well aware of the fact that surgeons who can see nothing else but appendicitis in cases in which the patients complain of pain in the right iliac fossa, have performed laparotomy, and these cases were not few in number, where as an excuse for their error in diagnosis, they have completed the operation by removing a normal appendix. Of the three cases of supposed appendicitis sent to the surgical ward, in only one the diagnosis proved correct, and this case was such a mild one that an operation was not deemed justifiable. One proved to be malaria, and the third typhoid fever.

Case 73.—Charles W. Dyer, age 19, Company K, Seventh Infantry, has been in the service only six weeks. He was taken sick September 11, and was transferred to the surgical ward three days later. The attack commenced with a chill and some fever, the following day pain in the right iliac region set in. Bowels constipated, no vomiting, loss of appetite. Had a similar attack a year ago, from which he recovered in a few days. On his admission to the surgical ward there was slight tenderness over the appendix and cecum, no tympanites and no palpable swelling or muscular rigidity, temperature only a degree above normal. Catarrhal appendicitis was diagnosticated, complicated probably by a similar condition of the cecum. Rest in bed, liquid diet and ounce doses of equal parts of castor oil and sweet oil, four hours apart, until the bowels move, constituted the treatment, under which the patient recovered in a few days.

Case 74.—James Reid, age 21, Company I, Seventh Infantry, has been in the service three months. Was admitted to the surgical ward September 1, with the diagnosis of appendicitis.

The clinical history, as well as his condition at the time of admission, warranted a change in the diagnosis from appendicitis to typhoid fever. The temperature was erratic, showing malarial complication, but the curve from day to day showed the typhoid part to our satisfaction. The tongue was brown and dry with red tip and margins. Pulse 100 and temperature at that time varied from 101 to 105 F. Abdomen tympanitic and great tenderness in the right iliac fossa. Numerous rose spots appeared on the abdomen next day. Under appropriate treatment the fever subsided gradually at the end of the third week of his illness. The great tenderness in the right iliac fossa undoubtedly led originally to a wrong diagnosis, but it simply indicated in this case deep typhoid ulcers in the lower portion of the ileum.

Case 75.—Martin G. Norman, age 27, Seventh Infantry, Company C, enlisted three months ago. On leaving Santiago he began to feel bad with headache, anorexia and malaria; became worse; lost sleep and complained of pain in the stomach; most severe on left side under costal arch; bowels constipated, tongue large, flabby, with indented margin. Spleen markedly enlarged. At times has had pain in cecal region which disappeared promptly after the administration of a laxative. Under quinin this patient improved rapidly.

STRICTURE OF THE URETHRA.

Case 76.—H. J. Ewing, age 54, Company A, Ninth Infantry, has been in the service twenty-eight years. Admitted to the surgical hospital September 12, and transferred the next day to a hospital in New York. Has suffered from stricture of the urethra for a number of years. Exploration with the olive pointed bougie reveals a small and tight stricture in the membranous portion of the urethra. The cause of the stricture is a fall upon the perineum he sustained in 1864. Denies venereal infection of any kind. Of late years he has had attacks of stoppage of the urine. The stream is small and micturition frequent. Patient transferred to New York for treatment.

Case 77.—Frank Hugh Banks, age 20, Ninth Cavalry, Troop D, enlisted three months ago. Has had several attacks of gonorrhea, the last, two months ago. The stricture for which he was admitted to the surgical ward September 1 involved the membranous portion of the urethra, was an old one and was much improved before he was transferred on the 8th to his command. By careful and prolonged attempts a No. 8 bougie passed the stricture. The treatment consisted of gradual dilatation.

Case 78.—T. C. Mark, age 29, Thirteenth Signal Corps, enlisted three months ago. Has stricture of the urethra dating back to gonorrhea two or more years ago. Examination made September 14 shows stricture half an inch back of the meatus

A 14; another just in front of the scrotum admitting A 12. Gradual dilatation was commenced, but patient was transferred to a hospital in Boston two days later for further treatment.

The few cases of gonorrhea, syphilis and stricture observed in Camp Wikoff speak well for the morality of our army.

ADDITIONAL CASES OF FRACTURE.

Two cases of fracture of the long bones occurring in men belonging to the Cuban Army are of interest in showing impaired nutrition as one of the causes of delayed or non-union.

Case 79.—Hillyard H. Felder, age 44, packer, not enlisted. Five weeks ago, in Cuba, fell from a freight wagon; jumped to save himself and landed on his feet in a small hole, twisting his legs. He sustained a transverse fracture of the right tibia about an inch above the base of the inner malleolus, and a transverse fracture through the middle of the external malleolus. He came to the surgical ward September 14, the left limb in lateral splints, the right in plaster of Paris bandage. None of the fractures of the right leg have united, and there are no signs of formation of provisional callus. Fracture of left fibula united with some deformity. Patient is over six feet in height and very much emaciated. Plaster of Paris bandage renewed on right limb; no dressing for the left one. Operation for non-union of fracture of tibia advised as soon as the patient's general condition is improved.

Case 80.—John Coleman, age 28, Irish, stevedore, employed at the dock, Montauk harbor. Admitted during the afternoon September 12, to the surgical ward. While handling lumber was struck on right side of face by a crowbar handle set in motion by the slipping of a wrench. The accident occurred an hour before his admission to the hospital. The patient was unconscious and very restless. Right side of face swollen. Two small wounds had been sutured before he entered the hospital. Exophthalmos of right eye caused by retro-bulbar hemorrhage, divergent strabismus and dilatation of pupil, which does not respond to light. Free hemorrhage from mouth; no hemorrhage or serum discharge from either ear. Through the swollen part of the cheek the malar bone could be distinctly moved and crepitus was distinct. Pulse 60. No paralysis. Fracture of the malar and superior maxilla with extension of lines of fracture through the base of the skull was diagnosticated. On the second day the patient's condition was very much improved but toward evening a rapid rise in temperature led to a careful search for the cause of the fever. Professor Delafield was called into consultation and found a right lobar pneumonia.

Since leaving the camp I have been informed by Dr. Greenleaf that the pneumonia terminated in a typic crisis at the usual time, and that the patient is recovering rapidly from the injury.

Case 81.—Charles Lubbas, age 44, German, engineer. Fracture of the clavicle. A week ago while at work as engineer on the *Vigilancia*, was struck on the right shoulder by a falling plank producing a fracture of the clavicle at the junction of the outer with the middle third. The fracture was oblique, the internal fragment displaced upward and forward and some overlapping. Reduction and Sayre-Velpeau dressing. Patient was transferred the same day to New York.

ADDITIONAL CASES OF GUNSHOT INJURIES.

Case 82.—Peter Carr, aged 40, sergeant Company F, Sixteenth Infantry. In service 16 years and nine months. Was wounded July 2 before Santiago. He fell down at once on receipt of the injury, and on trying to arise found that the left leg was paralyzed both as to sensation and motion. He was carried to the First Division Hospital where the wound was dressed and he remained four days, thence to Siboney where he staid three days before being taken on board Hospital Ship *Relief*. He was landed from the *Relief* at Governor's Island, has had a furlough of thirty days and on Sept. 16 reported for duty at Camp Wikoff, entering the surgical hospital Sept. 18. Examination shows a vigorous looking man with partial paralysis of left leg. There is a scar on the left side of the back $2\frac{1}{2}$ inches from the median line and on a level with the second lumbar vertebra. This marks wound of entrance of the ball there is no wound of exit. The patient says the wound healed very promptly with only slight discharge; further that four weeks elapsed before he could rest any weight upon the leg, but he has been improving ever since and can now walk with a cane. There is marked wasting of the extensor muscles of the left thigh and marked impairment of sensation of the left foot and leg. He says that occasionally the leg gives way in walking, especially if the toe strikes something above the level of the ground. He can not raise it when flexed and states that with much walking the knee swells. There has been no impairment of function of bowels or bladder and no priapism.

In this case the ball probably passed transversely producing contusion of the cord and bruising the roots of the spinal nerves very near their origin ; it is probably lodged where it will do no further harm. The man says the X-ray was used twice but the result of examination was not reported to him.

Case 83.—B. F. Frazier, age 24, Company B, Twenty-fourth Infantry, has been in the service eleven months. While in action July 1, before Santiago, he received a wound of the right hand, the bullet entering the web between the index finger and thumb, passing through the ball of the thumb and making its exit at the base of the adductors over the anterior row of carpal bones. No bone injury. The wound was packed with gauze. The wound of exit healed in two weeks, the wound of entrance has never closed completely and has discharged from time to time a small quantity of serous pus. The patient was admitted to the surgical ward July 15. Examination with the probe revealed the presence of a small metallic body. During the preparation of the hand for operation a small triangular fragment of metal was washed out of the fistulous opening. Under anesthesia next day the wound was again explored and the probe passed to a point underneath the scar of the wound of exit, detected another piece of metal which was removed by incising the scar, when a fragment of lead much larger than the first was extracted. On scraping out the fistulous tract with a small sharp spoon shreds of gauze were removed. The bullet that inflicted the injury must have been a deflected one, as otherwise no fragments of lead would have been left in the wound. The gauze undoubtedly belonged to the packing used at the first-aid dressing. The wound was dressed in the usual manner; no provision for drainage was made, with the expectation that it would heal speedily by primary intention.

Case 84.—John Marks, age 22, Troop D, Sixth Cavalry, enlisted five months ago. He was wounded in the charge on San Juan Hill, July 1. The bullet cut the margin of the upper posterior edge of the right ear, entered the scalp one inch above and one and a half inches behind the right external meatus, and emerged from the scalp three inches in a direct line from point of entrance, probably making a superficial groove in the external surface of the occipital bone. The patient says he was taken to Key West while in an unconscious condition, in which he remained two days. July 6 he was operated on, the wound being laid bare by a curved incision and a small piece of bone is said to have been removed. The wound healed in a month. Scars healthy and not sensitive to pressure. He complains now of attacks of throbbing pains from back of head to eyes, three or four times a week; the attacks last sometimes half an hour. He does not complain of vertigo or disturbance of any of the special senses. Whether the symptoms are purely of a neurotic nature or whether they depend on the injury must be determined by future observation. Potassic bromid was prescribed.

From the above report I have excluded minor cases that were treated as out-door patients or inmates of the surgical ward not of sufficient interest to have any material bearing on the subject of this paper. This communication has been written for the special purpose of pointing out to the profession, and more especially to the military surgeons, the nature and sphere of surgical work in field hospitals at the end of a war. This completes my surgical work of this war, and I return to civil life grateful to the authorities and my colleagues for the kindness and many courtesies I have received at their hands.

General Hospital, Camp Wikoff, Sept. 17, 1898.

EMPYEMA IN CAMP GEORGE H. THOMAS.

The short, decisive campaign with Spain just ended was characterized, from a medical standpoint, by the smallness of the number of those killed in the field, the prevalence of disease and the large number of deaths from this source. The brilliant victories on land and sea which forced Spain to sue for peace have cost us so far over three thousand lives—less than three hundred from the effects of bullets and over two thousand nine hundred from disease. The number of deaths from disease will be increased materially, as the different military hospitals at home and abroad still contain a large number of our sick, many of whom will succumb to the diseases contracted during the campaign. Even in case the hostilities are not renewed, it is impossible to predict the total loss of life at the present time, to say nothing of the thousands who will never recover the health they brought into the service. The unusual amount of sickness which prevailed among our troops, in our home camps and at the seat of war, can be attributed to various causes. The call to arms came at a time of the year when bronchial affections, pneumonia, pleuritis and rheumatism are prevalent. In the State camp of the Illinois troops cerebro-spinal meningitis made its appearance during the first days of their encampment. Typhoid fever had its origin in our State camps and followed our army to the National camps and to the seat of war in Cuba and Porto Rico. The accumulation of large armies and the prolonged encampments in localities which lacked a system of sewerage, could not fail in promoting the local spread of infectious disease. The invasion of Cuba occurred during the rainy season, which had a deleterious effect on the health of the unacclimated troops, rendering them more susceptible to the effects of the semitropical climate and the prevailing diseases. The transportation facilities for the unloading of the transports were utterly defective in furnishing the invading army at the proper time with the necessary supplies. The clothing of our troops was not adapted for the Cuban climate. And, lastly, the necessary precautions to protect the troops against yellow fever, which is always found on the Cuban coast, where the landing was effected, were not carried into effect. The commanding general had been fully advised by the Chief Surgeon of the Army in the Field, but the instructions were ignored in the haste and tumult of the brief campaign. A lack of a good knowledge of sanitation on the part of many of the medical officers, and especially the inadequate policing of the camps, had their influence in promoting the local spread of disease. Amebic dysentery and malaria, the two tropical diseases to which our troops were exposed in the southern camps and in Cuba and Porto Rico figured largely in the sick and mortality reports. The prevention of these diseases was beyond the control of the medical department. The ordinary camp diarrhea, from which almost every participant of the war suffered to a greater or lesser extent, I am satisfied, did much to increase the receptivity of our soldiers to typhoid fever infection.

Another matter of the greatest importance concerning the health of our troops was the regulation government ration. The food selected and furnished for the army in Cuba and Porto Rico was the same as that which had been used in the North. Every one who served at the front for any length of time must be convinced that the emaciated, starved condition of our soldiers who returned from Cuba, and who escaped disease, was largely due to the nature of the food upon which they had to subsist. The purchase of food at the seat of war was out of question. Investigation will undoubtedly prove that many of the canned meats did not contain the amount of nutriment claimed for them. Fresh meat and black bread furnished the continental armies are not only more palatable, but also more nutritious than the canned meats and hardtack furnished our army. A careful inquiry into the kind of food our occupation armies should be furnished, is one of the most important duties of those who are in charge of the commissary department. Another subject of special importance is the special diet for the sick.

It is to be hoped that the medical department will be consulted concerning these matters, and that the recommendations made will receive the well-merited attention of the military authorities. During my service, I met one of our soldiers who served under General Gordon in his advance on Khartoum, who informed me that during that campaign the British troops were supplied, on the whole, with much better food than was the case in Cuba. England has benefited by long experience how to conduct a campaign in a tropical climate; we are novices in this kind of warfare, but have learned enough during the last six months to enable us to take better care of our troops, should we again be called upon to conduct a war beyond the limits of our country.

I have deemed it appropriate and advisable, in accepting your kind invitation to deliver the address at this annual meeting, to discuss briefly and from the most practical standpoint, a surgical affection which I had an opportunity to study in a most satisfactory manner during my service at Chickamauga. It is my purpose to occupy my allotted time by relating my experience with empyema in Camp George H. Thomas. I was on duty as chief surgeon in that camp for nearly four weeks during the months of May and June. During that time the camp was occupied by nearly 40,000 men, representing nearly all of the States east of the Rocky Mountains. With the exception of one company of cavalry on guard duty, the army was composed entirely of volunteers. The days were hot, the nights cool; the midday temperature frequently reached 98 to 100 degrees F. The drouth which prevailed at that time rendered the roads dusty, the clouds of dust being only settled occasionally by showers of short duration. Camp diarrhea, dysentery, cerebro-spinal meningitis, pneumonia and typhoid fever were then the principal diseases we had to contend with.

It is one of the complications of pneumonia—empyema—as observed in Camp George H. Thomas, that I desire to discuss this evening. Empyema represents the pathologic product of suppurative pleuritis. Suppurative pleuritis is always the result of a pyogenic infection of the pleura sufficient in virulence to give rise to pus formation. In the absence of traumatic causes it appears clinically and pathologically either as an isolated inflammation of the pleura or as a more or less remote complication of pneumonia. Bacteriologically speaking, suppurative pleuritis can only result from the presence in and the specific action upon, the tissues of the pleura of pyogenic microbes in sufficient number and virulence to give rise to a suppurative inflammation.

Non-traumatic, suppurative pleuritis is a comparatively rare, isolated affection; in the great majority of cases it presents itself as a complication of pneumonia. Recent investigations tend to prove that the essential cause of pneumonia is either Fränkel's pneumococcus, Friedlander's bacillus of pneumonia (dipplo-bacillus) or the streptococcus pyogenes. Streptococcus pneumonia, occurring either as a primary or secondary affection, is characterized clinically by the gravity of the disease and pathologically by the tendency to pus formation. The microbes of pneumonia discovered and described by Fränkel and Friedlander are the bacteriologic agents usually found in the inflamed tissues in croupous pneumonia. Both these microbes possess feeble intrinsic pyogenic properties, and when, during the pneumonic process, abscess formation or suppurative pleuritis sets in, the complication occurs usually as the result of a secondary or mixed infection with pus microbes. Croupous pneumonia is a self-limited disease, and when febrile symptoms persist after a sufficient time has elapsed for the disease to complete its typic cycle, it is usually an indication that mixed infection has occurred, and in this event it becomes the urgent duty of the attending physician to look for, locate and determine, if possible, the nature of the complication to enable him to institute timely, appropriate therapeutic measures.

In suppurative pleuritis complicating pneumonia, the inflamed lung tissue is seldom involved in the suppurative process. Resolution may proceed in a satisfactory manner at the time and after the suppurative pleuritis has set in, a fact which would tend to prove that the parenchyma of the lung is more resistant to the action of pyogenic microbes than the tissues of the pleura, or that these microbes find their way more readily to the pleura than into the pneumonic focus after secondary infection has occurred. The complicating secondary pleuritis manifests itself usually about the time the crisis is expected or a few days later. It is evident that suppurative complications in cases of pneumonia would be likely to appear in cases in which the tissues are rendered susceptible to the action of pus microbes and under circumstances which would supply the bacteria for the secondary, mixed infection.

Both these conditions were present and operative in Camp George H. Thomas. The health of many of the men encamped at Chickamauga was impaired soon after reaching camp by the sudden climatic changes, change of food, malaria and camp diarrhea. Nearly all cases of pneumonia were characterized by the gravity of the symptoms and a tardiness with which resolution occurred. Camp Thomas was located on the government reservation ten miles south of Chattanooga. The ground is undulating and in part well wooded. Numerous clearings and open spaces furnished excellent facilities for the drilling and maneuvering of the troops. The National Park is traversed by a sluggish stream, the Chickamauga. Three regiments of cavalry and a number of batteries were in camp during the month of June, the time the five cases of pneumonia complicated by empyema came under my observation. The ground is intersected by numerous roads which during the season of drouth which prevailed at that time, became covered with inches of fine dust, which by driving of innumerable vehicles of all kinds, the marching of troops, the passage of cavalry and artillery would rise in dense clouds and by sudden gusts of wind would often cover the entire camp. This dust was contaminated by pathogenic microbes of all kinds, which could not fail in finding their way into the air-passages of the occupants of the camp. The dust was most abundant near the roads on which there was the most travel, that is, near headquarters.

It was not strange that most of the cases of pneumonia originated in localities where the dust clouds were densest, filling the tents and kitchens and covering the food supplies. The dust had undoubtedly some influence in the causation of pneumonia, and more particularly in determining the frequency with which it was attended or followed by suppurative pleuritis.

Many of the soldiers left their State camps affected by bronchial catarrh, which constituted a potent predisposing cause to pneumonia. This was particularly true of some of the regiments from Illinois. Naturally the first regiments arriving at Camp Thomas were quartered near the great thoroughfares of travel and those arriving later in more remote parts of the camp. It is a noteworthy fact that those regiments farthest away from headquarters were almost free from pneumonia, while those nearest the center of travel furnished the largest number of cases. The cool nights, the lying on the moist ground and the inadequate supply of blankets did their share in serving as potent exciting causes. Some definite information in reference to the distribution of the disease can be gained by considering the location of the division hospitals, and the number of cases of pneumonia treated in each one of them. The division hospitals were located as near the center of the respective divisions as possible.

The First Division Hospital was established on the Lafayette Road, about three-quarters of a mile from the headquarters of the corps. The Second Division Hospital was established about two miles from headquarters and about one-quarter of a mile from any principal thoroughfare, the Brotherton Road being the nearest one. But few of the regiments of this division were encamped on roads subject to much travel.

The Third Division Hospital was located at the junction of the Alexander's Bridge Road and the Jay's Mills Road, about two miles from headquarters. Some of the regiments of this division were quartered on roads which were used by the wagon trains hauling water, consequently frequently exposed to clouds of dust.

During the latter part of May and the month of June forty-six cases of pneumonia developed in the First Army Corps. These cases were distributed among the division hospitals as follows: Hospital at Headquarters, 4 cases; First Division Hospital, 32 cases; Third Division Hospital, 10 cases. The Second Division Hospital was not established until the middle of June, and from that time on until the end of the month not a single case of pneumonia was reported. Careful inquiry at the regimental hospitals failed in finding a case previous to the establishment of the division hospital. This was the division encamped almost entirely away from any of the principal roads, hence least subjected to dust-infection. It will be noticed that 32 cases, or nearly 70 per cent. of the entire number, occurred in the First Division regiments. Out of these forty-six cases six died, or a mortality of 13 per cent. The six fatal cases came from the First Division. In three of these fatal cases death was caused by the progressive extension of the septic pneumonia, and in the remaining three death was caused by complications. In one case death was attributed to a typhoid condition; in two to cerebrospinal meningitis. The septic nature of the cases of pneumonia which developed in the First Division is best shown by the frequency with which empyema attended or followed the pulmonary disease. In this division empyema complicated the pneumonia in nine out of the entire number of thirty-two cases, equal to 28 per cent. Four of these cases were treated at the Leiter Hospital and four at the St. Vincent's Hospital, Chattanooga. Five of these cases were operated upon by myself: four at the St. Vincent's Hospital and one at the Leiter Hospital. The following case represents the pathologic conditions found in these cases as well as the surgical treatment which was resorted to in meeting the indications of the empyemic complication:

W. F., private, Third Ills. Vols., was taken suddenly ill while on drill, May 30. The attack was initiated by nausea, vomiting, dizziness and a sense of great prostration. On the following day severe diarrhea set in, which, in connection with persistent vomiting and intense headache, influenced his physician to transfer him to the division hospital. At that time physical examination revealed a well-marked bronchitis. In the evening he had a decided chill; temperature 103.

June 1 he complained of severe pains in his chest and back, cough dry and hacking, sputum tinged a rusty color. Diarrhea continues; slight delirium; temperature 99 in the morning, 103 in the evening.

June 2. Chest pains not relieved, sputum more deeply tinged. Temperature varies from 101.5 to 103.

June 3. Diarrhea under control; cough and expectoration unchanged; delirium and temperature about the same.

June 4. No material change in the condition of the patient; tongue dry and dark brown.

Daily examinations of the chest did not reveal any signs of consolidation of the lung until June 6. At this time the middle and a part of the upper lobe of the right lung were found consolidated. Temperature 102.

June 7. Patient delirious most of the time; cough narass-

Record of variations of temperature beginning May 31, 1898, at Leiter Hospital.

ing, and copious expectoration of rusty sputum. Temperature rose rather suddenly to 105.

June 8. Cough less troublesome, sputum more scanty; subjective symptoms improved. Patient was transferred to the Leiter General Hospital, when on his arrival the temperature was found to be 102.4. The medication at this time consisted of strychnia in small doses, muriate of ammonia 5 grains every four hours, alternated with 3 drops of turpentine. Under this treatment the temperature was reduced $1\frac{1}{2}$ degrees during the first day, 2 degrees the second, and $1\frac{1}{2}$ degrees the third day, becoming normal June 11. Carbonate of ammonia was substituted for the muriate at this time.

From June 12 to 18 the temperature ranged one degree above and below normal. The pulse, which had been 118 beats per minute and feeble on his admission to the Leiter Hospital, became fuller and stronger and diminished in frequency to 80.

June 19. Temperature suddenly rose in the afternoon to 102, pulse 96.

June 20. Examination of chest showed absolute dulness on the right side, extending as high as the fourth rib. The appearance of fever after a few days of complete defervescence and the rapid increase of the area of dulness, displacement of the apex-beat to the right, as well as a marked bulging of the lower intercostal spaces, left no doubt of the existence of empyema. The symptoms indicating the presence of this complication were so evident that it was not deemed necessary to resort to an exploratory puncture to verify the diagnosis.

In all of the cases of pneumonia complicated by empyema that came under my personal observation, the disease pursued a very similar course to the one described. The clinical symptoms were characterized by their severity. The patient's general condition left little doubt as to the septic nature of the original disease. As in the case detailed, the suppurative pleuritis commenced two to three days after the pneumonic symptoms had subsided, its onset being announced by a rise of temperature and the appearance of local and general symptoms, suggestive of the existence of a suppurative affection.

It is more than probable that in most of these cases the pyogenic microbes, which eventually attacked the pleura and caused the suppurative process, entered the lungs at the same time and in the same manner as the microbes which caused the pneumonia. The bronchitis and diarrhea which initiated the disease were plain evidences pointing in this direction. In some of the cases in which the pneumonia pursued a more typic course, the subsequent suppurative pleuritis was caused by a secondary mixed infection. All cases of empyema which were subjected to operative treatment were characterized pathologically by the presence of an abundant fibrinous exudate, which covered both the visceral and parietal pleurae, and, in the form of large fibrinous masses, mixed with the thick cream-like pus. The purulent accumulation occurred rapidly, filling the pleural cavity in a very few days. Displacement of the heart, enlargement of the chest and bulging of the intercostal spaces were the most significant local signs indicating the presence of a large quantity of pus in the cavity of the chest. The right and the left sides were affected with about the same frequency. In one case the pleuritis was limited, leading to a circumscribed empyema in the left side. The abscess occupied the lower and posterior part of the chest. In performing the radical operation in this case, a section of the tenth rib, about three inches from the spinal end, had to be excised. The location of the empyema was determined beforehand by systematic exploratory punctures, the first two punctures yielding negative evidence. As a rule, expansion of the compressed lung followed soon after the operation, showing that resolution had occurred before or after the pleuritic complication appeared.

In some of the cases suppuration was scanty after the operation; in others it was abundant. In the former event a process of repair set in promptly; in the latter case it was retarded. The final process of obliteration of the pleural cavity was accomplished by granulation, cicatrization and cicatricial contraction. Evacuation of the pus and drainage were always followed by a fall in the temperature to normal, or nearly so, accompanied by symptoms denoting rapid improvement of the patient's general condition. In two of the cases the physicians in attendance were misled in their diagnosis by the absence of fever. The pleuritis was initiated as usual by a rise in temperature and other febrile disturbances, which subsided in a few days, the patients feeling well with the exception of the complaint of embarrassment of the respiration. In one case the respiration was so much interfered with by the copious pleuritic exudate that the lips were blue and the pulse almost imperceptible —conditions which necessitated the performance of the operation without an anesthetic. We relied in this case on strychnia and whiskey to counteract the immediate effects of the operation. In the absence of such contraindications ether was used as an anesthetic, aided by the administration of some heart stimulants immediately before the administration of the anesthetic.

OPERATION FOR EMPYEMA.

The existence of an empyema in the adult is a sufficient indication for the performance of a radical operation. Puncture and removal of the pus by aspiration may succeed occasionally in mild cases of suppurative pleuritis in the case of children; seldom, if ever in the adult. Operative treatment should be instituted as soon as a diagnosis can be made. Unless the signs and symptoms are conclusive, the diagnosis should be verified and the pus accurately located by an exploratory puncture, as was done in most of the cases operated upon in Camp Thomas. Nothing is gained and much is lost by postponing surgical treatment until the accumulated pus has increased to the extent of producing serious and often irremediable compression of the lung on the affected side. The plastic exudate, which is often copious, as in all the cases forming the basis for this address, is another source of danger in case the operation is not promptly performed, as it creates conditions unfavorable to the subsequent expansion of the compressed lung and extenuates indefinitely the infection.

In view of the pathologic anatomy presented by the cases of empyema which constitute the basis for this paper, it must be admitted that the only rational treatment consists in opening the pleural cavity freely and in establishing efficient tubular drainage. Intercostal incision and drainage do not enable the surgeon to remove the large fibrinous masses which play such an important rôle in maintaining suppuration and in preventing speedy obliteration of the pleural cavity. The fibrinous exudate contains pus microbes, and unless removed at the time the operation is performed, serves as a nutrient medium for their growth and reproduction and interferes mechanically with pulmonary expansion and speedy obliteration of the pleural cavity by granulation and cicatrization. One of the important modern indications in the surgical treatment of empyema is to remove the inflammatory product as thoroughly as possible, and this can only be done after opening the cavity sufficiently to remove by mechanic measures the infected exudate. In recent cases resection of two inches of one rib at a point where drainage will be most effectual will afford sufficient room to subject the pleural cavity to a thorough removal of the inflammatory exudate. With the exception of the case of circumscribed empyema, we opened the chest in the axillary line where the ribs are nearest the skin and usually resected the seventh rib. With one exception, aspiration was performed a day or two before the operation for the purpose of securing partial pulmonary expansion before admitting air into the pleural cavity.

Preliminary aspiration is of special value in the treatment of large empyemic cavities. The surface of the entire chest was thoroughly disinfected and every care taken to carry out full aseptic precautions during the operation. The opening of large pus cavities is attended by great responsibility, and this is more especially true in empyema, as secondary infection is liable to occur unless the operation is performed under strictest aseptic precautions. If an anesthetic is given, the greatest watchfulness is required to guard against accidents. I always prefer to perform the operation under partial anesthesia, and I am very partial to strychnia and alcohol as valuable adjuncts in minimizing its immediate and remote dangers.

I place the patient partially on the opposite side with the chest slightly raised, and the arm on the side to be operated upon raised to the side of the head for the purpose of increasing the width of the intercostal spaces. I expose the rib to be resected by a slightly curved incision with the convexity directed downward, beginning the incision at a point corresponding with the upper border of the rib, carrying it in a gentle curve to the lower border, and terminating it at the upper border at a point about four inches from where it started. By reflecting the cutaneous shallow, oval flap in an upward direction, the muscular covering of the rib is exposed. A straight incision over the center of the rib, about three inches in length, is then made down to the bone. With an elevator the periosteal envelope with the tissues attached to it is then separated, taking care to lift out from its groove the intercostal artery with the tissues to be reflected. After laying bare the rib to the extent of at least two inches, the rib is lifted forward with the elevator and excised with a strong pair of bone-cutting forceps. If the diagnosis is positive, all that remains is to make an incision with the scalpel in the center of the periosteal trough, large enough to admit the tip of the index finger.

The evacuation of the chest contents should always be done slowly; this can be done most effectually by interrupting the flow of pus from time to time by inserting the index finger into the pleural incision. After evacuation of the pus and loose shreds of fibrinous material, the pleural cavity should be carefully examined by direct inspection and digital exploration. Plastic exudates attached to either pleura must be removed as thoroughly as can be done with finger and a small gauze sponge held securely in the jaws of a pair of long, preferably slightly curved, forceps. The membranes should be removed by mopping and not by the use of sharp instruments. Scraping of the pleuræ with a sharp spoon is superfluous and occasionally detrimental. In acute cases I have often noticed quite free hemorrhage from the pleural surfaces even after gentle efforts to dislodge the adherent fibrinous exudate. Should troublesome hemorrhage follow the procedure, packing of the pleural cavity with one long strip of plain sterile gauze should at once be resorted to. The space below the drainage opening is packed first, and if the hemorrhage is not arrested, the balance of the cavity is packed from above downward.

Tubular drainage is the ideal method of draining a suppurating pleural cavity. I use for this purpose two fenestrated tubular drains, the size of the little finger, about four inches in length and securely fastend together with a large safety-pin. Drains have been repeatedly lost in the pleural cavity for want of resorting to this simple precaution. After inserting the tubular drain, the external wound is sutured in the usual manner. The curved incision, as described above, not only exposes the ribs more freely than the straight incision, as usually practiced, but it is also much better adapted for prolonged drainage.

I never irrigate the pleural cavity the day the operation is performed. I do so later, provided suppuration continues. In case irrigation of the pleural cavity becomes necessary, care is necessary in the selection of the antiseptic solution; carbolic acid and corrosive sublimate in the usual strength are dangerous, and should never be used. I make use of either a saturated solution of the acetate of aluminium or Thiersch's solution. Both of these solutions are efficient as an antiseptic and non-toxic even when used in large quantities. The value of the double drain is made apparent when it becomes necessary to irrigate the pleural cavity. By placing the patient on the opposite side, the fluid which enters the chest through one tube escapes through the other as soon as the cavity is full, thus washing it out thoroughly. By placing the patient on the affected side the cavity is emptied, when the same procedure is repeated until the solution returns clear. The solution used should always be heated to blood temperature, as irrigation with a cold solution is fraught with danger.

The external dressing should consist of a thick cushion of sterile gauze and absorbent cotton to absorb the fluid as fast as it escapes, and to provide the wound with a filter to prevent post-operative infection. The best way of keeping the dressing in place and to prevent the entrance of unfiltered air into the cavity, is to substitute for the ordinary bandage the rubber webbing bandage. Change of dressing and antiseptic irrigation become necessary as often as the dressing becomes saturated. For the purpose of obviating frequent changes, the dressings should be ample.

As the cavity diminishes in size the drains are shortened from time to time, and sooner or later one of them can be dispensed with. Premature removal of the drain is often followed by relapse. Drainage must not be suspended until the surgeon can satisfy himself by careful examination that the pleural cavity has become obliterated.

Should the lung fail to expand sufficiently in the course of a few months to place the cavity in a condition for definitive healing, Schede's thoracoplastic operation is the operation of choice, as Estlander's multiple rib resection has not yielded the expected results in the practice of many operators, including my own. It is well for the surgeon to keep close watch of the size of the cavity during the after-treatment. It has always been my custom, at stated intervals, to place the patient on the opposite side, then fill the cavity with one of the antiseptic solutions used for irrigation, then evacuating the chest by reversing the position and measure the quantity of fluid removed. By recording the results of such measurements, we are in a position to judge with mathematic precision the size of the cavity, and determine whether or not healing is possible without further and more serious operative interference. Prompt and progressive improvement followed the operation in all of my cases of empyema operated upon in Camp Thomas. In most of the cases suppuration was soon under control, followed by speedy pulmonary expansion and permanent healing of the empyemic cavity by granulation. In two of the cases a recent examination made by Dr. A. F. Lemke showed that the patients recovered their former health.

Our limited means of making a satisfactory bacteriologic examination of the inflammatory product made it impossible to ascertain in each case the nature of the microbic cause of the suppurative complication. In two of the cases, inoculation of proper nutrient media resulted in an abundant growth of the staphylococcus pyogenes aureus. I have but little doubt that in most, if not in all cases, the suppurative pleuritis developed in consequence of a secondary infection with pus microbes, probably in most instances with the staphylococcus, as indicated by the clinical course of the disease and the nature of the inflammatory product. The etiologic relationship of dust to pneumonia, and especially the pleuritic complication, must be regarded as established by the facts related above.

The influence of dust in the causation of pneumonia and suppurative pleuritis acts in two ways in the causation of these diseases: 1. The mechanical irritation of the bronchial mucous membrane resulting from the presence of ordinary dust renders the epithelial layer of the bronchial mucous membrane more permeable to the entrance of pathogenic microbes. 2. Pathogenic microbes, and in this case pus microbes, are suspended in the dust and find with it entrance into the air-passages.

The importance of early radical operative intervention in the treatment of empyema can not be overestimated. The only efficient treatment in such cases consists in opening the cavity of the chest freely by rib resection, removal of inflammatory product and establishing free tubular drainage, followed by safe and efficient irrigation, should subsequent suppuration demand it.

ESCULAPIUS ON THE FIELD OF BATTLE.

Esculapius on the field of battle! What an inspiring sentiment at this time and on this occasion! Esculapius, the fabled deity of medicine, engaged on the battlefield in directing his faithful disciples in bringing comfort to the dying and timely and efficient aid to the wounded, is indeed an idea conveying the loftiest, noblest, soul-inspiring subject. The disciples of Esculapius have followed and served every army since man has resorted to contest by force of arms to secure the real or imaginary rights of tribes and nations. Every battlefield bears testimony of their life-saving, humanitarian work. When battles were fought hand-to-hand, and by the use of the most primitive weapons of war, the Esculapians were there with their pots of boiling oil with which to stanch bleeding, with their crude instruments with which to extract arrows buried in the flesh of the wounded warriors, and with their bottles of wine and oil with which to dress the wounds. Their practice has kept more than pace with the rapid and wonderful improvements in the implements of destruction employed on the battlefield.

It is a long time since civilized nations abandoned the catapult for the cannon, and the small-caliber, repeating breech-loader has taken the place of the bow and arrow, but the disciples of Esculapius have more than counterbalanced the increased horrors of war by the marvelous advancements made in the science and art of surgery. The battlefield has witnessed many changes in the practice of military surgeons. It was on the battlefield that Ambroise Paré substituted the ligature for the cautery in arresting hemorrhage. It was on the battlefield that Hans Ryf, Baron Larrey, Pirogoff, Guthrie, Nussbaum, Langenbeck,

Esmarch, Stromeyer, Billroth, and a host of other worthy priests in the temple of Esculapius, achieved lasting fame.

Conservative surgery is the pride of the modern Esculapian on the field of battle. The stacks of amputated limbs that constituted such a gruesome and constant sight after every great battle during the Civil War, will never be seen again on the field of battle where modern surgery is practiced. Aseptic surgery has driven out of our military hospitals the four greatest enemies of the wounded soldier: hospital gangrene, secondary hemorrhage, pyemia and erysipelas. The probe, an instrument of torture, danger and fallacy, has been abandoned for the X-ray in locating bullets lodged in the body. The first-aid dressing properly applied at the right time constitutes, in the vast majority of cases, almost a sure protection against infection of the wound. Under aseptic precautions penetrating gunshot wounds of the large joints heal promptly, often without serious impairment of the function of the joint. Many cases of penetrating wounds of the chest and abdomen recover without operative interference. Prophylaxis has largely taken the place of operative surgery in the field. Our recent experience in Cuba and Porto Rico has demonstrated that the small-caliber rifle is a most humane weapon. If the wounded survive the immediate effects of the injury the prospects of recovery are good. Most of the wounds of the soft parts outside the three large cavities healed, with few exceptions, under one dressing in from ten days to three weeks. What a contrast with the experience of the surgeons during the Civil War only thirty-five years ago! This wonderful improvement in military surgery has been brought about through the labors of the disciples of Esculapius during the last thirty years.

Esculapius is unselfish and impartial in his work. His deeds of mercy are dispensed alike to friend and foe. He knows no creed, no politics. He is on the side of wrong as well as justice. He is loyal to every flag hoisted on the field of battle. He rejoices with the victorious, he sympathizes with the vanquished. He loves and respects the uniform of every nation. He is not anxious for war, but when war does come he is promptly on the field and remains there as long as a single soldier requires his services. He never sleeps. His thoughts, his actions, are devoted to the welfare and usefulness of the soldier. He is the adviser of the well, the comforter and physician of the sick and the good Samaritan of the wounded. His disciples have always proved worthy of their noble profession when engaged on the field of battle. They have served on every battlefield without any prospect or expectation of achieving undying fame, or even receiving the gratitude due them from those benefited by their services. Our histories of the world bristle with accounts of heroism and daring exploits of famous generals, but how little do we find of praise of the deeds of the disciples of Esculapius who faced all the dangers incident to warfare, besides doing battle daily with the Grim Reaper behind the fighting line.

The Esculapians on the field of battle belong to a noble, unselfish, learned profession. It requires years of hard study and a small fortune to acquire the necessary knowledge to prepare them for their work. They are men who in civil life would occupy a high social position and enjoy a handsome income from the practice of their profession. But the medical profession of all countries has always been intensely patriotic in times of war. The doctors always have been and always will be the salt of the population. Their education and training are of a nature to ensure qualities necessary to citizenship of the highest type. The practice of their profession, even in times of peace, is admirably adapted to prepare them for the emergencies of war. In the exercise of their duties they encounter dangers and hardships foreign to the lives of the average citizens. They brave epidemics far worse than bullets, as far as danger to life is concerned, without fear of death. In cities devastated by the scourge of yellow fever or cholera, when everybody else that can leaves for a place of safety, the doctors remain at their posts and minister to the sick and dying without any expectation of a substantial reward, or even the gratitude of their impoverished clients. Day after day and night after night the familiar modest conveyance, with its lonely occupant, can be seen in the depopulated streets, wending its way to the hovels of the poor on its errand of mercy.

No military surgeon has ever attained the fame of the innumerable heroes who distinguished themselves on the battlefield and whose deeds have been immortalized in prose and poetry. In rank, pay and social position he has always been at a disadvantage as compared with the leaders of armies. His greatest reward always has been, and probably always will be, the consciousness of having performed his duty to his fellow-men. Will you not agree with me that the doctrines as taught by Esculapius and as practiced by his disciples are akin to the teachings of the Great Master? If you do not, let us follow for one day and one night the work of our Esculapian on the modern battlefield.

The disciple of Esculapius is on the field before the expected battle. He is a non-combatant and modestly takes his place behind the fighting line. He knows what is expected of him during the next day, and makes the necessary preparations. During the night the troops are rushed to the front and the line of battle is completed. A deadly silence attends these preliminary preparations for the next day's conflict. From the commanding general down to the private a sense of responsibility, uncertainty and suspense prevails. With the dawn of the new-born day the deadly conflict begins. The batteries furnish the prelude to the impending battle, followed by the irregular firing of the picket lines. The more regular cannonading on both sides and the volleys of musketry announce that the day's bloody work has begun in earnest.

The uproar and tumult of battle has commenced. The line of battle is advancing slowly. Our Esculapian disciple is not idle for any length of time. He is near enough the fighting line to observe the movements of the troops, and within range of the fire. The singing, whizzing bullets do not disturb his calmness. Shells plow the ground around and about him, exploding with a dull but terrific noise and sending their messengers of death in all directions. He takes position in a sheltered place, where his patients will find protection from the fire of the enemy.

He is hardly ready for his day's work when the first victim arrives. He has been conveyed to the rear by friendly hands. A hasty examination shows that he has been shot through the thigh. The trousers on the injured side are soaked with blood. The garment is removed and a stream of red blood locates the bullet-wound. The patient's face presents a deadly pallor, his forehead is covered with a cold, clammy perspiration. The hands are cold and the pulse at the wrist is almost imperceptible. It is evident that the bullet has injured a large blood-vessel and that life is rapidly ebbing away from hemorrhage. The patient is conscious, but passive and listless. He does not realize his own danger. All he complains of is a torturing thirst and all he asks for is a drink of cold water. The experienced eye of the surgeon takes in the whole situation at a glance. He knows that prompt action is necessary to ward off impending death. In less time than is necessary to describe it, he applies an elastic constrictor above the wound which arrests the bleeding promptly, makes use of the first-aid package to protect the wound against infection, administers the necessary restoratives, pins the diagnosis tag to the lapel of the uniform, satisfies his thirst by administering the contents of his own canteen, and hands the patient over to the hospital-corps men, who bring him safely to the ambulance station.

Before he has disposed of his first charge his services are urgently demanded in his immediate vicinity, and he hastens to the new scene of catastrophe. A young soldier has been struck down by a fragment of a bursting shell which has almost completely severed both legs just below the knee-joint. The patient lies on the ground, motionless, with his sunken eyes directed stolidly toward the overhanging blue sky. He has lost but little blood, but his lips are pale and slightly livid, the nostrils dilated, the skin of the forehead thrown into deep folds. The hands are cold and the pulse at the wrist can not be felt. The respirations are irregular and sighing; a long and deep respiration is followed by a number of shallow, imperfect expansions of the chest. The mind is clear, but it takes repeated questions to elicit the simplest answer. The unearthly brilliancy of the otherwise expressionless, staring eyes clearly indicates the inevitable doom that awaits the wounded warrior. His life is but the flickering light of a tallow candle to be extinguished at any moment. The surgeon knows that in this case the terrible injury will result in death from shock. The patient is ignorant of the extent of the injury sustained, and if he should happen to see the cold, mangled, motionless legs, almost detached from the body, he would not realize that his life is in such immediate jeopardy. He makes no complaint and no requests. In an almost inaudible whisper he may ask for a drink of water. Home, relatives and friends have become to him but a pleasant dream. His mind is occupied by the experience of the day, his ears are filled with the din and tumult of battle, his eyes are still resting on yonder line of battle he was approaching but a few minutes ago with a firm hope of victory when he, with several comrades, was mowed down by the bursting shell.

The conscientious surgeon, recognizing the hopelessness of the case, feels that he has another mission to perform. He ascertains the name of the wounded and of the nearest relatives, and the address, and then calmly informs his patient of what awaits him. For a moment such information brings the patient's mind back to realities and, probably with a smile and look of gratitude, he responds calmly to the questions. He is made as comfortable as can be done under the circumstances, but before the setting of the sun his spirit has left the mutilated body and joined the peaceful army beyond the reach of human warfare. The next mail carries with it a letter from the surgeon, in which he details the date and cause of death of the gallant dead to his distant relatives. What such letters from the battlefield, conveying the last message of the dying soldier, mean to the relatives, can only be fully realized by those who have received them.

As the heat of battle rises the number of wounded increases rapidly. At the first dressing station they are lying, sitting, standing, walking, awaiting the first dressing. Our Esculapian is unmindful of the heat, thirst and hunger, and hastens from soldier to soldier to extend to as many as possible, and in the shortest space of time, the blessings of the modern first-aid dressing.

With the approaching twilight firing gradually ceases, without any definite decision of the fortunes of war on either side. On both sides the soldiers rest on their arms, and under the cover of darkness satisfy hunger and thirst. Tired to death from the day's conflict, sleep overtakes them and the naked earth is coveted as a luxurious couch. The work of the combatants has ceased for the day; that of the noncombatants now begins in earnest. Many of the wounded still remain on the ground, bleeding and suffering from pain and thirst. The veil of darkness is penetrated in all directions in search of them. The faint voices here and there serve a useful purpose in locating them. The dead remain where death reached them. Many a litter-bearer's steps are made uncertain by stumbling over the corpses which cover the field. The crowd of wounded behind the fighting line, at the ambulance station and in the field hospitals grows larger and larger, and the cries for surgical aid become louder and more and more imploring. Can the surgeon who has worked incessantly all day quiet his conscience and satisfy nature's demand for rest, follow the example of his combatant comrades, throw himself on the ground and seek repose by surrendering himself to the greatest of all charmers—sleep? No! As long as his brain will do its duty and as long as a single muscle will respond to his determined will power, he will serve the wounded.

There are cases in which a prompt primary operation will save life. These are the cases who receive his first attention. An operating-table is extemporized, assistants are pressed into service, and with the aid of a candle light the most difficult operations are performed in the silence of the night, broken only by the frequent moanings of the numerous wounded waiting their turn for the operating tent, mingled from time to time with the shrieks of those who have become raving maniacs, and the stertorous breathing of the dying. What an awful night for our poor Esculapian who forgets his own wants and strains every nerve to serve his fellow-men, and to do credit to his profession and the country and flag that he calls his own. Throughout the whole night he works faithfully and incessantly, and with the break of day he finds his task still unfinished, and the prospects stare him in the face of a repetition of the previous day's experience. The day work was hard and trying; the night work reached the limits of human endurance.

Can you give me a more striking example of genuine patriotism and heroism than the twenty-four hours' work performed by our disciple of Esculapius on the field of battle? If you can not, I can. It is the same Esculapian away from the bloody field in the fever camp. It requires courage to face the enemy on the field of battle. It requires courage to stand up in a rain of bullets and in an atmosphere torn asunder every few moments by shot and shell, but it requires more courage to enter the silent fever camp, with its myriads of invisible foes. The song of the bullet is sweet music compared with the silent, invisible microbes that cause yellow fever, typhoid fever, malaria, dysentery and camp diarrhea.

It is a privilege to die a glorious death on the battlefield; no such halo of glory surrounds the death-bed in the fever hospital. It is here that the greatest deeds of heroism are witnessed. It is here where the true manly courage of our Esculapian hero is put to the severest tests. Let me ask you a plain, simple question to test the correctness of the assertions I have made, a question the significance of which, I fear, is not fully understood: If left to choose for yourself, would you not be more willing to engage in a battle than to live and work in a camp filled with typhoid or yellow fever patients? It would take me or any other disciple of Esculapius not long to decide in favor of the battlefield.

During the war just ended, the disciples of Esculapius have taken an important and noble part. Cowardice is unknown in our medical department. Our surgeons have done their duty promptly and well. Esculapius has watched their conduct and their acts. On more than one occasion he shook his massive hoary head in disapproval, not because of what they did, but of what they could not do.

Esculapius has drawn his own conclusions from the lessons of the war, and now suggests to you and to the people of the United States and their representatives in Congress the absolute necessity of a complete reorganization of the Medical Department. He insists that the rank of our Surgeon-General should be that of a Major-General, that he should be clothed with more executive power, and that he should have his own commissary and quartermaster's departments. He is satisfied if these important changes in the organization of the Medical Department are made, that there will be less suffering and deaths from disease should we again be called upon to cross swords with another nation.

In conclusion, permit me to ask you to listen to the

voice of Esculapius in your efforts to effect a thorough reorganization of the National Guard. The new National Guard is destined to become the bulwark of the fighting force of our country, which will never imitate, much less adopt, the militarism of the tottering monarchies of the old world.

NURSING AND NURSES IN WAR.

One of the grave problems of modern warfare is the proper care and nursing of the sick and wounded.

Our recent experience during the war with Spain has brought the subject prominently to the attention of the military authorities and the people of the United States. The war just ended has furnished the most instructive and forcible object-lesson, in demonstrating the importance and necessity of making adequate preparation for the proper care and management of the disabled soldiers in war time. The motives which precipitated the war were of the purest, noblest kind, arising from the desire to bring freedom and liberty to the legitimate owners of our neighboring islands, who, under the iron rule of an effete, bankrupt monarchy, had been deprived of their liberty, happiness and prosperity for centuries. On our part, the war spirit was aroused by a sense of duty to our neighbors and to advance the cause of humanity on our own hemisphere, and not for gain nor conquest. It is not strange that our liberty-loving people responded so promptly to the call of the Chief Executive for volunteers. It required no special foresight to predict with certainty that a war with Spain, in Cuba, would result in greater loss of life and suffering from climate and disease than from the Spanish bullets. The result of the war has shown that this expectation has been fully realized.

The short, brilliant campaign on land and sea has taught the outside world the strength of our arms, and resulted in a victory over a foreign foe, which is well calculated to stimulate the pride and patriotism for our government and its various departments and institutions. The war just ended was characterized by the humane treatment of our vanquished enemy, and the desire on the part of the government and the people to provide the invading army with all the necessities and comforts compatible with active warfare. The war cloud came upon us so unexpectedly that a certain amount of confusion and unpreparedness in the management of the campaign had to be expected. Considering what has been accomplished, we have every reason to feel grateful that the prize secured was purchased at no greater cost of life and suffering. It was our first experience in fighting a foreign foe in a foreign land, and the many lessons taught and learned will prove of the greatest value should we again be called to cross swords with a nation beyond the limits of our country. Many of the well-founded complaints of the management of the war arose, not from any dereliction of duty of the heads of the different departments, but were due to a faulty organization, and this is particularly true of the medical department, which has been so severely criticised. The executive power of the Surgeon-General is indeed an extremely limited one. Everything of importance has to pass through the hands and by sanction of the Secretary of War. The Secretary of War is a busy man in keeping track of what is going on in his department outside the Surgeon-General's office. Again, the medical department depends entirely on the quartermaster's department in forwarding and distributing medical and hospital supplies. No wonder that many collisions between these departments occurred during the war with Spain. Our experience has taught us in a most forcible way that the medical department should have charge of everything pertaining to the care of the sick and wounded, in order to accomplish that for which it is intended. The Surgeon-General should be given higher rank and be clothed with more executive power, to enable him to discharge his duties with credit to himself and greater benefit to those who are now only nominally under his charge. The Secretary of War is not supposed to possess much knowledge of sanitation, medicine and surgery, or other wants of the sick and wounded, and yet the Surgeon-General is powerless in the execution of his orders without his co-operation. If the forwarding and distribution of the medical and hospital supplies were directly under the control and management of the medical department we would have heard less of criticism regarding the scarcity of medicines and hospital supplies. To make a department strong and efficient it must be independent, and invested with the necessary power it is expected to wield, and charged with a corresponding weight of responsibility.

The proper care of the sick and wounded in war is a subject as old as warfare itself. It is a subject that has attracted the liveliest interest of the most famous and successful commanders, and that has taxed severely the ingenuity and mental resources of the most famous military physicians. The soldier who risks his life in the defense of the honor of his country, when disabled from duty by wounds or disease, is entitled to the most humane treatment and the best of care on the part of those in whose charge he is placed. The moment he is disabled from performing his duty he comes under the care of the medical department, subject to its rules and regulations. The transportation and proper care of the sick and wounded are under the management of the medical department. The immensity of the labor which devolved upon the Surgeon-General and his limited staff of assistants during the war just ended must become apparent to the general public, when we consider the enormous number of the sick in an army of 300,000 men distributed from Porto Rico to Manila—nearly one-half the circumference of the globe. Hundreds of the recently enlisted men had to be detailed for hospital duty and were placed in charge of the sick. No wonder that among so many some proved absolutely useless in performing the trying duties of an army nurse. Nursing in the army in times of war is an occupation which is always attended by many difficulties, and particularly when the seat of war is in a foreign country. The unrest incident to the mobilization of troops, the moving and erection of hospital tents, the limited facilities for cooking and often for working, the occasional overcrowding of the allotted hospital space, the uncertainty of supplies, are some of the inconveniences which the army nurse must expect to meet and correct as far as lies in his power to do so. Patience, obedience, perseverance and devotion to duty are a few of the most essential virtues conducive to satisfactory and successful nursing in war. The army nurse, from the very beginning of his philanthropic career, places himself beyond the reach of any glory and distinction to be gained on the battlefield. His duties are more arduous and taxing than those of his comrades of the line. Being constantly in contact with infectious diseases he exposes himself to more danger than on the battlefield. It requires more courage to serve in a yellow fever or typhoid fever hospital than to face the enemy on the battlefield. The army nurse, with his inadequate pay and no rank, has little else to expect but a full measure of ingratitude. His greatest devotion and best efforts are never fully realized and appreciated. If he is competent and devoted to his work, his greatest satisfaction must consist in the consciousness of duty well performed. He is a Samaritan in every sense of the word, whose sole object is to serve his disabled combatant comrades. Few men are born with intrinsic qualities which constitute an efficient successful nurse. A true nurse is born, not made. Most male nurses lack the gentleness of manner and touch which exercise such a soothing influence over the fretful, nervous, impatient patient. The male army nurse should know something about cooking to enable him to prepare some special palatable dishes for the sick—an accomplishment which but few can claim. To utilize the ordinary army rations for this purpose requires tact and skill. It is wonderful what can be made out of bacon, beans, canned meat, hard tack, salt, spices and water in the hands of one skilled in the preparation of special diet. It is in this department of nursing that women excel men beyond comparison.

It must be conceded on all sides that the nursing in the field during the last war, as well as during any of the preceding wars, done almost exclusively by male nurses, leaves much to be desired. Many of the men enlisted for this special purpose, others detailed from the line for the hospital corps, lacked entirely the necessary qualifications by nature and training for such an important and responsible position. The haste with which the war was planned and finished precluded the possibility of making a careful selection. The tact to make patients comfortable under the most adverse circumstances is rarely found in men. To anticipate the wishes and carry out the directions of the attending physicians, requires more knowledge and training than belonged to the average hospital-corps men. The hospital-corps men of the volunteer forces, mostly new men in the service, did the best they could under the circumstances, but their work showed a decided lack of discipline and special training at a time when their services were most needed. With additional experience many of them would come up in a comparatively short time to the standard of requirements. An earnest willingness to learn and improve must be accorded to most of them. It takes months of hard work to make a soldier; it takes a much longer time to make a good nurse. The members of the hospital corps of the regular army are selected with great care, and are required to undergo a thorough and systematic course of instruction, hence they had an advantage over their comrades of the volunteer forces, and acquitted themselves more satisfactorily in the discharge of their duties. But every medical officer is conscious of the fact that even many displayed shortcomings which were too conspicuous to be easily overlooked. The average male nurse, in private, as well as in military life, works for money, and not for the dignity and good standing of his profession, or the welfare of his fellowmen.

The sunny side of the hospital-corps service was to be found in the transportation of the sick and wounded. No fighting army in the world ever enjoyed better ambulance facilities. No army is supplied more liberally and with better litters and ambulances than were in use during the recent war by our troops at home and abroad, and no better or more efficient men could be found anywhere than those who were placed in charge of the transfer of our sick and wounded. The manner in which our sick were conveyed from ambulance to hospital and from hospital to ambulance, commanded the attention and elicited the highest praise from our foreign visitors. After my return from Porto Rico, on my way from New York to Montauk, I was joined by Lieutenant Commander Tomatsuri of the Japanese naval medical service and two staff surgeons of the German army, who, upon arrival at the camp, watched with the greatest interest this part of the work of the hospital corps. One of the German surgeons freely admitted that our hospital corps men were far more efficient in this part of their work than those of the German army, and, what commended their work to him the most was the gentleness with which the patients were handled. He was astonished that a hundred or more patients could be transferred without hearing a rough or angry word, which he assured me was rather the exception than the rule in the German army. Hospital construction as witnessed by these distinguished foreign observers of our war, during the early history of Camp Wikoff, was another source of surprise and admiration to them. It was difficult for them to comprehend that in less than three weeks excellent hospital accommodations were furnished for nearly two thousand patients. I doubt if any of the old countries, always in a state of armed neutrality, could repeat what was accomplished by our medical department in this direction. Our foreign observers will never forget the impressions received in Camp Wikoff, with special reference to the transportation, care and treatment of the sick of our returning army from Cuba. Such object-lessons are best calculated to impress foreigners with the magnitude and resources of our country and the patriotism of our people.

A new phase in nursing was initiated during the last war by the use of hospital ships. The medical department of the Army and Navy recognized at the proper time the necessity of employing ships adapted for the transportation of disabled soldiers from the seat of war back to their own country, where they could receive better care and nursing and escape a prolonged stay in a malarial, semi-tropic country. The hospital ships *Relief, Solace* and *Missouri* were the means of saving hundreds of lives which, without such means of transportation, would have perished in Cuba and Porto Rico. The horrors enacted on some of the transports are more than balanced by the comforts, and even luxuries the sick and wounded enjoyed on these floating hospitals on their homeward journey. Nothing has done more in saving life and alleviating suffering than these messengers of mercy on their hasty errands to and from the seat of war. It was on these vessels that the nation's patients were in the care of competent female nurses. Ask any of the sick soldiers who returned on any of these ships, and you will find him ready to praise and bless the female nurse under whose care he was placed on his return from the seat of war. He will always remember with gratitude her gentleness and devotion to the sick under her care. During the four trips I made on the hospital ship *Relief*, to and from Cuba and Porto Rico, I had ample opportunity to compare the work of the male and female nurses, and I have no hesitation in speaking in decided terms in favor of the latter. Nursing is woman's special sphere. It is her natural calling. She is born a nurse. She is endowed with all the qualifications, mentally and physically, to take care of the sick. Her sweet smile and gentle touch are often of more benefit to the patient than the medicine she administers. The dainty dishes she is capable of preparing, as a rule, accomplish more in the successful treatment of disease than drugs. Her sense of duty and devotion to those placed under her care are seldom equaled by men. The sick soldier, far away from home, relatives and friends, realizes keenly the superiority of female over male nurses, and especially so, if his illness is tinged, as is often the case, with homesickness. It is under such circumstances that the professional female nurse is greeted in camp, on board ship and in the hospital as an angel of mercy, and every look and move she makes are of the keenest interest to the expectant sick. For the time being she takes the place of the deserted wife, the loving mother or the dear sister at the bedside. She watches the progress of the disease by day and by night, and her heart rises and gladdens with the approach of symptoms denoting improvement; deep sorrow and tender sympathy take possession of her when, in spite of all her exertions, the shadows of death advance. Woman is the natural nurse, and nowhere does she appear grander or nobler than when she is ministering to the sick and dying of an army in active warfare. The American woman, above those of any other nation, is peculiarly well fitted for such a post of duty. She is enthusiastic, energetic, tireless, devoted, and, more than all this, intensely patriotic. Our sick and convalescent soldiers owe a lasting debt of gratitude to the small army of female nurses who left their homes with no expectations of pecuniary gain and served their country in camp and field, in fever-stricken districts, and in common with them, suffered the privations incident to an active campaign without a word of complaint.

The demand for trained nurses during the war with Spain came suddenly and rather unexpectedly, owing to the prevalence of typhoid fever in the National camps and later by the return of the sick and wounded from Cuba and Porto Rico. From the very beginning of the war the Surgeon-General's office was overflooded by applications for service in the hospitals from all parts of the country. The material to select from was enormous, but the task of making a careful selection proved to be a difficult one. The Surgeon-General was overburdened with the various details of his important office and soon found it impossible to attend to this part of his duties in person or through his assistants. In his desire to supply the sick with competent nurses he assigned this duty to Dr. Anita McGee of Washington, who was commissioned acting assistant-surgeon, probably the first time this honor was conferred upon a woman in this country. The services of Dr. McGee proved of the greatest value in selecting from the thousands of applicants a sufficient number of trained, competent female nurses for duty in the hospitals at different points. The American Red Cross Society did excellent work, not only in furnishing supplies of all kinds where and when they were most needed, but also in supplying nurses when emergencies arose. Miss Clara Barton, the Florence Nightingale of this country, president of the society, has performed her onerous duties during the entire war with a devotion and earnestness that merit recognition at home and abroad. She has been tireless in her efforts to bring comfort to the soldiers at times when her service were most urgently in demand. The *State of Texas* and the little steamer *Red Cross*, under her command, made their appearance at Siboney at a time when outside help was most required. Ice, medicines, dressing and hospital supplies were freely distributed among the sick and wounded. Miss Barton and Mrs. Porter, wife of the secretary of the President, went to the front, a distance of eight miles, over one of the roughest roads imaginable, in an army wagon, and extended the work of the Red Cross to the very trenches before Santiago. A female nurse and a number of male helpers ministered to the sick in the Division Hospital in charge of Major Wood. I found representatives of the Red Cross in El Caney, in the vestry of the old village church, dealing out hardtack and flour to the hungry crowds of refugees. After the surrender of Santiago the *State of Texas* was the first vessel to enter its harbor on its errand of mercy in bringing food for the hungry Cubans, and medicines and delicacies for the sick of the victorious and vanquished armies. The Red Cross Society established supply depots in all of the large camps, and the good work done everywhere will live in the memories of all who were engaged in the conflict. I was told by a representative of this society that in Montauk alone for a number of weeks, supplies to the amount of $2000 were distributed daily. The Red Cross female nurses at Siboney did heroic work when the sick and wounded of our army were in the greatest distress. Several of these nurses were among the first of the yellow fever victims, and had to be taken to the first hospital for treatment. The sick and wounded Spanish prisoners at Siboney were almost exclusively cared for by the Red Cross.

Miss Barton has the confidence of the American people, and she has sustained it through the present war by the thoughtful and timely distribution of the innumerable and liberal donations to the society she so well represents. After peace was declared, Miss Clara Barton immediately sailed for Havana to bring much-needed aid to the starving reconcentrados of the long-besieged city, while her numerous helpers continued their faithful work in the home camps. The work of the Red Cross received the moral and substantial support of the charitably disposed citizens throughout the United States, and liberal donations from abroad. Recent experience has again demonstrated that this society is the most important auxiliary in war as well as other National disasters in bringing prompt relief to the sufferers. It seems to me that the Red Cross Society is the proper organization from which to recruit the nursing force should we be confronted by another war. This society should be made stronger and extend its influence to every part of the country. Under the supervision of its representatives, educated, trained nurses should receive additional training preparing them for military service and other emergency work. A list of names of nurses who had satisfied the proper authorities of their special proficiency for this kind of work should be kept, and the selection made from it, should a request be made by the medical department for service in the army. Provision for competent male nurses for army duty should be made by a more thorough training of the hospital corps of the National Guard of the States, a much neglected subject west of the Alleghany mountains. In addition to this, it would be advisable to establish training schools for young men in the principal cities of the United States, on the same plan and for the same purpose as the Samaritan organizations in Germany. The training of such men should be of the most practical nature, including the transportation of the sick and wounded, first-aid dressing. the art of nursing and cooking, with special reference to diet for the sick. An education of this kind would be of the greatest value and profit to the pupils as well as the respective communities, and would be the means of furnishing desirable material for the hospital corps in case of war and efficient aid in case of accidents and National catastrophies necessitating a sudden call for competent nurses. It appears to me that such a school of instruction for Samaritans could be made attractive and interesting to the pupils, and would become a reliable source from which to make selections for army nurses and the hospital corps.

The Sisters of Charity stood in the front rank of volunteer nurses in the Spanish war as well as in nearly all of the great wars during the last two hundred years. It is the oldest and best working order in the Catholic church. President McKinley became familiar with their efficient and faithful services during the Civil War and gladly accepted the offer of the Order to furnish nurses, made soon after the war broke out. All of the principal hospitals in charge of the

Sisters of Charity sent representatives to the front. They were on duty in nearly all of the National camps in Cuba and Porto Rico. The first six sisters were sent to the Naval Hospital, Portsmouth, Va., July 16. The whole number of sisters on duty September 24 was 232. The annex and the surgical wards and operating tent at Montauk were exclusively in charge of 100 members of the order. Their work in that great camp was a source of gratification to and admiration by the medical officers and all of the visitors and relatives of the sick. Several of these brave sisters have gone to their final reward in the service of their country, others are lying dangerously ill in the different hospitals. Too much can not be said in praise of this noble order, as it has always made itself felt in a modest but most efficient way in all of the great wars, without regard to nationality or creed of the contending armies.

Among the distinguished lay nurses special mention must be made of Miss Chanler of New York. I met Miss Chanler in Ponce, Porto Rico, where she did most excellent service in the military hospitals. Her numerous patients will always remember with deepest gratitude her arduous, unselfish work. The Misses Wheeler, daughters of Major-General Wheeler, accompanied their heroic father to Cuba, nursed him when he was ill and labored earnestly among the sick of his command. They continued their labor of love at Camp Wikoff, where many a sick soldier owed his restoration to health to their unremitting, tender care. Diet kitchens were established at Camp Wikoff under the supervision of Mrs. M. H. Willard of New York, which proved of the greatest benefit for the sick and convalescent soldiers. I take the liberty to quote from a letter recently received from Mrs. Willard, dealing with this subject: "For six weeks I was at Montauk, representing the Red Cross Society Maintenance of Trained Nurses, which, together with the Massachusetts Volunteer Aid Association, established diet kitchens in connection with the General and

Division Hospitals. On my arrival at Camp Wikoff I found the kitchen department in a very serious condition. The officers, doctors, nurses, orderlies and employees, as well as the patients, were procuring their food from a small wooden building, presided over by an army cook, and everything in and around the mess hall was in a dirty condition. Rice and oatmeal were the principal diet for the sick, and this was so often burned and badly cooked that the patients were unable to relish or retain it. The first diet kitchen was established August 27, and those at the three Division Hospitals soon followed, and this, with one at the Detention Hospital, made a system of five kitchens, covering a radius of three miles, with a force of fifteen cooks, several dieticians, ten volunteers and twelve detailed men. These kitchens supplied carefully and scientifically prepared food for the sick and convalescent, and the physicians and nurses were able to procure for their patients, not only liquid diets, but light and special diets as well. One of our prominent physicians remarked that his patients were better fed at Camp Wikoff than in any hospital in New York City with which he had been connected. The Government soon realized the value of the work, and two weeks after the opening of the kitchens they were turned over to the officials, and from that time, with no cost to private enterprise, the sick soldiers of all the hospitals were served, not only with home-made broths of beef, mutton and chicken, but also with oysters, broiled chicken, tenderloin steaks, chops, jellies, custards, etc."

This new enterprise in caring for sick soldiers deserves to be brought to the attention of the general public and should receive the strongest encouragement in the event of another war.

The different relief societies, National, State and local, did noble work in aiding the Government in properly caring for the sick and wounded. The names of Miss Helen Gould, Mrs. Ellen Hardin Walworth, and scores of other noble-minded, patriotic women will always be prominently mentioned in the history of the short, decisive war so gloriously ended. The charity that has been practiced so bountifully and so generally, must satisfy our victorious army that the patriotism they carried into the field has been cultivated at home in words and action to a degree and extent unparalleled in the history of the world. War in a just cause begets patriotism, and nothing can demonstrate this more clearly and forcibly than our experience in the field and at home during the last eventful six months.